SCHOOL ADMISSIONS AND ACCOUNTABILITY

Planning, choice or chance?

Mike Feintuck and Roz Stevens

First published in Great Britain in 2013 by

The Policy Press
University of Bristol
Fourth Floor
Beacon House
Queen's Road
Bristol BS8 1QU
UK
Tel +44 (0)117 331 4054
Fax +44 (0)117 331 4093
e-mail tpp-info@bristol.ac.uk
www.policypress.co.uk

North American office:
The Policy Press
c/o The University of Chicago Press
1427 East 60th Street
Chicago, IL 60637, USA
t: +1 773 702 7700
f: +1 773-702-9756
e:sales@press.uchicago.edu
www.press.uchicago.edu

British Library Cataloguing in Publication Data
A catalogue record for this book is available from the British Library.

Library of Congress Cataloging-in-Publication Data
A catalog record for this book has been requested.

ISBN 978 1 44730 622 1 paperback
ISBN 978 1 44730 623 8 hardcover

Cover design by The Policy Press
Front cover: image kindly supplied by www.istock.com
Printed and bound in Great Britain by TJ International, Padstow
The Policy Press uses environmentally responsible print partners

Contents

List of statutes

Academies Act 2010
Disability Discrimination Act 2005
Education Act 1944
Education Act 1976
Education Act 1980
Education Act 1981
Education Act 1991
Education Act 1993
Education Act 1996
Education Act 2002
Education Act 2011
Education and Inspections Act 2006
Education Reform Act 1988
Equality Act 2006
Equality Act 2010
Human Rights Act 1998
Local Government, Planning and Land (No 2) Act 1980
Race Relations Act 1976
School Standards and Framework Act 1998
Sex Discrimination Act 1975
Teachers' Pay and Conditions Act 1987

List of cases

Associated Provincial Picture Houses v Wednesbury Corporation [1948] 1 KB 223

Bromley LBC v Greater London Council [1983] AC 768

Brown v Board of Education, 347 US 483 (1954)

Choudhury v Governors of Bishop Challoner Roman Catholic Comprehensive School [1992] 3 All ER 277

Council of Civil Service Unions v Minister for the Civil Service [1985] AC 374 ('*GCHQ*')

Cumings v Birkenhead Corporation [1972] Ch 12 ('*Cumings*')

R v Bromley LBC ex p C and others [1992] 1 FLR 174

R v Cleveland County Council ex p Commission for Racial Equality [1994] ELR 44, CA

R v Commissioner for Local Administration, ex p Croydon LBC [1989] 1 All ER 1033

R v Greenwich LBC Shadow Education Committee ex p John Ball Primary School (1989) LGR 589 ('*Greenwich*')

R v Lancashire County Council, ex p West, 27 July 1994

R (on the application of Ahmad) v Waltham Forest LBC [2007] EWHC 957

R (on the application of Governing Body of Drayton Manor High School) v Schools Adjudicator [2008] EWHC 3119 ('*Drayton Manor*')

R (on the application of Omotosho) v Harris Academy, Crystal Palace [2011] All ER (D) 161

R v Richmond upon Thames LBC and Education Appeal Committee, ex p JC [2001] ELR 21

R v Rotherham MBC, ex p LT [2000] ELR 76

R v Sheffield City Council, ex p H [1999] ELR 511 ('*Sheffield*')

Secretary of State for Education and Science v Tameside MBC [1977] AC 1014 ('*Tameside*')

Watt v Kesteven [1955] 1 QB 408 ('*Watt*')

Wood v Ealing LBC [1967] Ch 364

List of abbreviations

AA10	2010 Academies Act
AJTC	Administrative Justice and Tribunals Council
APS	Assisted Places Scheme
CLA	Commissioner for Local Administration
CTC	City Technology College
DDA	2005 Disability Discrimination Act
DCSF	Department for Children, Schools and Families
DES	Department of Education and Science
DfE	Department for Education
DfEE	Department for Education and Employment
DfES	Department for Education and Skills
ECHR	European Convention on Human Rights
EA44	1944 Education Act
EA80	1980 Education Act
EA93	1993 Education Act
EA02	2002 Education Act
EA11	2011 Education Act
EIA06	2006 Education and Inspections Act
ERA	1988 Education Reform Act
GCHQ	Government Communications Headquarters
GLC	Greater London Council
GM	Grant Maintained (schools)
HOC	House of Commons
HOL	House of Lords
HRA	1998 Human Rights Act
ILEA	Inner London Education Authority
IPPR	Institute for Public Policy Research
LA	Local Authority
LEA	Local Education Authority
LMS	Local Management of Schools
NAO	National Audit Office
NFER	National Foundation for Educational Research
NUT	National Union of Teachers
NASUWT	National Association of Schoolmasters/Union of Women Teachers
OE	Open Enrolment
OECD	Organisation for Economic Co-operation and Development
Ofsted	Office for Standards in Education
OSA	Office of the Schools Adjudicator

RRA	1976 Race Relations Act
SATs	Standard Assessment Tests
SDA	1975 Sex Discrimination Act
SEN	Special educational needs
SMF	Social Market Foundation
SSFA	1998 School Standards and Framework Act
TES	*Times Educational Supplement*
TUC	Trades Union Congress

Notes on authors

Mike Feintuck is Professor of Law at the University of Hull. He was the author of the well-received *Accountability and Choice in Schooling* (Open University Press, 1994), in which he explored, from a socio-legal perspective, issues arising out of the introduction of Grant Maintained schools; some of the same themes are returned to in the present work. He has since written extensively, primarily on issues relating to regulatory theory and practice. Other publications include *The public interest in regulation* (Oxford University Press, 2004) and *Media regulation, public interest and the law* (2nd edn, with Mike Varney, Edinburgh University Press 2006). He has taught a wide range of undergraduate law subjects, including, as an accredited mediator, mediation and alternative dispute resolution.

Roz Stevens, after spending a substantial portion of her career working in the field of leadership and management development in a variety of sectors including IT, investment banking and the media, developed an interest in education policy during a period of employment with the Centre for Educational Leadership at the University of Manchester. Here she worked closely with school leaders during a period of intense policy change between 2006 and 2008. She pursued this interest further by completing a PhD on New Labour's Academies policy and its relationship with democratic values and constitutional practice, at the University of Hull from 2008 to 2011.

Acknowledgements

We are both very happy to have the opportunity to thank our friend and colleague Professor Mike Bottery, of the Faculty of Education at the University of Hull, who was instrumental in bringing us together for this project, and during discussions with whom the early gestation of this project took place. In addition, we thank all those who attended and contributed to seminars which Mike Feintuck gave at the Institute for Learning at the University of Hull, and at the Law School of the University of Manchester. Roz Stevens would like to thank Vernon Coaker, MP, Fiona Millar and David Wolfe QC for granting permission for some extracts to be quoted from research interviews conducted in 2010/11, originally undertaken for other purposes but which proved highly relevant to the subject matter of this book.

We would both like to thank the staff at The Policy Press for their consistently professional approach to all stages of the publication of this book and also those academic readers who kindly reviewed the initial proposal and the final draft, and offered insightful suggestions for improvement and focus. Above all, we owe enormous debts of gratitude to our spouses, Lisa and Paul, who offered continuous support on which we relied.

Preface

In this book we address key questions relating to admission to secondary schools, but we recognise that though education determines every child's future chances, it sits within a still broader social policy context. If radical social reform is the outcome, intended or not, of the processes and changes we have considered here, or the broader processes of reform of which they form a part, it will be important for focus to be maintained on the values and claims which attach to these reforms, individually and collectively. It seems to us that fundamental claims and values are far too rarely made explicit in relation to government policy in the modern era, yet all such policies do have some such justificatory values, even if recent reformers may be unwilling to specify them. While we have tried to remain focused on one very specific policy area, we hope that the task we have undertaken here, of engaging simultaneously in immanent critique of a range of competing approaches while scrutinising them also against background democratic and constitutional norms, offers a rigorous process for the scrutiny of current and future policy reforms relating to schooling, both individually and as a whole.

In writing this book we have tried to ensure that the points we have raised are supported by reasoned argument and analysis, and we want to avoid lapsing too far into speculation or assertion here in the Preface. We feel it necessary, however, to project forward our thinking on some important themes that have been central to the approach we have adopted and to point, very briefly, towards planned legislative developments relevant to school admissions that have occurred since the completion of the main typescript.

Through the 2010 Academies Act and the 2011 Education Act, the Coalition government has now put in place a structure and system of secondary education where entry to school will be largely determined at a meta level by the ambitions and views of the Secretary of State for Education and at a micro level by individual headteachers and college leaders, and, if an Academy chain, by the guidelines and goals set by the particular charity, organisation or company involved, albeit within the strictures (such as they are) of the 2012 School Admissions Code. Whether a General Election is called at the appointed time in 2015, or earlier, the Coalition government has argued that it is concerned to address the lack of social mobility in English society and that part of its mission in its social policy reform programme is, in part, intended to make positive inroads into reducing such inequalities. If this is a claim the government continues to highlight, we would suggest that, at the time of the General Election, in the case of schools policy, there will be one key question to answer: has social segregation in state secondary schools increased or decreased as a consequence of its legislative and ministerial actions? As will become clear for those engaging with the arguments made in this book, there is room for doubt that the increasing emphasis on introducing further 'freedom' and 'independence' into the school system, while simultaneously reducing the apparatus for accountability, will increase social mobility.

A school admissions system based on a hierarchy of successful and less successful schools will inevitably dispense education in an asymmetric manner, and of particular note in this crucial period of reform is the effect that the new arrangements will have on the most vulnerable group of school pupils – those with disabilities and special educational needs. The Coalition government plans to introduce legislation in early 2013, forming part of the Children and Families Bill, which aims to provide parents of children with disabilities and special educational needs 'greater control of the services they use and receive' and to 'prevent the unnecessary closure of special schools and remove the bias towards inclusion' (DfE, 2011a, pp 11 and 3). These proposals have met with a mixed reception during the Green Paper consultation period and, while outside the time frame of our work, the new legislation may well add to the concerns that we have expressed in this book. The proposed legislation is to be accompanied by a revised SEN Code of Practice and it remains to be seen how the revised Code and the relevant sections of the future Children and Families Act will combine to support or inhibit admission to mainstream schools and access to an appropriate and developmental curriculum for such children.

As we completed the very last work on the typescript, media reports suggested that Michael Gove was considering a proposal to review qualifications taken at age 16 and that this might include a desire to shift away from a unitary examination model to a binary model somewhat akin to the historic distinction between O-level and CSE. The argument which immediately emerged, as much between the Coalition partners as elsewhere, served to illustrate vividly a theme which has been central to our study of school admissions: the enormous potential for reforms in education policy and practice to serve different agendas in relation to challenging or reproducing social hierarchy, and restricting or furthering social justice. The relevance of the agenda we pursue in this book, of identifying with clarity the values which underlie policies related to schooling, and the relationship between such values and the outcomes of the implementation of policies, could not have been more clearly reconfirmed.

Mike Feintuck and Roz Stevens
June 2012

ONE

The admissions question

1.1 Introduction

Schooling is crucial, in its accreditation function, as a means of accessing employment and in its other tangible and intangible benefits for the individual and society. The path of our future life will be heavily determined by the quality of education we receive as children. Therefore, understanding the way that families access secondary schools for their children and the effectiveness (or not) of the school admissions systems and safeguards that the state puts in place is of profound importance. The significance of schooling is recognised explicitly in the Universal Declaration of Rights – the United Nations' 'common standard of achievement for all people' – which includes the right to free education up to elementary and standard level (Article 26). But beyond such grand statements of intent or aspiration, the legal and administrative frameworks that individual states use to guarantee and deliver access to such educational provision may choose to be explicit (or not) about the expectations or entitlements its citizens will have.

In the English school system that evolved following the passing of the 1944 Education Act (EA44), the allocation of places within a tripartite system of secondary schooling was certainly contentious, with the obtaining of a place at a grammar school being seen as offering an enormous increase in subsequent life chances. Despite the sentiment expressed in EA44 that all types of schools would have 'parity of esteem', from the 1960s to the early 1980s debate persisted, varying only in level of intensity, about the place and role of selective admission to grammar schools or the perceived non-selective alternative of a genuinely comprehensive school system. From the late 1980s, with the introduction of a range of quasi-market forces, initially under the 1988 Education Reform Act (ERA), the way in which school places are allocated has become a vitally important issue, relating to an increasingly diverse range of forms of organisation for state schools. Throughout this period, questions of social justice and social mobility have come in and out of focus in the context of 'the admissions question' and, along with expectations and claims relating to meritocracy, egalitarianism and citizenship, have dominated debate at different times. Many excellent studies have been undertaken on the nature and effects of admissions practices in different types of state secondary schools in England, but less attention has been paid to the constitutional and legal factors that have influenced the environment in which school admissions take place, and it will be part of this book's purpose to focus on this latter area.

Given the range of issues involved, it will quickly become apparent that any serious consideration of 'the admissions question' implies necessarily a broad-ranging inquiry, responding to what is, in reality, a series of related questions. Beyond considering the individual sense of disappointment and grievance for a minority arising from the denial of a place at a school for a particular child, there are also the questions of social justice, and arguments about notions of equality – equality of worth, of opportunity, of treatment and of outcomes. Such arguments remain as relevant and prominent now as they did under the 'settlements' (Jones, 2003) brought about by the landmark legislation of 1944 or 1988, or under the post-1997 'New Labour' education system. If we are to understand and progress debate about school admissions, and move beyond simple reiteration of established and entrenched political positions, it is necessary to consider a series of issues and assumptions that underlie apparent questions about how school places are allocated, and whether processes and outcomes are consistent with conceptions that citizens have of their right to access resources supplied by the state in a 'fair' or 'equal' way. However, what is 'fair' and 'equal' in society carries many meanings (see, for example, IPPR, 2007, p 10) and will be returned to later in this chapter.

Broadly speaking, in this chapter and the next the range of issues that underlie debate about school admissions will be clarified in order to establish the basis for analysis in the later chapters. These chapters will survey and review the range of possible claims – purposes, expectations and priorities – that might be attached to a system of schooling in a modern democratic state, and which might be expected to be reflected in the arrangements for admissions to its schools. Arguments about such claims must also be viewed in a broader context still, for they do not exist in some otherwise value-free vacuum, but rather are intimately connected with broader debate about the values associated with democracy, our constitutional arrangements, and our legal system. All of these sets of institutions and claims offer implicit or explicit promises, both procedural and substantive, about the values that they will serve and protect, and this institutional framework provides the necessary context in which debate regarding school admissions needs to be viewed. It is intended that by combining a process of immanent critique of three distinct approaches to school admissions (asking, simply put, 'Does each deliver what it promises to deliver?') with a thorough evaluation of the different approaches against the underlying democratic, constitutional and legal values, a rounded analysis will emerge, permitting robust conclusions to be drawn.

Given the diverse readership of this book, with expertise in one or more of the various disciplines implicated in this study, it is necessary to spend some time in this first chapter setting out the basic positions apparent in relation to the purposes of the school system, the broader democratic and constitutional values involved in debate in this field, and the roles of the legal system in this context, both in relation to a human rights jurisprudence and more generally. This groundwork is necessary to permit subsequent discussion structured around three very different, and competing, approaches to organising school admissions which will be introduced very briefly in this chapter and expanded upon in Chapter Two, and which will then form the basis of the analysis undertaken in Chapters Three to Six. In the most general terms, the three paradigmatic approaches to school admissions to be considered here can be labelled as 'state planning', 'quasi-market mechanisms' and 'random allocation'.

In the period from 1944 to 1988, the first of these approaches – state planning – predominated, with Local Education Authorities (LEAs) playing a central role in determining the number and type of school places available in a locality and how they should be distributed. However, in 1988, ERA introduced a range of quasi-market mechanisms of competition between schools for pupils (the 'unit of resource'), simultaneously increasing the autonomy of individual schools and the influence of central government over crucial matters such as the curriculum, hence substantially disabling LEAs from engaging in their previous roles (see, for example, Maclure, 1988; Lawton (ed), 1989; Chitty, 1992). In this context, the shift in statutory language by which reference to 'Local Education Authorities' (LEAs) has been changed simply to 'Local Authorities' (LAs) (2006 Education and Inspections Act, s 162) may be thought to be symbolically significant.

In part as a response to an ongoing lack of consensus regarding allocation of school places, surviving from the planning era into that of the quasi-market, and in part arising simply as a pragmatic response to ongoing oversubscription in popular schools, though also with some roots in a free-standing approach to the allocation of social goods, the consideration and use of random methods to allocate school places has become an increasingly debated issue, and forms a distinct third approach beyond traditional planning approaches or the mechanisms of choice and competition. Lotteries, generally in a limited form, have already been employed in practice for some time, and their practical implementation and potential utility will be considered further in Chapter Six. Some Academies have been using lotteries, mainly in tie-breaking scenarios, for several years, while in Brighton and Hove the local authority has used them extensively, though at the time of writing it is consulting on future practice. The idea of random allocation has received support from a range of sometimes surprising sources such as the Social Market Foundation (SMF, 2004) and Sir Cyril Taylor (2009), limited approval from Education Ministers in the New Labour administration, and a sanguine response from the Chief Schools Adjudicator (OSA, 2009a), though the Coalition government's 2012 School Admissions Code (DfE, 2012a) allows much less scope for their use. The use of random methods for allocation of school places cannot be characterised as a 'system' such as the LEA-planned model under EA44 or the quasi-market approach under ERA but, as will be argued in Chapter Six, consideration of their use may serve as a useful heuristic and a mechanism for challenging the validity of the other approaches: if these latter approaches cannot produce outcomes which meet expectations of fairness to at least as great an extent as random allocation would, their claims to legitimacy must be seriously questionable.

Before progressing further it is necessary to make explicit some limitations to this work. In order to maintain focus and keep the project manageable in terms of scope, the book will focus on issues related to admissions to secondary schools in England. Though some parallel concerns exist in relation to primary schools, the full range of issues often does not appear at primary school level, with local geography tending to predominate over all other factors. The scope of this book does not include the other constituent parts of the UK, where devolution has resulted in different agendas and statutory foundations for schooling, and differing degrees of variance from the English pattern. In discussing the general context of admissions questions and debate about the system of secondary education generally, awareness must be maintained of the place and roles of private schools, often referred to as 'independent' schools; an option generally available only to those parents with the financial means to buy into it. Coverage of these matters is largely confined to Chapter Two; the specifics of admissions arrangements to such schools, and detailed discussion of their place in the school system as a whole being beyond the central theme of this book. Given the focus of this book on the specifics of the English system, only occasional and limited comparisons will be drawn from other overseas systems, and then with a significant degree of caution due to the very substantial differences in the legal, constitutional and political frameworks within which they operate. The voluminous cases and statutes relating to special educational needs (SEN) and to the reorganisation and closure of schools are only addressed in as far as they are directly relevant to admissions-related questions. This book considers developments up to February 2012, so encompassing the early period of the Coalition administration and coverage of the 2010 Academies Act, the 2011 Education Act and the 2012 School Admissions Code (DfE, 2012a).

1.2 Purposes, priorities and expectations for schooling and admissions

In any discussion of the purposes of schools, and hence the processes for determining admission to them, it is necessary to emphasise from the start the contested and contentious nature of all such visions of purpose for education. Finch (1984, p 4), discusses how social policy in this context could pursue agendas as diverse as 'action designed by government to engineer social change; as a mechanism for identifying human needs and devising means for meeting them; as a mechanism for solving social problems; as redistributive justice; as the means of regulating subordinate social groups', while Lawton (1977, p 5) identifies as an obstacle to developing education policy which effectively offers good quality schooling to all children, 'the difficulty of providing an acceptable theory of education in a pluralistic society'. In pursuing a sociology of education policy, Ball (2008) demonstrates how vulnerable to capture, and susceptible to redefinition, the purposes of the school system are. Indeed, a strong awareness needs to be maintained of the constantly shifting nature of 'the political focus and ideological purposes behind educational change' (Tomlinson, 2005, p 2). Nonetheless, it is possible to identify in education policy a periodic process of 'the making and remaking of settlement' (Jones, 2003, p 9), in which can be observed 'Limited and conditional reconciliations of different interests' (Jones, 2003, p 9, quoting Clarke and Newman) and policy priorities determined in 'policy settlements reflecting prevailing economic, political and social circumstances' (Jones, 2003, p 8). The landmark EA44 is perhaps the prime example of such a phenomenon, seeming to chime with a genuine readiness of society, or at least a strong and vocal majority within it, to give effect at that time to a certain range of values and policies within the school system. In contrast, ERA may be thought to represent an example of 'capture', with the education system being reshaped according to a particular political vision with few concessions to competing views. While it can be observed that from 1944 to 1979, 'Education policy was largely based on a social democratic consensus that governments should regulate and resource education to achieve redistributive justice, and provide equal opportunity' (Tomlinson, 2005, p 3), as evidenced by legislation from 1988 onwards, the Conservative governments, and then their 'New' Labour successors, increasingly placed emphasis on forms of market forces and individualistic drivers to deliver outcomes considered desirable in relation to perceived national economic interests. Tomlinson (2005, p 2) concludes that 'it was clear that social democratic values were to be subordinated to neo-liberal values'. In the interests of clarity, the discussion thus far has emphasised a sense of distinct stages, but it is important to recognise that 'legacy thinking' and sometimes the actual practices of earlier phases in English education policy tend to seep into later phases, and the effect of this phenomenon is illustrated later; in particular in our coverage in Chapter Three of the influence of pre-War thinking on EA44, and in Chapter Two and in passing in later chapters when considering the impact of the simultaneous presence of planning and quasi-market approaches on policies regarding school admissions and SEN.

Despite its emphasis on the ability of market forces to deliver desirable outcomes, the post-1988 era is also noteworthy for a general trend of increased quantity and frequency of policy making and change – what Ball (2008, p 2) refers to as 'policy overload'. Thus, while the rhetoric of market forces remained wholly dominant in high policy debate, constant change and intervention was imposed on those involved with the delivery of schooling, via, among other means, a greatly increased use of delegated powers by Ministers (see Harden and Lewis, 1986, pp 112 and 154; Seaward and Silk, 2003, pp 162–5; Walters, 2003, pp 220–3). Such increased activity and political intervention may be related to the phenomenon of 'policy ratchetting' identified by Ball (2008, p 97 but also see Ball, 1990) where major agendas or developments viewed as politically impossible by previous generations of politicians can eventually be addressed more easily because of foundations laid earlier in the form of small-scale developments. A classic example of this kind of process might be thought to be the rapid development of Academies being pursued by the Coalition government, building on a much narrower agenda for Academies developed under New Labour, which in turn had drawn on aspects of the City Technology College (CTC) and Grant Maintained (GM) schools policies introduced by the Conservatives.

In the same period, as 'a diminished emphasis on redistribution, equity and social justice' (Tomlinson, 2005, p 3) took hold, there developed in parallel a very clear connection in policy debate between education policy and the national economy in a global context. Ball (2008, p 3) points towards the manner in which, post-1997, Prime Ministers Blair and Brown 'signalled in a variety of ways the increasingly close-knit relationship between the processes of education and the requirements of the economy'. In a similar vein, Tomlinson (2005, p 3) talks of 'A language and practice of managerialism, of accountability, inspection, testing and targets [which] precluded debates about the purposes of education beyond preparation for the economy'. Such priorities, of course, stand in stark contrast with the social democratic emphasis of the 1944 settlement.

In such discussion, it is necessary to avoid seeming to hark back to any apparently golden age in which there might seem to have been wholesale social agreement on priorities and during which such priorities were consistently met – even the settlement brought about under EA44 must realistically be viewed as being of the limited, conditional and pragmatic kind suggested by Jones (2003, pp 8-9), with competing visions elided rather than reconciled, as, for example in failing to offer or impose any resolution to the later stark divisions between Conservative and Labour parties over grammar schools. As will be discussed and illustrated in Chapters Two and Three, there are plenty of doubts to be expressed and questions asked about the extent to which the school system between 1944 and 1988 was successful in fully achieving its social democratic objectives. Indeed, it is plausible to argue that one of the reasons why the Conservative governments from 1979 onwards were able to implement policies which radically restructured public services such as education was because they were able, in conjunction with supportive elements of the media, to represent such services as having manifestly failed to deliver promised or desirable outcomes, and hence as having lost legitimacy. This seems to confirm the observation that 'policy is vulnerable to claims that it cannot resolve an inbuilt conflict between private interest and social need' (Jones, 2003, p 172), even if it may seem that policies on education such as those of New Labour may seek to, or appear to, elide the two (see Shaw, 2007). It is this dichotomy which is at the heart of competing visions of the values which should inform education policy. Broadly, the visions, which compete, tend to originate from, and emphasise the values of, either individualistic or collective positions, and this is arguably the key distinction in origin and orientation between the various settlements and re-settlements.

We will consider now, briefly, the broad purposes for public education before scrutinising the institutional arrangements, and location of power, in the next chapter. Few more explicit examples exist of a statement of a specific set of purposes for the enterprise of public education than that set out in the White Paper *Educational Reconstruction* (Board of Education, 1943) that preceded EA44. The objectives of the education system were described as:

> to secure for children a happier childhood and a better start in life; to ensure a fuller measure of education and opportunity for young people and to provide means for all of developing the various talents with which they are endowed and so enriching the inheritance of the country whose citizens they are. (Board of Education, 1943, p 3)

In establishing the LEAs as the primary mechanism through which such objectives would be delivered, EA44, s 7 identified a 'duty of the local education authority ... to contribute towards the spiritual, moral, mental and physical development of the community by securing that efficient education ... shall be available to meet the needs of the population of their area'. The contrast between such language and the conceptual basis for promoting EA44 and that associated with ERA could not be clearer. In the former case, we find an emphasis on community, citizenship and personal development, while in the latter these three informing concepts are essentially replaced by an emphasis on, respectively, individualism, consumerism and the needs of the economy. Maclure (1988, chapter 10) provides an excellent summary of the landmarks along the road from 1944 to 1988 on which it proved possible to implement in education policy 'a framework of political ideology which substituted an individualistic "enterprise" culture for the once-fashionable collective virtues and imperfections of the Welfare State' (Maclure, 1988, p 149). Within the paradigm established in ERA and developed by subsequent governments, any egalitarian expectations relating to opportunity and treatment within a sphere of social solidarity have been marginalised in a revised set of values that instead emphasises meritocratic arguments as part of an atomised view of society, and contrasts markedly with the attempts at consensus building inherent in the development of EA44 and the apparently genuine, if possibly naïve, aspiration to 'parity of esteem' across a school system which had selection by examination at its heart.

While it is tempting to emphasise this shift from collective to individualistic orientation, and even to present this as the key shift, the distinction here is often not clear cut, for there is a range of claims and values that can push in either direction. A necessarily multi-faceted understanding of citizenship is established by Marshall (1950), who identifies three aspects of citizenship (civil, political and social rights) which emerge in turn as a society such as Britain moves towards its modern form, and in this context it is obvious that claims relating to citizenship incorporate both collective and individualistic aspects – while the individual will have expectations as individual citizen in that capacity, the rights associated with citizenship exist only because of, and in the context of, membership of a collectivity known as society. In a similar fashion, the discourse of 'human rights' as applied to education (see Harris, 2007) will also have individualistic aspects, including expectations relating to self-development, but will often be formulated in respect of, and in relation to, diverse groups within society. Indeed arguments about diversity can arise from, and be made in pursuit of, individualistic claims but can also equally be located within a vision of diversity within a social collectivity. The different implications of approaches to school admissions deriving from citizenship and from human rights will be returned to in later chapters. Meanwhile, arguments about the relationship between education and employment can also be played out as arguments about individual needs for, or expectation of, paid employment or as servicing the economic and industrial requirements of society. In popular terms, the arguments about education and access to it are often referred to in relation to 'fairness', but this also can have individualistic and meritocratic orientation (relating to the worth of the individual) or collective undertones which emphasise equality of treatment between all members of a group.

Despite such complications arising from the language used to express the range of values implicated in debate about the purposes of education, there are some areas in which the move away from a collective or social orientation can be clearly observed. Most conspicuously, instead of the development of community and society and their educational foundation bases, emphasis on serving national economic interests can be seen. Instead of an emphasis on collective aspects of citizenship which imply active membership of, and contribution to, society, there is a shift towards emphasis on individual expectations and claims associated with citizenship. Thus, the role of education in supporting social solidarity is diminished and marginalised. Recently, in the run up to the 2010 General Election, any understanding of social justice in its broader sense seemed to be replaced across the political spectrum by a narrower vision of 'social mobility', implying perhaps an acknowledgement of and acquiescence with the existence of a structurally stratified society.

1.3 Constitutional and legal perspectives

Underlying the various settlements and re-settlements of the school system are not only differing political priorities, but also differing understandings of the democratic expectations attached to schooling. The democratic assumptions and visions which inform different perspectives on education, and its reform, have both substantive and procedural implications.

The expectations of citizenship which apply to education, both individualistic and collective, exist within the context of a set of values associated with democracy. Central to such expectations, and indeed arguably the key characteristic distinguishing democracy from other systems of government, is a promise that no body or office will exercise unlimited or arbitrary power. Crucial to ensuring delivery of this expectation, and to maintaining confidence in it, is an expectation that those exercising public power will do so subject to mechanisms of accountability.

'Accountability' here refers both to being required to give an account of one's actions and being liable to sanction should actions be found to fall short of required standards. It includes mainstream political mechanisms such as elections and parliamentary scrutiny, and the potential for legal challenge, but also, in the modern context, a wide range of devices of scrutiny and participation such as those that Keane (2009, p xxvii) associates with 'monitory democracy'. In addition, consideration must be given to a 'deliberative' aspect of democracy (see, for example, Sunstein, 1990), which emphasises a role for the citizen in formulating and discussing policy options, going beyond the 'citizen-as-consumer' perspective of the individual as simply the recipient of the outcomes of a policy-making process from which they are largely excluded. Though meshing more easily with a Civic Republican approach than the Liberal-Democratic vision which predominates in the British polity, a deliberative approach does incorporate a more expansive view of citizenship, importantly distinguishing between citizen (properly so-called) and the more limited concept of 'citizen-as-consumer', encouraging consideration of non-commodity values, and emphasising collective purposes and values beyond those of individuals. The expectations of deliberative democracy imply an active rather than passive mode of citizenship, and import more explicitly values such as inclusion, equality and rationality, contrasting sharply with what might be termed aggregative approaches (see Young, 2000, chapter 1), in which values to be protected are no more than the sum of the individual interests of the majority at a particular point in time. This 'more ample liberalism' (Stewart, 1983, p 1537), implies that, in Sagoff's terms, 'When society seeks to respond to or act upon its members' opinions, arguments and principled beliefs, it must turn from economic calculation to political deliberation' (Sagoff, 2004, p 15). In the present context this seems to imply looking beyond concerns relating to how individual school admission decisions are taken, acknowledging a need to consider the systemic consequences of school admissions processes.

It is clear that the ever-evolving constitutional settlement implies, assumes, and indeed is centrally premised upon, the existence and effectiveness of mechanisms of accountability. However, in the context of Britain's uncodified constitution, it can sometimes appear difficult to be certain or confident regarding other values which are fundamental to the polity, and as a result resort to weakly defined and/or essentially contested concepts such as 'the Rule of Law', or 'the public interest', or simply 'fairness' is frequently seen. In such a context 'fairness' should be read as referring to both substantive and procedural concerns. As Tomlinson (2005, p 3) has suggested, an emphasis on accountability to the extent that it marginalises discussion of substantive values would be problematic, but if we are to be able to challenge the practice as well as the policy of school admissions, it is vital that effective accountability mechanisms do exist. In an era of relocation of power within school systems, as part of a 're-settlement', it is necessary to be certain that appropriate consideration is given to ensuring that adequate mechanisms of accountability are introduced alongside structural reforms. The relocation of power which was brought about by the introduction of GM schools and CTCs under ERA was subject to criticism in terms of the questionable adequacy of the accountability of those exercising power within these quasi-autonomous institutions (Feintuck, 1994). Though this example is now essentially of historical interest, similar questions should also be asked about the management of Academies and Free Schools in the modern context.

Accountability is central to conceptions of democracy and the constitutional arrangements that we should expect to be involved in the governance of institutions within a liberal-democratic state. Though such expectations can sometimes seem nebulous and slippery, it might be expected that one mechanism of accountability, via legal rules and process, might be clearer than others. In part this is true, in so far as the relevant legal rules can generally be discerned via scrutiny of statutes, secondary legislation and case law. But it should also be made clear that the influence of law, though arguably growing in relation to decision making regarding education, remains marginal in relation to the inception and development of policy, which rests essentially in the political realm. Dale (1989, p 98) describes the settlement under EA44 as having 'cast central government as its guardian, the maker and keeper of the rules, conventions and limits of educational policy making', and while the power co-ordinates have shifted under subsequent arrangements, political power vested in the Executive remains a dominant force, arguably a still more dominant force, in establishing the framework within which debate about education policy will take place. In such a context, law and legal processes do not, and should not be expected to, provide an answer to all the issues which might arise, and must be viewed in their proper context of a tension between individual and collective interests (see Adler et al, 1989, chapter 1).

In part, the limited potential for the law to resolve questions relating to decisions on school admissions relates to a traditionally deferential position adopted by the courts in relation to scrutinising the decision-making powers of the Executive in Britain. Throughout much of the 20th century the British courts adopted a somewhat self-denying and defensive position within the constitution, construing fairly narrowly the scope of their powers to review decisions of public bodies, especially those of central government, under broad headings which came to be known, as summarised by Lord Diplock (in *Council of Civil Service Unions v Minister for the Civil Service* ('*GCHQ*') [1985] AC 374, at 410), as 'illegality, irrationality and procedural impropriety'. Of these heads, the first and especially the third are based upon moderately clear legal rules of interpretation that are reasonably readily explicable. However, they are also rather limited, perhaps being viewed best as re-modelled versions of a historical focus on ensuring simply that bodies did not exceed the powers granted to them by statute or in common law, with an emphasis on adherence to proper procedure, rather than scrutinising actions in relation to any pre-established set of substantive standards. In relation to the second head of review, irrationality, the application on occasion of a rather extreme test of 'reasonableness' (deriving from *Associated Provincial Picture Houses v Wednesbury Corporation* [1948] 1 KB 223; for discussion see Bradley and Ewing, 2011, pp 679–80) in relation to the actions of public bodies led to the likely absence of judicial intervention save in the most egregious examples of abuse. Certainly, courts were more willing to scrutinise the activities of local authorities, whose powers derived almost entirely from statutes, as opposed to the organs of central government, where much greater latitude was offered (see Leigh, 2011, pp 237–46; also Loughlin, 1996). The classic example arises in the case of *Bromley LB v GLC* [1983] AC 768, in which the Greater London Council's (GLC) 'Fares Fair' policy to support the use of public transport across London, part of an electorally mandated manifesto commitment, was outlawed by the courts, ultimately on a narrow construction of the word 'economic' in the relevant legislation. The modern context, in which the pivotal role for local government has been replaced by a combination of central government influence and fragmented local decision making being undertaken in individual schools, poses a particular challenge to the efficacy of a legal system coming from a historical position such as this.

Even so, on the whole, the impact of the law in relation to education generally, and admissions specifically, was restricted by a narrow vision taken by UK courts in relation to their role as guardians of substantive constitutional values, when compared say, with the more dynamic role adopted by the judiciary in a country such as the USA. The British position is partly explained by the still dominant concept or rhetoric of the Supremacy of Parliament, despite what Harden and Lewis (1986, p 57) identify in the modern era as 'the *realpolitik* of executive omnicompetence'. In addition, the absence of as clear a statement of constitutional values and principles as is found, say, in the Bill of Rights and Constitution of the USA, distinguishes Britain from most other democratic states. While the constitutional stability in the UK, arising from a high degree of continuity and incremental change over the last 350 years or more might be a strength, it has also led perhaps to a less clear set of constitutional arrangements and values than is apparent in countries where revolution or 'regime change' following revolution, conquest, or liberation after defeat in war has led to moments of wholesale constitutional change and the necessity to reassess and restate fundamental values.

Through the 1980s and 1990s, UK judges began to develop some new techniques in response to the far greater activities of government than had been in existence in the 19th and early 20th centuries when our 'modern' public law had developed. Doctrines of 'legitimate expectation' (see Jowell, 2011, pp 29–30) and proportionality (see Bradley and Ewing, 2011, pp 680–2; also Lester and Beattie, 2011, p 84) began to emerge, which, though contentious, justified judicial intervention in a somewhat greater range of circumstances. In part a growing presence and understanding of the jurisprudence of European Union law and the European Convention on Human Rights (ECHR) and the judicial bodies that oversee these separate institutions influenced this development. A landmark development which gave the British judiciary a very different route into reviewing the actions of public bodies came with the effective incorporation of the terms of ECHR into UK law via the 1998 Human Rights Act (HRA), permitting the judiciary to scrutinise UK measures for compatibility with ECHR provisions (see Lester and Beattie, 2011). While some might argue that HRA represents a quantum shift in UK public law, it is important not to overestimate its significance in relation to school admissions, where the direct impact of HRA is strictly limited (see Harris, 2007, chapter 2). Specifically, while the Act does confer a right of access to education, this does not extend to securing a place at a particular school.

It is worth noting at this point the very different conclusions adopted pre- and post-HRA by Neville Harris. In 1993, Harris was able to observe how education-specific legislation from 1944 onwards reflected and re-established power relationships within the education system, and particularly in the form of ERA gave effect to a shift in the power relationships as between 'producer' and 'consumer' within the school system. That said, appeal processes, both within the education system and in the courts, tended still to approach the subject from an administrative law perspective which emphasised procedural rather than substantive rights. By 2007, Harris was able to focus on a new body of law relating to education, substantially developed following a change of legal climate brought about by HRA, though perhaps resting more on legislation focused on specific forms of discrimination, relating to race, gender, and disability rather than HRA in itself. This law and practice revolves around claims of diversity and locates education law not only within a traditional approach focused on administrative appeal, but also within debate around substantive human rights and expectations related to diversity and equality. These issues are returned to in particular in Chapters Two and Five in the context of the experience of parents with children with disabilities or SEN in the school admissions process, and more generally in relation to questions of social segregation in schooling. But, it should be noted that individual decisions relating to matters such as school admissions will ultimately have systemic consequences. In Tweedie's terms, 'The consequences of rights in social programmes reach beyond the decision of individual cases and the treatment of individual clients. The focus on individual cases neglects the cumulative effect of case level decisions and procedures' (Tweedie, 1986, p 408), and this important theme will be returned to repeatedly through this book.

Thus, in the immediate post-1944 era, we see a system of education law which asserted the centrality of LEAs to the school system, granting them wide-ranging discretionary powers, with the limited potential for legal appeal and intervention in relation to individual cases reflecting this allocation of power. Post-1988, however, a marked shift can be observed, reflecting an increasing tendency to view school pupils and their parents as 'consumers' with a distinct set of legal expectations that arise from this position. Such a shift reflects the phenomenon noted earlier of the changed orientation of education policy, with the shift in emphasis from the values associated with the welfare state to those of the market economy. More recently, HRA and legislation targeted at inequality and discrimination have served to establish an aspect of the legal system relating to schools which overlays this consumerist perspective with a series of expectations reflecting a vision of human rights. Though this more recent approach could be premised either on a collective or an individualistic aspect, unsurprisingly, given the more general tendency of the British legal system to respond to disputes primarily in individualistic terms, in practice it has tended strongly towards the latter (see Goodie and Wickham, 2002; and Feintuck, 2005).

In relation to school admissions, Harris (2007, p 250) observes how both Conservative and Labour governments, while adhering to a rhetoric of individual parental choice, have been forced to acknowledge the impossibility of ensuring all parents are happy with the outcomes of admissions processes, given the relative popularity or perceived desirability of some schools compared with others. Under the New Labour administration, local appeal processes to panels established by the local admissions authority still existed. The provisions of Part III of the 1998 School Standards and Framework Act established the statutory framework for admissions and appeals with limited scope for further appeal, though with the potential for reference to the Local Government Ombudsman in relation to maladministration, with legal challenge via judicial review still available as a further possibility. These routes of challenge will all be discussed in later chapters. Also added to the admissions landscape via s 25 of the same Act was the Office of the Schools Adjudicator (OSA). Though without a role in relation to individual appeals against admissions decisions, the Schools Adjudicator does have a duty to consider the compliance of school admissions arrangements with the legislation and the School Admissions Code. Interestingly, under the New Labour government's School Admissions Code (DCSF, 2009a, section 4.2), the OSA role could extend to the effect of admission arrangements 'in the context of all the admission arrangements in the area'. The clear implication of this provision is an acknowledgment of systemic consequences of the admissions processes at any one school, or group of schools, for educational provision across a locale, and this acknowledgement requires reflection in any discussion of the competing models which may be employed in allocating school places. This and other potential responses to the fragmentation of pre-existing local systems for school admissions, and the Coalition government's 2012 School Admissions Code, are subjects that will be returned to in later chapters.

What is visible in recent and current admissions arrangements is the significant degree of fragmentation, mirroring the broader approach of education reform post-1988, highlighted in the diminishment of the influence of the local authority in running schools. The disabling of local authorities in this regard is potentially of much more than symbolic significance or partisan political import. Returning to a theme referred to earlier – the fundamental constitutional expectation of accountability in the exercise of public power – it becomes clear that any restructuring of school admission processes must be accompanied by robust mechanisms of accountability for the exercise of power in any forums which will be operating outside the traditional mechanisms of local democratic structures and the processes associated with such public bodies. Here we encounter a clear and concrete example of how procedural concerns can be of considerable constitutional significance in relation to a substantive issue such as allocation of school places. In October 2011, the Administrative Justice and Tribunals Council (AJTC) raised substantial concerns regarding the operation of appeal panels at the level of individual schools. The Report (AJTC, 2011, paras 68–9) noted that the School Admissions Appeal Panels operate outside the management oversight of Her Majesty's Court and Tribunals Service, and that 'concerns remain about the recruitment, operation and independence of these panels, brought about by the locally-based nature of the panels; the absence of procedural rules; and the fact that their operation is subject to Ministerial decisions through statutory Codes of Practice and Secretary of State guidance'. The Report noted also that the former Council on Tribunals had recommended the establishment of a national admission appeals system. Of course, the context in which these concerns arise is not yet fully developed, so the concerns regarding a fragmented appeal systems operating outside democratic and constitutional frameworks may yet acquire still greater significance. As the Report continues,

> Unfortunately, the increasing number of schools that will be outside Local Authority control (including Academies and Free Schools), and which will therefore act as their own admission authorities, is especially troubling. It is uncertain whether such schools will easily be able to find independent and trained panel members to deal with admission appeals properly, impartially and promptly. (AJTC, 2011, para 70)

The concerns regarding accountability which underlie the AJTC's Report, arising from the fragmentation and de-democratisation of the school admissions and appeal processes, should be viewed as of fundamental constitutional concern whatever party political perspective is adopted. Such themes are central to this book, and will be returned to throughout.

1.4 The key lines of argument

The changing legal framework, from 1944 to the present, is clearly of some significance in terms of understanding the issues and priorities implicated in the practices and outcomes of decisions relating to school admissions. The law can be seen to establish the framework, in more detail or less, within which the decisions are taken. While sometimes it is plausible to claim that legislation such as EA44 represented something approaching political consensus or compromise, the legislative framework for education can often be viewed as reflecting and manifesting the political values and preferences of the party dominating the Westminster parliament, and as such can be subject to regular, and on occasion radical and highly controversial, reform.

While the legal framework may be subject to reform, contributing to 're-settlement' of the school system, it can be argued that certain values and expectations transcend individual statutes and case law, and survive above and beyond the vagaries of party politics. What is being suggested here is that there is a set of values that are constitutional in nature and which overarch the legal and political systems. These values include, but extend beyond, the sort of interests protected by instruments associated with human rights protection that can often encourage an approach based on individualistic claims. Rather, the constitutional values, in underpinning the social settlement in which we exist, can be viewed as inherently collective in nature, informing the collectivity that we refer to when we talk of society. These values, likely to be central to both citizenship and human rights discourse, would include expectations of some constructs of fairness and equality of treatment in relation to those activities in which the state is involved. They may take a substantive form, for example requiring that a school place be made available to all children of a certain age, or they may be procedural, relating to the manner in which decisions are taken. But they may also include an expectation of deliberation relating to decisions with systemic consequences as well as proper reasoning in relation to individual cases. Thus it is likely that close scrutiny will reveal what values underlie the system in place, and though the institutional structures associated with decision making may be reformed from time to time, certain fundamentals can be expected to remain in place; deriving directly from the founding expectations of the liberal-democratic state, they should be able to survive such 're-settlements'.

In later chapters, the different approaches adopted under the planning, quasi-market and random allocation approaches to school admissions will each be scrutinised in relation to such fundamental constitutional values. Central to these values is that of accountability, implying both a requirement to give an account of one's actions in decision making, and liability to sanction should one's actions be found to fall short of required standards. In a fragmented school admission environment, detached from the local democratic system, questions of accountability become especially significant. An aspect of the fundamental democratic expectation of ensuring that power be not unlimited, accountability can take on a strongly procedural flavour within a legal system such as Britain's in which the judiciary has not had recourse to a modern constitutional settlement or bill of substantive rights. However, in the requirement to give an account of how decisions are taken, often facilitated via practices related to transparency in decision making, light should be shed on the substantive factors that have been taken into account in reaching decisions. In this sense, procedural accountability can also bear on substance, and the democratic legitimacy of decision making in relation to a public service such as education derives substantially, indeed crucially, from effective accountability. An entirely procedural approach to accountability would be meagre in the extreme; and it can be argued that substantive values for the operation of the school admissions system might be gleaned both from the immanent promises implicitly or explicitly associated with the various approaches, and in the constitutional values which form the context in which the various systems operate.

In the chapters that follow, the various approaches to school admissions will be scrutinised from this perspective. It will already be apparent that the planning model, operating within a historically conventional structure of local government, fits most easily into a traditional view of the accountability mechanisms associated with public administration. But this does not mean that the mechanisms were, in theory or practice, adequate to lend full legitimacy to the processes relating to admissions within this system. The post-1988 admissions system, with its emphasis on responsiveness to quasi-market forces might be thought to replace legitimacy based on traditional visions of accountability with a new model premised on the outcome of individual choices. But fundamental questions remain regarding whether decision-making power in relation to school admissions (and other matters) had in fact been 'privatised', having been removed from traditional mechanisms of accountability which were not replaced with any adequate alternative, leaving doubts over whether the post-1988 system fulfils the fundamental democratic expectation relating to accountability. The third approach identified, relating to the use of random methods in allocation of school places, raises a very different set of issues. Here the problem encountered is that one of the basic methods for holding decision makers to account for their actions is to require them to give the reasons for their decisions, and it is immediately apparent that 'blind chance' is an unusual answer within our scheme of public administration, and one which is not readily amenable to challenge or review on grounds of reasoning. This may be seen as a strength or weakness of the approach but the absence of reasons for decisions, while not necessarily leading to a conclusion that the decision is necessarily 'irrational', gives very little beyond procedural matters for the legal system to engage with in terms of seeking to challenge or review decisions made in this way.

In relation to all three approaches to decision making relating to school admissions, it might be expected that accountability mechanisms would reveal reasoning pertaining to and consistent with a set of specific values and objectives which the political system has incorporated into and prioritised within the then current education system, while also showing adherence to the broader expectations deriving from the constitutional settlement and human rights. In the next chapter an overview will be taken of the changing structures, values and processes relevant to school admissions, while Chapters Three to Six will examine more deeply each of the three different approaches.

TWO

The changing policy context

2.1 A framework of analysis

By tracing the history of themes and variations within reform of the school system over the last 60 years it is possible to shed some light on the underlying tensions which bear upon the current construct of 'the admissions question'. The essential position adopted here is that issues relating to school admissions must be viewed in the context of the broader processes of school reform. Offering a narrative history here of the reforms that have taken place could be useful and interesting, but it is important that this does not become an end in itself, as excellent examples of such work can already be found elsewhere (see Simon, 1991; Carr and Hartnett, 1996; Tomlinson, 2005). Rather, this chapter will focus on those landmarks that signify most clearly the changing power relationships within the system. In practice, this means focusing on the locus of decision-making power and, given the agenda set in the previous chapter, the accountability arrangements relevant to the deployment of such power.

What will become apparent is that, unsurprisingly, it is political debate and political power that has shaped the various settlements and re-settlements pertaining to education policy. It might therefore be expected that this would have also resulted in a set of values that would underpin the arrangements, but the processes of conflict and compromise inherent in the political fray have arguably left the value base much less strongly built than might be desirable. Indeed, the story that will emerge in this chapter is one of repeated compromise, the gravitational pull of pragmatism and the failure of political nerve and conviction in relation to the school system, at least as regards embedding a coherent set of *educational* values. While structural reforms have been introduced with commitment and vigour, much less movement is observable in terms of the introduction of a clear system of fundamental values for schooling. At the broadest level, a shift in emphasis is evident from the 1944 Education Act (EA44) to the 1988 Education Reform Act (ERA) and later, when schooling as a civic and personal good in itself was increasingly superseded by a priority placed on education in the service of the national economic interest. While EA44 may often be presented as denoting consensus over the future of the schooling system, it can also be suggested that it did little to address or challenge underlying class tensions, while simultaneously allowing a privileged position within the system for certain religious groups. Later, active pursuit of the introduction of comprehensive schooling in England under Labour administrations might be considered to represent a failure of nerve, in never managing to grasp the nettle of grammar schools and hence leaving a still divided system. Later still, when the Conservative government introduced its choice and quasi-market reforms from 1988 onwards, though clearly oriented towards competition via market forces, they declined to go quite as far as introducing a fully-fledged voucher system as more radical proponents of reform had advocated.

Writing shortly after the passage of ERA, Ranson (1990, p 1) makes an interesting point about the 1988 reforms, that 'the principal shift in direction – towards public involvement and accountability – is to be acclaimed, although the means chosen are often to be derided'. Though Ranson's point should not perhaps be accepted wholesale or uncritically, given the relatively narrow sector of society engaged, and the limited forms of accountability developed under ERA, it helpfully directs our thoughts to an important set of issues, and indeed hints that the reforms of 1988, like those before and after, may well have contained substantial inconsistencies. All of the programmes of policy reform might be seen as missed opportunities to establish robust long-term settlements in terms of educational values, even if each of the re-settlements imposed a new educational power structure which in some cases had substantial longevity. Such compromises on (or avoidance of) principles relating to educational values might be seen as an acceptable and far from unpredictable situation within the processes and traditions of liberal-democracy, which might be thought to frown upon absolute solutions. On another view, however, this position renders processes of political accountability rather problematic; when the values on which a settlement is established are less than absolute, or lack clarity, it is difficult for the political system to hold to account those who are charged with the management or administration of the system.

In such a situation, an alternative line of accountability via judicial mechanisms might be thought attractive. As will become apparent, legal challenges to decisions relating to education in England often tend to focus on procedural aspects of the decision-making process, and may as a consequence fail to address, amplify or illuminate any inherent values. Like the legislation that results from political debate, there is a tendency for judicial intervention to emphasise structure and procedure rather than substantive values. Though procedural values and questions of structure are clearly relevant in debate about an area of social policy such as education, it is equally clear that they do not represent the full set of issues at stake, potentially marginalising matters of substance. In addition, as noted in Chapter One, legal challenges and judicial decisions are prone in England to be based chiefly on individualistic concepts, responding to the particularities of the instant case rather than broader, perhaps more collective issues underlying a situation. As will be discussed shortly, the provisions of the 1998 Human Rights Act (HRA) relevant to education seem to incorporate, rather than resolve, the tensions between potentially competing values. If we assume for the moment that there are some collective values incorporated within the school system, this situation would be problematic. If the legal system does not respond readily or effectively to collective and value-laden issues involved in schools, and if the political system, essentially conflictual and partisan in nature, tends to produce outcomes as a result of 'winner takes all' political processes occasionally supplemented with reluctant compromise, there is a real risk that development and protection of a coherent value base for the education system might be neglected. Though it is naïve to hope for whole-hearted consensus across the political system on something as inherently contentious as the values that should inform the school system, and allocation of places within it, it does seem reasonable to expect that those who engage in the reform and administration of schooling should believe that there are substantive values in play, and that once the democratic processes (however imperfect), have approved them, these values should be protected via the democratic and legal procedures which form the accountability devices within our constitutional settlement. Doubtless these values will be inherently contestable – such is the nature of political values! But that is not to deny that from time to time a set of values is given the democratic endorsement, and, as will be discussed later, it seems that the value set approved for the school system should be expected to contain, in addition to procedural expectations, a series of substantive and collective values which are constitutionally protected. In the absence of a clear statement of such values, or any long-term agreement as to them, the best that can be attempted is to scrutinise the various settlements against the promises they make for themselves – a process of immanent critique, which is essentially the task undertaken in Chapters Three to Six.

2.2 The role and limits of the law

Beyond the scale of grand policy disputes between political parties or between central and local government relating to reorganisation of schooling, the law is also implicated in resolving individual grievances in relation to the operation of schools on a day-to-day basis, admissions disputes being perhaps the most immediate concern to many parents, though, with matters relating to discipline, exclusions and special educational needs (SEN) coming close behind. As will be discussed in Chapters Three to Five, whether in review by the courts, local appeal processes, Local Government Ombudsmen or Adjudicators, the tendency has been, again, to focus on adherence to proper procedure rather than substantive rights, though this is hardly surprising given the lack of substantive rights granted to parents under the relevant legislation.

A wide range of differing criteria used by admissions authorities across different types of schools adds complexity to a system already hampered by oversubscription for the most popular schools, and Ruff notes a risk that in an area with oversubscribed schools, 'the variety of admissions criteria can result in some children not satisfying the admissions criteria for any of their local schools' (Ruff, 2002, p 199). How different approaches operate will be examined in some detail in Chapters Three and Four, but it is important to stress here that under no circumstances, whether under EA44, the 1980 Education Act (EA80) (see Harris, 1993, pp 130–5), ERA or subsequent legislation, have parental rights in reality amounted to more than a right to express a preference. This situation was expressed most explicitly in EA80, which allowed local education authorities (LEAs) to deny parental choice/ preference for a place at a school which was full to capacity, where compliance with it would 'prejudice the provision of efficient education or the efficient use of resources'. As Harris noted (1993, pp 159–60), the 'open enrolment' provisions of ERA sought to maximise the number of places available at popular schools, and to re-emphasise the significance of parental choice, though, inevitably, as will be seen in Chapter Four, this was far from wholly successful in removing disappointment and dissatisfaction in relation to admissions.

Disputes concerning school admissions under the specific legislation in force relating to schools have since the mid-1970s in particular been subject to an overlay of discourse regarding broader social and human rights. Reflected in the 1975 Sex Discrimination Act and the 1976 Race Relations Act were particular visions of equality which school admissions authorities were required to adhere to, and could form the basis for legal challenge. Of course, racial segregation in education proved a historic landmark in American jurisprudence in the 1950s, when, in *Brown v Board of Education* 347 US 483 (1954) the US Supreme Court found racial separation in schooling to be unlawful. As Harris noted (1993, pp 140–5), however, the UK courts as recently as 1992 were seeking to give priority to parental preference over principles of non-segregation, with the decision in *R v Cleveland County Council ex p Commission for Racial Equality* [1994] ELR 44, CA (see Harris, 2007, p 279) indicating that an LEA which rejected a parental request for transfer of school on grounds of race would be acting in breach of the then current legislation. While the legislation and guidance relating specifically to schools admissions has, of course, altered since that time, of potentially greater significance is the arrival of HRA which incorporated in UK law the provisions of the European Convention on Human Rights (ECHR).

In Harris's terms, 'The right to education is a social right that arises from, and is correlative to, a positive duty to provide a child with learning that, while assumed by society and associated with the principle of parental responsibility, rests with and is carried out by the state' (Harris, 2007, p 35). This statement of the position demonstrates the complexity of the relationships involved in the 'right' to education, encapsulating the potentially very diverse interests or positions of state, society, parent and child. Though established and stated expressly in ECHR, the Universal Declaration of Human Rights, the UN Convention on the Rights of the Child, and the Charter of Fundamental Rights of the European Union, this does not mean that the practical application and interpretation of the 'right' is easy. Article 2 Protocol 1 of ECHR states that nobody must be denied the right to education, but also that 'the State must respect the right of parents to ensure such education and teaching in conformity with their own religious and philosophical convictions'. At the same time, there is scope for debate about the extent to which, and at what age, the children themselves should have a significant voice in expressing their preferences (see Carroll and Walford, 1997; HOL, 2010). In addition, universal and equal access to education for all arises and must be read alongside provisions seeking to support diversity and to outlaw discrimination (ECHR, Article 14). The tensions between the potentially divergent interests and positions should already be apparent, with resulting pressures on the education system, and ultimately the legal system, to resolve such conflict as arises in this context. The way in which human rights legislation plays out in the specific context of school admissions will be considered further in Chapter Five, but for the moment we note Harris's views on 'the difficulties inherent in the realisation of a right of the individual that arises out of a duty on the state that is essentially collectivist in nature'. He concludes that,

> The state has wide social and economic goals to achieve through educational provision to all children. While it undeniably owes a duty to the individual child, in part as a consequence of its assumption of the responsibility for a child's education, these wider social and economic goals predominate. As a consequence, the state's authority and power over education results in a fairly severe curtailment of the individual's rights, and the state education system as a whole is generally fairly unresponsive to the wishes of individual parents or particular groups. (Harris, 2007, p 85)

While human rights provisions can play an important role in signposting the range of, sometimes conflicting, interests that need to be considered in the context of decisions about education, they do not in and of themselves necessarily provide comprehensive answers to the questions that will arise. Rather, it might again be concluded that some clearer and unambiguous statements regarding the orientation, objectives and priorities of the education system itself are needed before reliably authoritative and legitimate answers can be found via the legal system.

2.3 The rise and fall of consensus?

EA44 can be considered remarkable, not least for its longevity. The basic framework it established remained in place, albeit subject to regular amendment, for 40 years; an outcome which we would be unlikely to expect of any equally significant piece of social legislation in the modern era. The fact that it was amended, but continued to form the fundamental basis for education administration throughout the period until 1988, bears testimony to a degree of social and political consensus at the time of its creation and the high level of consultation with the interested institutional and professional parties in the three years it took to draft the Bill. It represented, in Rab Butler's terms, an opportunity to 'harness to the educational system the wartime urge for social reform and greater equality' (quoted in Chitty, 2009, p 19). The longevity of the 1944 framework indicates a degree of continuity in expectations, and relationships between citizen and state throughout much of this period (notwithstanding the 'social revolution' of the 1960s), but without doubt it is also a consequence of the particular style and form of the legislation, establishing a framework rather than seeking to impose a detailed prescription.

As Jones (2003, p 16) observes, quoting the 1943 White Paper that preceded the Act, it 'seemed to promise a free and universal system of education that involved students ... in a common system, based on the idea that the "nature of a child's education should be based on his capacity and promise, not by the circumstances of his parents" '. Yet the way in which this promise was to be fulfilled was not set out in a detailed formula laid down in the primary legislation or prescribed either by parliament or central government. It might be viewed as politically expedient for legislators to avoid any attempt to spell out values on such a contentious issue – expedient, but potentially problematic from the point of view of future scrutiny, challenge and accountability. Rather, the Act itself established a framework in which the precise structures for delivering on these general promises was to be determined primarily through the LEAs, a branch of local government and therefore with some claims to democratic legitimacy, alongside some influence and direction being provided by central government via secondary legislation and guidance, and some influence maintained by the teaching profession as represented by the trade unions. Dale (1989, p 98) quotes Middlemas as referring to 'the 1944 arrangements as a political contract to which all parties, even governments, could be held', though the precise terms of the 'contract' were clearly subject to interpretation and revision, and in the British constitutional schema it was clearly central government that had the ultimate power to vary the terms. That said, the position for much of the 40 years following EA44 is captured by Ranson: 'Whitehall was to promote education, Town and County Hall was to plan and provide, teachers were to nurture the learning process so as to meet the needs of children and wishes of parents' (Ranson, 1990, p 3).

Within this framework, education could, viewed positively, be described as a national service, locally delivered, with the potential for democratic responsiveness to local needs built strongly into the system. While the presence of such responsiveness can be readily considered as a potential strengths, with the benefit of hindsight it is clear that such a system may in time become subject to criticism for creating real or apparent inequalities in provision or outcome across different localities; it is a relatively short step from here to accusations of a 'postcode lottery' in terms of the quality, type or range of schooling available. Likewise, the synergies which existed between a professional group of education administrators in LEAs, whose existence, like the Whitehall civil servants and the teaching professions, continued beyond changes of political administrations, might be deemed a real strength of the post-War settlement. But in an era in which the dominant political philosophy, under the administrations of Thatcher and later Blair, shifted its emphasis from the collective to the individual, from state to market, and from citizen to consumer, and in which corporatist relationships involving the state and the labour movement become de-legitimised, the education system established by the 1944 Act was peculiarly vulnerable to accusations of representing an establishment- and state-centred approach.

From the perspective developed within the radical Conservative school of thought in the 1970s and 1980s, the state's arrangements for schooling in England and Wales could be represented as too prone to local systemic differences. Simultaneously, though, it could be presented, or represented, as a model which was too unresponsive to individual needs or preferences, too heavily controlled by the teaching profession and the local state, and therefore too open to abuse by radical local authorities. Never was there a more obvious target for the proponents of a Thatcherite agenda, who pursued a society based around what they offered as the only two legitimate loci of power – the individual operating within markets, and a strong central state (Gamble, 1994). Inevitably, 'the education establishment' came to be viewed as one of the tribal enemies of proponents of Thatcherism and their successors.

Yet the education system was never quite as monopolised by local bureaucracy and unionised teaching professions as it at first glance appeared. As Jones (2003, pp 16–19) notes, it is possible to identify at least two influences on the education system which rendered it far less monolithic than it might otherwise have seemed, and which both formed part of, and reflected, sources of underlying tensions between meritocratic and egalitarian approaches to schooling, and between central planning and parental preference.

In the 1950s, and the two decades which followed, fundamental questions were raised and ongoing and deep-rooted debate took place about the presence of selective state grammar schools and in particular their role as an obstacle to the comprehensive systems introduced by many LEAs. Selection by ability for entry to grammar school contributed to hiding a potentially more fundamental division within the education system. The 1944 settlement had also left in place a small, but very significant, private education system (that is, independent schools, often referred to, very confusingly for outside observers, as 'public schools'), and if the school one attended had a significant bearing on future chances of entry into the higher echelons of a class-structured society, as it did in England, the ability of those with sufficient financial means to buy places at desirable private schools represented a clear potential for schooling to contribute to reproducing social hierarchy and division. While studies of the significance of private schooling to future life chances abound (see Mellors, 1978; Halsey et el, 1980; Adonis and Pollard, 1997; Beetham and Weir, 1999), it is worth noting some figures emerging from research conducted by the Sutton Trust (2010a, p 2) on the backgrounds of MPs elected to parliament following the General Election of 2010. Of these, over one-third attended independent schools and nine in ten MPs had been to university, with just under a third having studied at Oxford or Cambridge. From this data, the Sutton Trust concluded that 'the creation of the country's social elites is largely the result of educational inequalities exhibited in the school and university system. Children at leading independent and state schools dominate entry to the country's most highly academically selective universities, which in turn produce the lion's share of graduates in the professions' (Sutton Trust, 2010a, p 3). Worth highlighting, in terms of the reflection it offers on life chances and the over-representation of privately educated people in high status activities such as being an MP, is that the percentage of the overall population that is privately educated is only 7% (Independent Schools Council, 2011). Jones (2003, p 17) notes how the question of private schooling was carefully avoided in parliamentary debate about EA44, though the matter was hotly contested outside Westminster by left-wing reformers during the War years (see Simon, 1991, pp 38–46). Though relatively small in terms of overall numbers, it is clear that the private education system, left untouched by EA44, remained, and remains, a significant factor in what is sometimes represented as a settlement of the education system as a whole.

The second source of tension pulling against any monolithic or uniform state-dominated system of schooling was the existence of, and structures for embedding and supporting, schools that are in receipt of public funding but that are established and directed to varying degrees by religious organisations. Religion was structurally engineered into the school system by virtue of state support for denominational schools. Writing in 2007, Harris (2007, p 430) notes that approximately one in three state schools had denominational affiliation with the Church of England, Roman Catholic, Jewish or Muslim faiths as voluntary controlled schools, voluntary aided schools, or foundation schools with a religious character. Despite any trends towards secularism that have flowed in and out of fashion in the period since 1944, it is clear that the existence of such schools, with their distinctive ethos, offers some substantial potential for children to be educated in accordance with the religious beliefs of their parents, in schools which, when compared with their non-denominational counterparts, have been subjected to reduced state/democratic influence. When we consider (as we will briefly later in this chapter, and in Chapter Four) the potential for new Academies and Free Schools to be established by religious groups, the extensive and expanding potential influence of religion over the education system becomes still more apparent. The presence of faith groups as significant players within the school system indicates a degree of a particular form of diversity within the post-1944 settlement, continuing in revised form through to the present. Though representing a particular version of diversity, the religious sector in schooling represents a clear manifestation of tension between expressions of parental preference, and state planning and control of a school system.

To summarise at this point, it might be said that EA44 sidestepped the question of private education, while granting a privileged position for religious beliefs within the state-funded school sector. As arguments regarding meritocracy and egalitarianism, secularism and faith, diversity and uniformity, and between parental preference and state-planning, have taken place over the period since 1944, the private and religious sectors have largely been accepted features of the schooling scene. It is tempting to describe the arrangements in place as representing more-or-less successful examples of compromise, but if compromise is about consciously seeking to reconcile and reach agreement on two conflicting positions, with each party giving ground in order to reach a mutually acceptable and rationally justified solution, it is possible instead to characterise the approach adopted by legislators as being one of avoiding these issues altogether. Yet, as can be seen from the increasingly high-profile clamour of faith groups for their views to be recognised, such causes do form a source of challenge to, and require restatement and re-evaluation of, the fundamental value system on which an educational settlement is based. In this context, 'avoidance' might not be expected to be a wholly successful, viable, legitimate or desirable strategy in the long run.

2.4 'Half way there'

If the place of private schools and religious schools remained relatively marginal to education debate for much of the post-War period, the same certainly could not be said in relation to the place of grammar schools as an obstacle to moves towards a system of comprehensive schooling from the 1960s onwards. As an outcome of a broader struggle relating to the power to organise and reorganise local school systems, the end product could be conceived of as a compromise solution, but this would serve to hide the reality that the outcome was the result of local and national political and legal conflict, rather than any conscious, value-driven compromise process. Just as the 1944 legislation might be viewed as only a partial re-settlement of the school system, given its failure to address the issues relating to private schools and those informed by religious faith, 'Half way there' proved a wholly apt title for Benn and Simon's 1972 report on the process of comprehensivisation.

Arising out of debate regarding the appropriateness and/or effectiveness of the tripartite model of secondary education established by EA44, the well-documented, patchy and incomplete move towards comprehensive schooling started in the 1960s, with the Labour government's Circular 10/1965 seeking to provide some impetus for reorganisation along comprehensive lines. In many areas, a policy of co-existence was adopted, with selective grammar schools continuing alongside schools of comprehensive intake. The existence of 'Direct Grant' schools and the absence of sixth-form provision in early comprehensives denied the spirit of the comprehensive movement from the very start. For these reasons, and more noticeably in some local authority areas than in others, such schools were not necessarily viewed by some parents as the most desirable choice.

Though it would be over-simple to characterise the debate about selection versus comprehensivisation as a straightforward conflict between the Conservative and Labour Parties, this was certainly part of the context. The other part, however, was the relationship between central and local government in Britain. Here we find a curious position, whereby local authority autonomy in England enjoys relatively limited constitutional protection, given its traditional basis in statute rather than any more fundamental constitutional device or document (Loughlin, 2003, pp 548–50). Given the elected basis of local authorities, there was considerable scope for argument over the location of legitimate power to take decisions about the organisation of schools in a scenario where the actions of a local authority did not match the priorities of a central government of a different political persuasion, that sought to impose its will upon local councils.

An example of the arguments underlying such a situation was played out in court in the case of *Secretary of State for Education and Science v Tameside MBC ('Tameside')* [1977] AC 1014 (see Leigh, 2011, p 240) in which the legality of a situation was determined, but in a way that arguably failed to address the underlying question of legitimacy. From the mid-1960s onwards, the Labour Party formally supported a policy of comprehensivisation, seeking to address perceived problems within the school system arising from the selective nature of grammar schools. Rather than pursuing this controversial agenda via legislative means, Labour governments chose to use administrative routes, issuing Circulars in 1965, 1970 and 1974, in an attempt to 'persuade' LEAs to move towards a comprehensive model of schooling. In 1975, Tameside MBC, then Labour controlled, submitted proposals for the abolition of the five grammar schools in that LEA area; a proposal subsequently approved by the Labour Secretary of State. Before the proposals had been fully implemented, however, local elections resulted in Tameside falling under Conservative control, and the local authority submitted fresh proposals which included the retention of the grammar schools. The Secretary of State rejected the new proposals and required the local authority to implement the original plan submitted when under Labour control. The Secretary of State was exercising powers under EA44, s 68, which granted him powers to give such directions as appeared expedient when satisfied that an LEA, school or governing body was acting unreasonably. This decision was challenged by the local authority, and the House of Lords (then the highest court of appeal) found that the Secretary of State's decision had been unlawful – while he might believe that the second proposals were misguided, he had no grounds in law for finding them 'unreasonable' within the definition of this term applied in administrative law. Ultimately, legal determination of such questions turns on the judicial construction of specific statutory terms and a general view of the court's role in reviewing administrative decisions rather than any broader considerations of constitutional principle, or even close scrutiny of attempts at 'government by Circular', whereby more-or-less informal influence is exercised by central government over local authorities. The consequences of the court's decision in *Tameside* was addressed head on by the Labour administration's 1976 Education Act, which granted explicit powers to the Secretary of State to require LEAs to introduce comprehensive schooling, but the project remained incomplete, and the election of a Conservative government in 1979 ended any likelihood of comprehensive schemes being imposed by central government.

In Chapter One the case of *Bromley LB v GLC* [1983] AC 768 was considered, where the court had found that the GLC's local democratic mandate could be overridden by virtue of a particular interpretation of a statutory term, indicating the weak constitutional position of local government in England. In *Tameside*, the court ultimately found in favour of the local authority, but not on grounds of the local democratic mandate or on constitutional grounds, but rather on a narrow, technical interpretation of the Secretary of State's actions. Again, there is little if anything here to provide confidence in or security for the constitutional position of local government. In addition, the government's response to the court's decision in *Tameside*, passing legislation to override directly the court's decision, serves to confirm how constitutional and administrative law will take for granted the superior constitutional authority of central government in a jurisdiction in which local government, though able to claim a democratic mandate, is a creation of statute, and as a result is subject to reform or abolition by statute, and hence is highly vulnerable within the constitutional scheme. In the absence of any statement at a higher constitutional level of general rights, expectations or values attaching to schooling and school admissions, British courts are likely to reach decisions on such matters without regard to educational factors or arguments but rather by reference only to general legal principles. More specifically, it needs to be understood that unless such principles are expressed in statute in explicit terms, the legal process will generally serve to emphasise procedural considerations and to marginalise in legal debate any implicit substantive principles and policies underlying the school system, which might be thought to be the fundamental matter at stake in a case such as *Tameside*.

As a result of frequent changes in the party of government, much more common in the 1960s and 1970s than from 1979 to 2010 (when only one change of party of government took place, in 1997) but also perhaps as a result of lack of political conviction in the Labour Party, 'Half way there' remains an appropriate summary of the comprehensive schools project. The resulting inconsistencies and outcomes, which appeared to be 'unfair' or hard to justify, left it weak and vulnerable in terms of legitimacy. Thus, the system of secondary schooling administered by LEAs remained difficult to defend in the face of persistent reactionary criticism, and some of the more high profile, ambitious, progressive or *avant garde* policies and practices adopted by certain LEAs became easy targets for the political Right and the popular press. These themes will be returned to in Chapter Three, but it was not only from the Right that the education system came under criticism. Seeking to join the critique of the education profession and its methods already cultivated by the earlier right-wing Black Paper writers, the 1976 Ruskin College speech by Labour leader James Callaghan started a 'Great Debate' on education, challenging any possibly complacent assumptions about the roles of education within society. It was within this space that sections of the Conservative Party were able to develop the policies which were first given concrete manifestation in ERA.

2.5 The 1988 Education Reform Act: towards choice and diversity

At the time when the Conservative government came to power in 1979, headed by Margaret Thatcher (a former Secretary of State for Education), the ideology that later became identified as 'Thatcherism' had not been fully developed. In relation to education, while proponents of utilisation of social market methods were prominent, the first Secretary of State for Education under the new administration was Mark Carlisle, whose outlook seemed closer to the more traditional, paternalist wing of the Party. Though the early Conservative legislation did have an apparent intention of enhancing parental choice, via revisions to appeal processes relating to admissions and exclusions, more radical moves considered by some ministers, such as Keith Joseph and Rhodes Boyson, towards a system of 'education vouchers' were left to one side at this stage. Moves towards enhancing parental influence on governing bodies, combined with a range of central government driven initiatives (Feintuck, 1994, p 14), began gradually to shift LEAs out of the central position in education administration. More radical reform was not brought about until the ideological struggle between the more traditional, moderate Tories and the free-market, authoritarian-populist 'Thatcherites' had been won decisively by the latter group. While Keith Joseph, as Secretary of State, after lengthy consideration, had concluded that it would not be possible to deliver such a radical idea as a voucher scheme, the arrival of the politically pragmatic Kenneth Baker as the new Secretary of State for Education in 1986 brought a new era of reality to the delivery of a genuinely Thatcherite prescription for education. In many ways, however, this lacked the decisive simplicity of parents arriving at the school gate, voucher in hand, demanding their 'right' for their child to be educated at that school. Though it also lacked the crucial market element of differential pricing between suppliers (schools) that a fully marketised model might imply and require, the fundamental nature of the reforms introduced in 1988 is unquestionable. Avoiding the risk of policies being scuppered by civil servants, or influenced by those beyond the Thatcherite inner circle, in Maclure's terms,

> What eventually emerged in the election manifesto – and therefore ultimately in the Act – was assembled in secret in the nine months before the 1987 General Election. There was a determined effort not to consult either the DES or the civil servants or chief education officers or

local politicians. Under the discreet eye of Brian Griffiths, head of the Prime Minister's Policy Unit, the outline of a radical reform was set down in bold lines from which there was no going back. The transition from 1944 to 1988 was complete: so complete that there was no longer any need to seek consensus. (Maclure, 1988, p 166)

Whether it is right to characterise the 1944 settlement as consensus has already been questioned, and, as just indicated, the 1988 settlement could have taken an even more radical direction. However, there is, as Maclure indicates, a clear sense in which the inevitability of a fundamental break up of the settlement brought about in 1944 was determined by, even if not completed by, ERA. In particular, the focal place of local government was challenged directly by the package of measures contained in ERA, some of which served to shift powers to school level while others moved powers to central government.

In examining the nature and extent of reform it is necessary at this point to exemplify the two key trends evident within the Act. An 'open admissions' policy was introduced, removing the ability of LEAs to restrict the number of pupils at any one school in order to further any local planning objectives. Funding would follow pupils to schools managed by the headteacher and governors under Local Management of Schools (LMS), while parental 'choice' in relation to schools was to be informed by the publication of league tables rating schools against their pupil's performances in nationally set Standard Assessment Tests (SATs). At the same time, a National Curriculum was introduced, standardising to a previously unprecedented level what was to be taught in core areas of the school curriculum across the whole country. The claim was that this combination of measures would introduce a new and much increased level of accountability for schools, now required to respond to, or pre-empt, parental criticism by demonstrating their levels of performance against national standards.

At the same time as the mechanisms of choice were introduced, informed by greater and more accessible information, channelling money and decision making directly to school-level management, LEAs powers to plan a local system of schools were further eroded by an additional stream of reform. Beyond the 'voice' powers and influence granted to parents via the choice/preference mechanisms just outlined, the power to 'exit' (Hirschman, 1970) the local system was brought about via the ability of schools, subject to parental ballots, to opt out of the local authority system entirely by moving to Grant Maintained (GM) status. Again, the controversies and sometimes brutal campaigns that ensued over opting out are well charted (see Feintuck, 1994). Alongside GM schools came the development of a small number of privately sponsored but chiefly publicly funded City Technology Colleges (CTCs), their structure being the forerunner of the Academies introduced by New Labour and pursued in much revised and accelerated form by the 2010 Coalition government. Though originating from a statutory basis, the presence of the CTCs and the GM schools raised new constitutional questions regarding the effective accountability for these schools that reported to central government and their quasi-autonomous agencies – not the local authority. Meanwhile from 1994, suitably qualified secondary schools could apply for 'specialist' status in technology, language, sports or the arts if they were able to attract substantial private sponsorship, which would then lead to the award of further government grants. Such schools were allowed to select 10% of their intake. In the state sector, a number of school types held early advantages in gaining the benefit of additional government funding on a per pupil basis. The first specialist schools tended to be in more advantaged areas where active parents with good social capital found it relatively easy to generate the necessary private sponsorship (Whitty, 2001; Ball, 2008, pp 123–4). By the time of the 2010 election, 88% of secondary schools carried specialist status. Though the Coalition government discontinued the scheme and placed the funding into the general education budget, the plethora of school structures already in place meant that Tomlinson's (2005, p 103) identification of a hierarchy of 13 kinds of schools, 12 within the state sector, remains a significant indicator.

Diversity of provision can be viewed primarily as an end in itself, or as a simple pre-requisite for the exercise of meaningful choice within the education system. It may be about facilitating and responding to the diverse strengths, needs and wants of society as a collective, or about delivering the ability to choose schools in pursuit of individual self-interest in the context of a market economy, but the absence of a single shared vision of the values underlying pursuit of diversity has, inevitably, produced once again what can be viewed as an uneasy compromise outcome.

In Harris's terms, 'like other universal services to which all are guaranteed access by right, [the provision of education] has a redistributive effect' (Harris, 2007, p 35). While diversity may well be presented as a good in itself, its advantages may be questioned by some if it simultaneously produces results which lead to social, racial or religious segregation within the school system, if the arrangement does not permit or facilitate the equal and/or equitable exercise of choice by all parents, or if it simply tends to confirm and reproduce social hierarchy. The final point is not one of mere assertion – Tomlinson (2005, p 175) is able to quote an OECD report from as long ago as 1994 which concludes that 'a major result of choice policies globally had been to increase social class segregation in schools'. Jenkins et al (2006), in a statistical study assessing data from the OECD's Programme for International Student Assessment, collected in 2002 and 2003, compared social segregation in schools across 27 'rich industrialised' countries and found England to be in the middle of the rankings in contrast to the Nordic countries and Scotland positioned at the least segregated end of the spectrum. The researchers considered that England's position appeared 'surprisingly high for a country with a state school system which is primarily comprehensive'. In the case of England, the researchers argued that 'its segregation is mostly accounted for by unevenness in social background in the state school sector [and that] cross-country differences in segregation are associated with the prevalence of selective choice of pupils by schools' (Jenkins et al, 2006, pp 15 and ii).

There must remain substantial concern about increased diversity in school provision having the potential to serve an agenda which contributes to the reproduction of educational and social separatism, or parallel social arrangements, rather than one of social integration. If popular, oversubscribed schools, with a high degree of autonomy over their admissions arrangements, and not integrated into a locally planned system of schooling, begin to recruit pupils 'in their own image', there is a significant possibility that they will serve to reproduce or increase social and economic inequality. In the terms used by Woods et al (1998, p 212, quoting Walford, 1996), 'Greater diversity "may decrease social integration and mutual understanding" – a possible consequence of more schools serving distinct value communities (through greater religious/philosophical diversity, for instance) or social groupings (as a result of market specialisation, for example).' Put slightly differently, 'A key question is whether more socially advantaged parents place greater emphasis on academic standards. If so, school choice would tend to increase social segregation across schools, with advantaged pupils concentrated in schools with the highest academic standards' (Wilson, 2010, p 11, summarising Burgess et al, 2009). Such a situation would appear likely to be in direct opposition to any agenda of equality of educational opportunity that is found perennially in the rhetoric of debate about schooling. Given the added factor of general preferences for minimising distance of travel to school, especially perhaps for those with less access to private transport, and given the strong relationship between socio-economic status and neighbourhood, the potential for school 'choice' to serve to reproduce or increase social separatism and stratification (see IPPR, 2007, pp 16–17) is re-emphasised. In such a situation, within a 'quasi-market' in schooling (a concept explored further in Chapter Four), a very high premium needs to be placed on ensuring the quality and equity of procedures adopted for admitting or recruiting pupils, given the mutual interest of school and parents in seeking to ensure that the most desirable schools attract the 'most desirable' pupils.

The flagship policies on school diversity just discussed served to reinforce an impression that the era of a local *system* of schools, administered by a LEA, subject to some scrutiny and accountability via mechanisms of local democracy, was to be replaced by a more atomised model, in which schools acted independently, in competition for resources in pursuit of their own perceived institutional self-interest and that of their pupils. In the field of education, local authorities, left only with residual powers in relation to schooling, were faced with the challenge of 'losing an empire and finding a role' (Audit Commission, 1989).

At a more fundamental level still, the reform of the education system in England and Wales brought about in 1988 represents the imposition of a particular 'Thatcherite' vision of society, in which the only apparently legitimate forces are seen to be individuals acting within the market and a strong central state, with all intermediate bodies such as local government, de-legitimised and marginalised (see Gamble, 1994). Of course, the extent to which meaningful choice was delivered to parents remains controversial, as does the possibility that some parents will be much better able to exercise such choice as exists to much greater effect than others, potentially furthering social division and inequality within and via schooling. For some parents, preference rather than choice remained the reality. Despite parents voicing disappointment when their hopes of 'choice' of school had been dashed, the ERA reforms established a foundation that was built upon rather than challenged by the New Labour governments from 1997 onwards, and then extended by the 2010 Coalition government. In Maclure's terms (Maclure, 1988, p ix), ERA 'altered the basic power structure of the education system', and while subsequent reforms have resulted in substantial revisions to the patterns established by ERA, there has been no attempt to change the fundamental pattern of power co-ordinates established in 1988.

2.6 Special educational needs in the admissions context

Specific sets of issues relating to diversity and integration or segregation arise in the context of allocating school places to children identified as having special educational needs (SEN). Questions relating to special education have often appeared daunting due to the myriad legal and technical material (see Harris, 2007, chapter 6; Harris and Riddell, 2011), and there is a tendency in the literature to keep the subject within its own boundaries. But there is clearly a strong case for 'mainstreaming' this subject in the current context, as, given the rapid increase in schools becoming their own admissions authorities, there is a substantial risk that those pupils identified as having SEN, particularly the most complex, will become even more vulnerable in an admissions environment where parents compete for places in oversubscribed secondary schools. Chapters Three to Five deal separately with the two predominant paradigms of running schools, and entry to them, through mechanisms of planning or choice but the discussion of school admissions for those with SEN is better presented as part of an integrated discussion because it usefully encapsulates some of the most pressing issues and themes concerned with school admissions, namely: the lack of an agreed set of values underpinning policies regarding the admission of pupils to state-run schools and the consequent difficulty in arriving at any definitive political resolution in schools policy; the more negative aspects of planning (the interplay of bureaucratic, professional and sectional interests and variation of resources and opportunities across the country); and the negative and unintended outcomes of choice (selection, social segregation and competition).

Currently pupils identified as having disabilities or SEN are 'disproportionately' from disadvantaged backgrounds (Ofsted, 2010); they are more likely to experience discrimination in admissions, especially if schools are their own admissions authorities (NFER, 2006); they are eight times more likely to be excluded from school, they are less likely to be entered for formal examinations, and they face poorer employment prospects (Burchardt, 2005; Crowther, 2011; Roulstone and Prideaux, 2012). It was not until the passing of EA44 that a statutory duty was placed on LEAs to identify and secure appropriate 'treatment' for all affected children in their area and to establish 'special schools' to cater for those whose 'disability is serious'. As EA44, s 33 made clear, the LEA was expected to determine with its professional advisors, the 'treatment' required and 'give parents notice' of its decision; there was no conception that parents should participate in the decision-making process. Further, consistent with the general attitude of the time, government saw parental choice in selecting suitable education for their disabled children as a possibility 'only if compatible with efficient instruction ... and [the] avoidance of unreasonable public expenditure'. Compared to pupils without such needs, the entry criteria of 'compatible with efficient instruction' posed an additional barrier to entry to mainstream schools. Those parents seeking redress if they disagreed with diagnoses and/or 'treatment plans' emanating from the LEA stood little chance of altering the original findings. Between 1951 and 1960, for instance, only four of 4,000 appeal judgments made by local committees set up for the purpose were decided in favour of parents (Roulstone and Prideaux, 2012, p 28, quoting Barnes, 1991).

Assessing the approach taken by LEAs to the identification of appropriate educational opportunities for the disabled and those requiring 'educational treatment', Roulstone and Prideaux's (2012, p 11) view is that 'notions of mild, moderate and severe subnormality were applied uncritically throughout the 1940s through to the early 1980s' and that, in its worst aspects, the placement of children in special schools was seen as a form of 'warehousing'. In the 1970s, LEA provision for children with SEN and disabilities extended in an informal way to include a category of children considered 'disruptive'. Using the statutory route made available in EA44, s 56 to make educational provision for children 'other than at school', two-thirds of LEAs created 'referral units', neatly avoiding the lengthy process of formal pupil assessment (Tomlinson, 1982, p 64).

In 1978 Baroness Warnock, in a government-commissioned report, criticised 'the unacceptable marginalisation' of children with disabilities from mainstream schooling and recommended that the existing 11 medical and quasi-medical categories of disablement be replaced by a broader description of 'special educational needs'. It is important to note, however, that Warnock recommended (and later gained government acceptance for the idea) that children moved into referral units should also be included in the formal categorisation of SEN. At a stroke this incorporated 'non-normative' categories of 'maladjusted' and 'disruptive' pupils where diagnoses sometimes relied not so much on medical precision, but rather on the potentially less objective judgements of teaching and educational professionals (Tomlinson, 1982, pp 56, 65–6). For the first time in a government-sponsored document, the Warnock Report included an aspiration that the role of parents should be seen as active 'partners of professionals' in the work required to assess needs (Todd, 2011, p 69). The Conservative government included many of Warnock's recommendations in the

1981 Education Act, an Act dedicated to making provision 'with respect to children with special educational needs'. Later the 1991 Education Act, s 4 stipulated that a Code of Practice for assisting children with SEN, which included admissions to schools, should be distributed to headteachers and LEAs and that a tribunal should be established for parental appeals. Despite these legislative steps forward, Borsay (2005, p 14) considered that progress towards inclusion in mainstream schools was slow and inhibited by the special interests of the various medical, psychological and teaching professionals involved with assessing needs, who deployed 'spurious scientific criteria for demarcation' and who 'disempowered families in the determination of needs'.

Though Borsay thought that progress towards inclusion was slow, there was a detectable, though gradual, decrease in the number of pupils attending special schools between 1981 and 1991 (Audit Commission, 2002) but this progress stalled in the following decade. In searching for possible reasons for this trend, the Audit Commission (2002) implied that the introduction of LMS in 1988 might provide some explanation for this phenomonen. Presumably, the Audit Commission thought that headteachers and governing bodies with more control on financial decision making may have been influenced by the cost to the school of taking on pupils with disabilities and SEN. Apart from the introduction of LMS, the concurrent increase of GM schools in the period, with such schools becoming their own admissions authorities, could provide an additional explanation. By the mid-1990s concerns were being expressed that 'moves to exclusivity in schooling' (Feintuck, 1994, p 63) meant that some GM schools were prone to weed out 'problem' children. Feintuck (1994, pp 119–20) refers to the example of Barnet London Borough requesting the Secretary of State to investigate a claim that the headteacher of one GM school in its area had pursued a campaign to 'shed problem pupils and those underachieving'.

In 2001, Estelle Morris, Secretary of State for Education and Skills, produced a Code of Practice for Special Educational Needs (DfES, 2001), the fundamental principles of which included the aim that 'the special educational needs of children will normally be met in mainstream schools', that parents 'had a vital role in supporting their child's education', that the 'view of the child should be taken into account' and that such pupils should have 'full access to a broad, balanced and relevant education'. Further, the Code of Practice stated that pupils with statements (the most demanding category of need) should attend mainstream schools unless 'there is overwhelming evidence' why not; such evidence to be based on cost efficiency and impact in the classroom and the consequent level of 'disruption' (Leslie and Skidmore, 2008, p 3). The Labour government also made clear its intention to reduce the dependence on special schools but, although 9,000 places in special schools were shed between 1997 and 2006, Roulstone and Prideaux (2012, p 73, quoting Rustemier and Vaughan, 2005) noted 'an increasing trend in a third of local authorities for increasing segregated provision between 2002 and 2004'.

Labour's creation of the Department for Children, Schools and Families (DCSF) in 2007 and the consequent merging of education and social care in each local authority under the new badge of 'Children's Services' was intended to bring a more holistic approach to policy intervention in the lives of children. This, together with an emphasis on parental choice and the introduction of new 'rights-based' legislation including HRA, the 2005 Disability Discrimination Act (DDA), and the 2010 Equalities Act (replacing major parts of DDA) put in stark legal relief the contradictions created by multiple agencies approaching SEN through 'rights-based' and 'resources-based' approaches. Despite New Labour's wish to increase inclusion, Booth et al highlight the implications of this scenario:

> Policy and legislation relating to disabled children have broadly developed in three core areas of education, care and disability discrimination. The result has been the emergence of parallel approaches to provision for children. In education, the law takes a resource-blind, rights-based approach, and in care, the law takes a resource-led approach, which balances the entitlement to support services with the pressures on local budgets. (Booth et al, 2011, pp 25–6)

As Haines and Ruebain (2011, p 2) argue, this presents a 'paradox [that] goes to the heart of the current system where a "jigsaw of provision" framework both asserts the rights of disabled students, largely aiming towards the goal of inclusive education, and seeks to meet their needs within the established resource-based structure'. As Booth et al (2011, p 24) state, this presents a challenge for public lawyers: 'In the current system parental choice is undermined by the way in which policy frameworks and legislation are structured'.

Despite all the policy and practice interventions in the New Labour period to promote the inclusion of pupils with SEN in mainstream schools, the Lamb Inquiry on *Special educational needs and parental confidence* (DCSF, 2009b) found that a significant proportion of parents still saw the process of identifying needs and securing appropriate school places as 'a battle to get the needs of their children identified and for these to be met'. Lamb also found that 'the legacy of a time when children with SEN were seen as uneducable' pervaded the minds of some professionals; that their attitude was to sideline rather than challenge children to 'be the best they could possibly be'; and that 'too many schools still focus the best teachers on those children with the highest abilities' (DCSF, 2009b, p 2). In a study of classroom practice, Bangs et al (2010, pp 18–19) noted that children with SEN were often seen as 'invisible' in schools and that, in their view, New Labour's introduction of workforce reform had resulted in the tendency for teaching assistants to be assigned to this category of pupil and for them to use 'nurturing' rather than developmental approaches to 'protect' the children in their charge. Additionally, an Ofsted review (2010) of SEN provision considered that having a 'statement' (the strongest of three categories of special educational need) did not guarantee that schools were providing the services required and opined that for the least severe form of special need, defined as 'School Action', as many as half of the pupils identified in this way would not be in this category if better goal setting and improved teaching was provided by schools.

While governments have made efforts through legislation to reduce barriers to entry to English schools for children with SEN and disabilities, an emphasis 'on place over instructional substance' (Gerber, 1996, p 157) does not guarantee equality of outcomes in terms of academic development. That is not to expect that all children reach identical levels of academic achievement but it is to say that an expectation, from the perspective of social justice, is that schools should ensure the maximum possible development for each child in their charge. Christensen and Rizvi (1996) criticise what they see as 'a narrow conception' of social justice based on the right to access mainstream schools and develop their argument as follows:

> Recent reforms in special education have been limited to issues of access and equity. But what has become increasingly clear is that these distributive concerns are not sufficient to account adequately for either contemporary politics of difference, or the various complex ways in which exclusion and discrimination are now practised. ... While access and equity politics enable individuals to gain entry into mainstream institutions, they often leave the institutions themselves unaltered.

In a departure from New Labour's emphasis on inclusion, the Coalition government has re-emphasised the use of choice and diversity policies and, in March 2011, published a Green Paper, *Support and aspiration: a new approach to special educational needs and disability*, with the intention of introducing the proposals as part of the Children and Families Bill early in 2013. The stated ambition of the proposed legislation is to 'provide parents with children with disabilities and SEN 'greater control of the services they use and receive' and 'prevent the unnecessary closure of special schools and remove the bias towards inclusion' (DfE, 2011a, pp 11 and 3). To create more choice, it wishes to extend the range of options for parents through the increase in the number of Academies and the opening of Free Schools. At the time of writing it is not possible to anticipate with certainty the likely effects of the planned legislation. But, from the perspective adopted in this book, questions should be raised about the effects of a further increase in the use of diversity and competition; how a move away from inclusion might affect the legal rights of children who may wish to be educated in a mainstream school when their parents may prefer a special school environment; and also the effect of the government's proposal to publish league tables to show the progress of pupils who are working below Level 1 of the national curriculum which, it could be argued, may place pressure on school management teams in both mainstream and special schools to seek to favour those pupils with the best chance of academic achievement.

The way the state and society treats children and young people with disabilities and SEN raises questions about definitions of equality. In a school admissions' context, securing equality of entry is one thing but ensuring provision of appropriate educational resources post entry in a way that takes into account the principles of social justice is quite another. Later chapters in this book will suggest that the former democratic ambition has not been achieved and so it follows that this must compromise the achievement of the latter. Brighouse (Brighouse et al, 2010, pp 41–4) adopts a notion of a society that seeks to 'benefit the least advantaged'. Here he puts forward a values-based social policy argument that 'it really matters that social institutions should be designed to benefit those who have the lowest prospects for having a flourishing life'. In looking at those who have 'severe disabilities', Brighouse argues that 'whereas within a cohort it is reasonable to see occupational opportunities and opportunities for income and wealth as being zero sum, the opportunity to live a rewarding life is not. The opportunities of the less advantaged … might be enhanced by distributing education in ways that violate the meritocratic conception of educational equality'.

2.7 New Labour, new era?

The 1997 General Election brought New Labour to power with education and social inclusion central to their manifesto. The social democratic aspirations which had been prominent in Labour thinking from the Party's inception had been substantially revised by Tony Blair and his advisers when he became leader of the Labour Party with a modernising agenda in 1994, and though the rhetoric differed substantially from that of the Conservative Party (unsurprisingly considering the strong loyalty to comprehensive education within Labour's rank and file) the practical realities of New Labour in government indicated little diversion from the direction established by ERA.

In his account of New Labour's approach to education policy, Jones (2003, chapter 5) observes how competition between schools was seen as an appropriate and effective driver to best serve economic growth within the British economy via preparing pupils for 'the knowledge economy'. Such an emphasis seems far removed from the historical positions adopted within the (Old) Labour Party in relation to education – Jones contrasts 'one oriented towards equal opportunity and decentralization' with the new approach based around 'choice based reforms and centralization' (Jones, 2003, p 156). The New Labour claim was of having 'synthesized the right's programme of diversity with the left's aspirations to social justice' (Jones, 2003, p 159). Jones describes the resulting system as embodying a belief in 'selective universalism', 'open to students from all social groups, but structured in ways that supported different types of schooling, qualification and outcome, probably according to some important extent to social origin' (Jones, 2003, p 145). Shaw (2007, p 60) considered that Blair's view was that 'A just society was not one which levelled income and wealth but one in which all people could compete equally in the labour market for the positions which conferred the greatest prestige and the highest rewards: in short a meritocratic social order where advancement was based on effort, qualification and ability, not inherited wealth or family background'. Ball indicates that, under New Labour, 'education policy [was] almost entirely subsumed within an overall strategy of public services reform' (Ball, 2008, p 101), a likely implication being that structure and procedure could readily take priority over clearly stated educational aims *per se*. Most striking is how, in contrast to previous (Old) Labour policies for education, New Labour is found to have 'designed a new institutional pattern, and a new symbolic order of schooling in which "ability", "aptitude" and "differentiation" are central principles, and Conservative legacies a powerful influence' (Jones, 2003, p 166).

Central to the New Labour agenda was a continuing emphasis on raising school standards, with the rhetoric promising both the carrot by way of support and the stick by way of pressure. The new government's first significant legislation on education was the extensive 1998 School Standards and Framework Act (SSFA), which, as Tomlinson observes (2005, p 99), in marked distinction to previous Labour emphases, included no reference to 'comprehensive school' or 'comprehensive education'. Beyond a new system of nomenclature for LEA maintained schools ('community', 'voluntary' and 'foundation'), all schools were to have a delegated budget, confirming the emphasis inherited from the Conservatives of viewing schools as individual enterprises. Meanwhile, re-emphasising the Conservative agenda of individuals within the market and a strong central state, marginalising and delegitimising intermediate bodies such as democratically accountable local government, SSFA 'gave the Secretary of State the unprecedented power to intervene in local authorities, effectively ending any notion of democratic pluralism and partnership between central government and locally elected councillors' (Tomlinson, 2005, p 109). Now viewed by New Labour as 'delivery agents of central government policy', LEAs had a statutory duty to secure high standards in their schools, but were 'not to meddle in the day-to-day running of individual schools' (Tomlinson, 2005, p 109, quoting School Standards Minister Stephen Byers). Later, New Labour policy makers applied a statutory duty on local authorities, through s 72 of the 2006 Education and Inspections Act, to 'have regard to … the legislative guidance for intervening in schools causing concern'. In terms of addressing admissions-related issues, SSFA, ss 84–89 required LEAs to establish admissions authorities and to facilitate parental expression of preference, with the establishment of appeals panels and school adjudicators, all operating subject to a Code of Practice on admissions issued by the Secretary of State.

As Tomlinson charts (2005, pp 119–20), New Labour's second term in office saw no slackening of the pace of reform, via primary and secondary legislation, despite reports, including one from the House of Commons Select Committee on Education and Skills (HOC, 2004), which 'cautioned the DfES against introducing further initiatives until earlier ones had been properly evaluated' (Tomlinson, 2005, p 117). Despite any such cautions or concerns, the 2002 Education Act took forward the Academies agenda but more generally the pursuit of further autonomy for individual schools, (Tomlinson, 2005, p 123) while requiring each LEA to have in place a Schools Forum relating to budget planning, and a School Admissions Forum. Such a system implies a range of schools available to enable parents to make practicable choices, and implies informed parental choice as well as effective, fair and accountable mechanisms for the selection and rejection of pupils when demand exceeds supply and the most popular schools become oversubscribed. All of these matters are addressed in Chapters Four and Five, and for the moment it is sufficient to note that many commentators offer evidence pointing towards the extent to which it is specifically sections of the middle classes, who may lack the means to fund private education but who have the knowledge and skills to best make use of the opportunities of choice available, who are most likely to utilise effectively, and benefit from, the mechanisms of choice/ preference provided (Tomlinson, 2005, p 171 et seq).

Some major themes of education reform in the New Labour years coalesced in the context of Academies. In Tomlinson's words (2005, p 127), 'Academies were to be "independent" semi-privatized schools sponsored by business, faiths or voluntary bodies ... partly modelled on the charter schools in the USA'. Quite aside from debates about whether such schools delivered improved pupil performance, or any arguments of principle over the extent to which private commercial bodies and faith groups should have such a prominent role in 'state education', as will be seen in Chapter Four, the policies of Academies on admissions and exclusions, especially in the context of threats of judicial review, persuaded ministers to iron out some of the irregularities of practice caused by the individualised nature of the funding agreements (see Wolfe, 2010, pp 19–38, and Wolfe in interview, quoted in Stevens, 2011, pp 79–80), which had proved highly controversial. With Academies acting as their own 'admissions authority', and seen as desirable and popular in many areas, the policies and practices on selection of pupils in the case of oversubscription had the potential to 'privatise' school admissions in a way which threatened constitutional expectations of accountability in relation to 'public' bodies, and could significantly distort pre-existing local systems of schooling. Notwithstanding Labour's introduction of the School Admissions Code of Practice and the development of Local Admissions Forums, the House of Commons Select Committee on Education and Skills (HOC, 2004) was directly critical of the stated and the covert admission/selection practices utilised by some such oversubscribed schools (Tomlinson, 2005, p 129). Parental choice, the supposed driver of the quasi-market, could often readily be seen to be little more than a right to express a preference, with choice actually being exercised by those responsible for admissions arrangements at the most popular schools.

2.8 The 2010 Coalition – more of the same?

2010 saw the formation of Britain's first Coalition government since the Second World War. Consisting of Conservatives and Liberal Democrats, the Coalition was the result of a hung parliament following the General Election of May that year. It was clear that the new government's policies in education did not differ in direction from that pursued by the Blair governments, and continued to build on the foundations laid in ERA some 22 years earlier. This was hardly a great surprise for anyone who followed the political debates in the 2010 General Election campaign, in which education had, inevitably, a high profile, but there was little to distinguish the policies of the major political parties, all of which sought to operate within the dominant paradigm of choice and diversity as a pathway to raising educational standards, even if there was some variation with regard to the role of local authorities. The new government quickly demonstrated the route it intended to take in relation to schools by emphasising a substantial extension in the Academies programme and announcing its intention to establish 'Free Schools'.

Funded by central government, though supported by a private sponsor, Academies had been introduced by New Labour with the stated aim of addressing the problem of 'failing' schools in deprived areas. The Coalition's Secretary of State for Education, Michael Gove, turned these intentions in the opposite direction, by offering almost immediate transfer to Academy status to schools rated as 'outstanding' by Ofsted. The Academies Act 2010 (AA10) dramatically extended the Academies scheme, allowing maintained schools (secondary, primary and special) to acquire Academy status, allowing those schools currently operating selection policies to continue to do so post-transfer to Academy status. It also empowered the Secretary of State to require schools designated by Ofsted to be in special measures to convert into Academies. At the end of the Labour period in government, 203 Academies had opened. By February 2012, 1,580 such schools were operating in England, the majority being secondary schools, and constituting 45% of that sector (DfE, 2012b). Given the arguments already presented in this chapter, the rapid increase in the number of schools able to control their own admissions raises potential concerns on matters of equity, social justice and accountability.

At the same time as pursuing the extension of the Academies scheme, the Secretary of State, Michael Gove, announced a new programme encouraging the establishment of 'Free Schools', with the first batch of 24 opening in September 2011 (DfE, 2012c). Inspired by the models of

Charter Schools in the US and Free Schools in Sweden, the plan was to encourage businesses, charities, universities, teachers and groups of parents to start new schools, with the government easing bureaucratic requirements in order to assist their foundation. A New Schools Network, granted £500,000 for its first year (letter, Michael Gove to New Schools Network 18 June 2010, DfE, 2012d), was established to offer assistance and advice to those seeking to establish a Free School but 'without the time or experience to set one up' (DfE, 2012e). Described as 'non-profit making, independent, state-funded schools', the DfE states that all Free Schools will 'meet rigorous standards', but also that 'Free Schools will have some additional freedoms. For example, teachers will not necessarily need to have Qualified Teacher Status' (DfE, 2012f). As regards admissions, 'The admissions arrangements of any Free School must be fair and transparent. Free Schools are expected to be open to pupils of all abilities from the area and cannot be academically selective. Free Schools will need to take part in their local coordinated admissions process, and so parents apply for places for their child in the same way as any other local school' (DfE, 2012g).

At the time of writing it is premature to reach conclusions on the extent to which the rapid extension of the Academy scheme, and/or the introduction of Free Schools will have positive or negative impacts on educational outcomes. But what can be fairly concluded is that the effect will be to further marginalise local authorities, and traditional models of local democratic control within education, and to further reduce any sense of a 'system' of local schooling. The same range of issues need to be considered as have been relevant to GM schools, CTCs and existing Academies – as examples of the privatisation of publicly funded education, how successfully do they fare in terms of questions of educational hierarchy and integration, and are they adequately and properly accountable in relation to exercising the powers and pursuing policies, such as on admissions, that they exercise within the freedoms they have been granted?

2.9 Conclusions

Earlier in this chapter it was suggested that ERA, like other major education-related legislation, was a compromise, in the specific sense that it did not make the radical shift to a voucher system properly-so-called, but rather introduced quasi-market forces into schooling. What is clear, with the benefit of more than 20 years' hindsight, is that ERA did fundamentally change the structure of the system of schools in England, moving the main power to organise and reorganise away from the LEA-centred position established in 1944. As will have become apparent in this chapter, though subjected to further reform by Conservative, New Labour and now Coalition governments, the foundations laid down by ERA remain the basis for the education system, with little likelihood of any major diversion from this approach in the foreseeable future. Thus, it can be said that the structural reforms introduced by ERA are firmly established, though no greater clarity as to the fundamental values or objectives of the education system has arisen as a result of ERA or its subsequent variations.

Despite the diversity of types of school developed from 1988, the exercise of choice (or preference) in relation to schooling continues to feel like an unpredictable process for many parents and their children, and indeed is often characterised colloquially as 'a lottery'. On various bases, parents have preferences for some schools over others, and some parents have greater ability than others to exercise such choice effectively. The exercise of such 'choice' has consequences for other parents, and for the ecology of what used to be thought of as a local 'system' of schools. The quasi-market model of ERA continues to influence fundamentally the management of our publicly funded schools. The post-ERA structure of the education system reflects closely the priority placed on individualism within the institutions of the market and a strong central state, in the absence, or marginalisation, of influence for any other intermediate bodies such as the local authorities or the teaching profession. Seen in this light, the reform of the school system since 1988 has been much more about fulfilling a broader vision of the appropriate relationship between citizen and state, rather than anything focused on the purposes of schooling. In Chapter Three, the historical position of LEAs in the context of school admissions will be reviewed, and problems and weaknesses will be observed. Often, the local democratic structures were presented by central government as being an obstacle to reform, and lacking legitimacy as a result of electoral apathy. As such, they were obvious and easy targets for criticism and attack, especially given the weak position of local authorities as statutory creations, within the British constitutional system.

Yet it is pertinent to ask whether certain functions previously located with LEAs have been adequately fulfilled within the structures devised in the wake of their empire being removed. Most obviously, the ability to plan a local system of schools has been fundamentally challenged. Since the reduction of power of LAs in relation to schooling, the establishment of the Funding Agency for Schools and also the School Admissions Forums (though removed as a mandatory requirement in the Coalition government's 2012 School Admissions Code, DfE, 2012a) seemed to reconfirm the need for certain planning functions to be fulfilled, even if they now operate outside of a local democratic framework. There is also no doubt that within our constitutional schema, there remains a requirement that those that exercise public power do so accountably – this is one of the essential distinctions between democracy and other forms of government. It is therefore crucial, if the arrangements in place are to be viewed as constitutionally legitimate, that those who exercise power to manage the budgets of publicly funded schools, and who determine admission to them, are properly accountable. Even where control over public money is 'privatised' into the hands of more-or-less autonomous schools, perhaps with private stakeholders involved in their funding and management, the public nature of the money implies that meaningful accountability over its use must still exist if such activity is to be democratically legitimate. Though subject to justifiable criticism on occasion, it is clear that LEAs, as an aspect of local government, could at least fall back on a claim of legitimacy via the democratic mandate and the political and legal scrutiny to which they could be subjected. In the privatised world of quasi-independent state schools such as Academies and Free Schools, operating outside traditional mechanisms of local democratic control and, as will be discussed in Chapter Four, operating through individual contracts with the Secretary of State, it is crucial that adequate mechanisms of accountability are in place. In addition, Harris (2007, p 1) notes that, 'In the way that it responds to and engages with diversity, public policy has the potential to underscore or reduce social divisions and the tensions that can arise from them'. There are significant doubts (to be returned to in Chapters Four and Five) about whether the policies, as implemented via the legislation from 1988 onwards, have contributed to the reduction of such divisions, or whether the de-systematisation of schooling in local areas, and the exercise of parental preferences within a marketised system has actually encouraged, or has the potential to produce, increased divisions.

What should also be clear is that the reforms from 1988 onwards have been less focused on the establishment and pursuit of educational aims *per se*, and more focused on the structural reform of education as an aspect of much broader reform of public service and society generally. While the desire for improvement of educational standards has been the persistent rhetoric of all governments, the reasoning behind this has not related to education as a good in itself, but rather has been increasingly limited to faith in forces of competition and the pursuit of educational attainment as a function of servicing the economic well-being of the country, and in particular the pursuit of economic growth within 'the knowledge economy'. Servicing the economic needs of the country can certainly be viewed as a legitimate objective for the education system, but it is reasonable to challenge any implicit assumption that it should be the only or pre-eminent objective.

It should be clear from this account of the changes of emphasis in the reform and administration of schooling that there is no single agreed set of values relating to education that has been established for the schooling system in England. Rather, governments of different political persuasions have sought to impose their stamp upon it. While recent governments, from 1979 onwards, have largely pursued a similar approach, this has generally related to structural reform, and a view that sees education as part of a broader social and economic issue, rather than looking at the internal values of schooling itself. This must be understood as the necessary context in which the three very different approaches to school admissions discussed in the chapters which follow must be seen, and, in the absence of any clear or uncontested set of values, each of the systems will, of necessity, be judged primarily against their immanent promises.

THREE

The rise and fall of the planning model

3.1 The 1944 settlement: the backdrop

Under the 1944 Education Act (EA44), for the first time in English history, all parents could access secondary education free of charge for their children up to the age of 15, with all schools funded by the state required to work within the same legislative and regulatory framework. This constituted a step-change from what had been, before 1944, a far more confused and inconsistent environment of educational provision.

In this chapter, it is argued that pre-existing and long-standing attitudes about schooling based on selection and differentiation contributed to the post-war development of a tripartite system of secondary schooling based on the division of pupils into different types of secondary schools via use of a test of intellectual aptitude at age 11; EA44 had suggested but not required that such an approach be adopted. Within the post-1944 system, local authorities had a clear mandate to organise secondary education according to the requirements of the locality and to account to their electorates for their actions. This chapter will track how problematic aspects of the tripartite system, with its promised 'parity of esteem', became increasingly apparent, and how changes in the relationship between central and local government, highlighted on occasion in the form of judicial decisions and legislation, eventually led to a shift in the relative rights and powers of the local authority, of parents and of central government, and laid the ground for a new system of parental 'choice' run through quasi-markets.

In the post-War period up to the 1970s, Dale (1989, p 78) characterised education policy as conducted on 'non-partisan' and even 'bi-partisan' terms, and Ranson (1990, p 5) thought that the 'partnership' established by EA44 'formed a cross party consensus for a generation'. This is testament perhaps not just to a unifying post-War spirit but also to the broadly drawn nature of the powers and structures within the non-prescriptive legislation. This consensual style chimed with a pluralist view of democracy whereby different interest groups engaged with government decision-makers (and each other) in a way that respected other parties' views and values, including democratic values, in order to arrive at a pragmatic and sustainable solution (see for example Dahl, 1967; and Held, 1996). The drafters of EA44 might be thought to have anticipated this approach in envisaging that education would be run through a partnership incorporating a degree of 'creative tension' between local authorities, the central government department, and the teaching profession. Kogan's research (1975, pp 78–124) into the relationship between the five main local authority associations, the Teachers' associations and the Department of Education and Science (DES) suggests an era of constant dialogue and consultation which will seem remote from the more assertive policy-making style of the Thatcher years and thereafter.

Despite general enthusiasm for the reforms introduced by EA44, some educational historians identify a strong legacy of pre-War attitudes influencing its formulation and policy in practice. For instance, Baron et al (1981, pp 59–61) suggested that while the securing of universal provision was a major victory for the Labour Movement, the Act itself was 'constructed in predominantly conservative forms'. This partly arose from the unresolved conflict within the Labour Party between those who wanted a school system based on common access and those who favoured differentiation; in other words, those who wanted to see a system founded on principles of equality and those who wanted a system founded on meritocracy. Baron et al (1981) note that the TUC disputed the desirability of the emerging ideas concerning tripartite education on the grounds that 'social divisions would be maintained by the separation of schooling along the lines of the division of labour'. In similar vein to Baron et al, Simon (1991, p 64) considered that although 'a clear radical policy of educational change' emerged during the Second World War within the Labour movement outside Westminster, the 'democratic programme' was 'beaten back' by the Labour leadership and Conservative backbench influences in the Coalition government of the time. While in 1938, the TUC and many of the teaching unions wanted to see the end to the dual system of church and local authority schools, and the abolition or integration of public schools, the Labour Party in Westminster voted for the 1944 Education Bill without mounting 'serious opposition' to a measure that offered far less than this. Although the system was modified to bring church schools more in line with council schools, the wording of s 8 of the Act 'with its emphasis on the provision of secondary schooling according to the pupils' "ages, abilities and aptitudes" was based on the ideological thinking of the 1930s' and 'implicitly … appeared to legitimate a tripartite structure of secondary schools'. For Simon, EA44 was marked by 'concern for the preservation of the existing social order' and that, 'after all the discussion and legislation, the country emerged with a hierarchical educational structure almost precisely planned and developed in the mid to late nineteenth century' (Simon, 1991, p 53 and pp 73–4). Finch (1984, p 11) also observes how 'features of the system after 1944 were recognisable as continuations of, modifications of, or in some cases reactions against, prewar (*sic*) educational provision', indicating some potential for inconsistency in overall effect. Lawton (1977, p 4) comments on how 'The framework itself was incomplete and the terminology ambiguous', but despite such reservations, like many others, he states that EA44 'was a major step forward in declaring publicly that all children had a right to secondary education'.

For the first time, a Ministry of Education was established, replacing the Board that had existed since 1899, implying a greater degree of central government interest in, and potential influence over, schooling. Wide-ranging powers and duties were delegated to LEAs under the broad terms of s 7, which established that:

> The statutory system of public education shall be organised in three progressive stages to be known as primary education, secondary education, and further education; and it shall be the duty of the local education authority for every area, so far as their powers extend, to contribute towards the spiritual, moral, mental and physical development of the community by securing that efficient education throughout those stages shall be available to meet the needs of the population of their area.

For those involved in education in England at any time from the passing of EA44 until the early 1980s, the settlement formed what may have seemed to be an apparently permanent basis for the administration of schooling. Though non-prescriptive in terms of curriculum, aside from its specific requirement of religious education, EA44 set out clearly the power co-ordinates for decision making relating to schools. At the heart of this structure was the LEA, where lay the power and duty to plan a local system of schooling and put in place appropriate admissions arrangements. While potentially a source of friction, where LEAs of different political persuasions to central government sought to push in different policy directions (as illustrated vividly in the *Tameside* case, discussed in Chapter Two), the allocation of powers to LEAs was premised on the democratic legitimacy deriving from their position as a branch of a locally elected authority, formally established by statute.

While an electoral mandate can be viewed as a source of strength for local authorities, a marked reduction in local political activism, and even in voting at local elections, which was seen over a 40-year period after 1944 ultimately proved to be one of the bases on which politicians began to challenge the legitimacy of local government activity. When the first Thatcher government came to power in 1979, with an agenda based on the free market and on a strong central state, local government proved an obvious and relatively easy target for challenge and reform by the centre. Ultimately, its statutory foundations would not prove strong enough to defend its position within the constitutional schema.

Each LEA exercised power over planning in their area, while headteachers and other senior staff enjoyed considerable professional autonomy (see Bush and Kogan, 1982), with the curriculum chosen to reflect local specifications rather than one prescribed by central government. The statutory framework permitted, indeed seemed designed to permit, a degree of influence, via more or less formal means from central government, in the form of Circulars and Guidance over matters such as selective education, with the response to these at a local level being a political decision for local authorities. Ranson (1990, p 3) describes a 'polycentred' structure in which 'Whitehall was to promote education, Town and County Hall was to plan and provide [and] teachers were to nurture the learning process so as to meet the needs of children and the wishes of parents'. In broadly parallel terms, Dale (1989, p 99) refers to how 'LEAs and their teachers were the major means of putting flesh on the bones of the educational framework implied in the 1944 settlement and were trusted by central government to do so, with its power in reserve to police the boundaries rather than to prescribe the content of education'.

In at least one sense, the intention of EA44 was unambiguously progressive, in that, for the first time in England, 'The Act established the universal right to personal development through education', regardless of the 'material well-being, status and power of [children's] parents' (Ranson, 1990, p 4) Within the broadly drawn parameters established by EA44, central government, LEAs and teaching professionals were granted sufficient authority and autonomy to contribute in partnership to delivering education for the young people for whom the system was intended to benefit. Parents were treated as relevant but not powerful in the new arrangements. The Thatcherite idea of 'parent power' would have seemed incongruous at the time.

Within the Labour Party leadership, there was a view that, released from the requirement to pay fees, the grammar school system would help any able working-class pupil to succeed and that it would be merit not money that would be the basis of entry to selective schools. This notion prevailed as a dominant belief until research reports began to identify a number of problems with the system of selection to grammar schools. For example, the Newsom Report, *Half our future*, published in 1963, concluded that the country was wasting talent because early selection based on the eleven-plus examination was not a reliable predictor of future success. Floud, Halsey and Martin (1957) identified that pupils from working-class backgrounds were losing out to their middle-class compatriots when it came to grammar school entry. In 1969, Douglas reported that 54% of 'upper middle' class children attended grammar schools compared to 11% of 'lower manual' working class children and concluded that 'Those who still support selection, despite the evidence, have to face the fact that they are also supporting rejection – rejection of four out of every five children' (quoted in Mauger, 1970, p 137). Wooldridge found that 'Educational selection was to a disconcerting degree, a process of social selection disguised as academic selection. Instead of determining social stratification, education was effectively validating distinctions which had their origins elsewhere' (Wooldridge, 1996, p 244). In addition, with uneven resourcing, there was a wide variation in the number of grammar school places available in different locales (Walford, 1994, p 20).

The foregoing has indicated that the post-War 'consensus' had limitations, was in itself unhelpful at times to large sections of the school pupil population and that the difficulties in the system were becoming apparent by the early 1960s. Given this backdrop, it is unsurprising therefore that, on occasion, a high degree of tension and conflict was readily observable within the system. The potential for conflict between the 'partners' to be fought out in the courts has already been noted in Chapter Two, in the context of *Tameside*. But the extent of conflict between central and local government also went beyond the specifics of education policy. While attention is paid most often to Thatcher's fight with the teaching unions and the New Right's dislike of 'modern' teaching methods and practices, it was the Conservative government's decision to demand tighter control of local government finance that perhaps most influenced the demise of the power of the LEAs. As Simon (1991, p 480) states: 'A central concern, to dominate through the 1980s, was to cut local government expenditure and, above all, to bring it under control. The ability of local government to fund developments relatively autonomously through raising the rates was a prime target'. In Dale's terms, 'Crudely put, the replacement of Keynes by Friedman as the guiding light of the government's political economic strategy entail[ed] both quantitative and qualitative changes for education'

(Dale, 1989, p 91). The 1980 Local Government, Planning and Land (No 2) Act introduced a new 'block grant' where central government would assess the level of expenditure required to produce a standard level of service and thus constrain the freedom of a local authority to apply funds according to their view of the educational needs of their area. This reform was but one part of a wider and lengthy campaign by the Thatcher governments to transform central-local government relations (see Leach and Stoker, 1988) with the position and functions of LEAs inevitably being changed in the process.

A prolonged teachers' pay dispute, that started in February 1985 and was not resolved until 1987, damaged relations between the profession and their local government employers, resulting ultimately in the imposition of a settlement by central government in the form of the 1987 Teachers' Pay and Conditions Act. More significantly, however, in terms of the agenda for reform, which was to be manifested in the 1988 Education Reform Act (ERA), schooling had become one battleground in a much broader conflict between central and local government. What Maclure (1988, p xi) describes as 'the steady deterioration in the relationship between central and local government' became especially apparent in certain cases where local authorities became briefly dominated by 'the hard Left' in an era of what might be characterised as a central government of an increasingly 'New Right' persuasion.

3.2 Judicial, legislative and constitutional perspectives

The education settlement established by EA44, like any partnership, needed some basis on which disputes could be resolved legitimately as and when they arose, as they inevitably would. But, it can be suggested that the broadly drawn terms of the Act, established in a context of wartime solidarity and some degree of post-War agreement as to aspirations, and which survived relatively unchallenged through the 1950s and 1960s, did not anticipate such conflicts, and were not designed to facilitate their resolution. In such a scenario, and where the political process does not offer a ready or effective solution to such conflict between 'partners', this will necessitate recourse to constitutional and legal mechanisms which underpin and legitimate the relationships to resolve authoritatively such disputes.

What might look strangest to eyes more familiar with the modern, post-1988, position in English schooling, is the absence in the account so far of any significant role or powers for parents in decisions regarding the education of their children. In many areas the strong presence of selective grammar schools meant that the most desirable school places were allocated via academic selection at age 11. For non-selective schools, under EA44, the wishes of parents regarding choice of school for their child were to be taken into account, but, by virtue of s 76, only 'so far as is compatible with the provision of efficient instruction and training and the avoidance of unreasonable expenditure'. Stillman and Maychell (1986) point out that it was never the intention of Rab Butler, the President of the Board of Education to offer parents open-ended choice. In fact, in the White Paper leading to the 1944 Education Bill, no mention was made of parental preferences but pleas by various MPs and Peers that parents should be able, where feasible, to ask that their children be sent to a school of their own religious denomination resulted in s 76, though direct mention of religion was carefully avoided in the wording. Stillman and Maychell quote Butler clarifying the background, in a later debate on education: 'The origin of Section 76 was rather different from what people imagine. ... The object of that settlement and of Section 76 was to give Roman Catholic and Anglican parents a choice of school' (HL Deb, Vol 353, col 590: 10 July 1974). No matter what the intention of s 76 may have been, parents began to challenge admissions decisions made by the LEAs in appeals to ministers. As an indicator of evolving policy, in 1950, the Labour Government released a Manual of Guidance, *Choice of Schools*, in which it suggested three 'strong' parental justifications for asking that their children attend an alternative school, not of the LEA's choosing: denominational, specialist educational provision and linguistic (English or Welsh) reasons, and a further five reasons including medical grounds and single sex school (Stillman and Maychell, 1986, pp 11–12). Walford's (1994, p 25) view on the power differentials present in this arrangement was that the formula of 'parental preferences being taken into consideration' still favoured the LEAs and that 'it should be noted that there was no idea of giving parents complete freedom of choice'. The ability of LEAs to utilise this provision to override the wishes of parents was confirmed by the courts in cases such as *Watt v Kesteven CC* ('*Watt*') [1955] 1 QB 408 and *Cumings v Birkenhead Corporation* ('*Cumings*') [1972] Ch 12. Again, the primacy of the LEA in the 1944 settlement was confirmed, and remained in place until the ideological challenge of free-market individualism came to the fore in Conservative Party thinking during the 1980s.

Two rather different groups of legal cases need to be considered here. One, which will be familiar to many readers, relates to appeals processes against individual decisions relating to school admissions. Though important as regards outcomes for individual children and their parents, and illustrative of questions regarding the administration of admissions processes in particular LEAs, such cases tell us relatively little about broader issues relating to school admissions. The second group consists of judicial review decisions, challenging the lawfulness of the actions of a public body. While relatively few judicial review actions have been brought which bear directly on the question of school admissions, judicial review actions involving local authorities acting in their capacity as an LEA are much more common, and offer important insights into how English law responds to the constitutional and democratic questions about the extent and exercise of power arising in this context. While the overall message might seem likely to be that legal processes have played relatively minor roles in shaping matters relating to school admissions, that in itself would be an important conclusion to reach when considering different approaches, actual or potential, to admissions. For the moment, concentration here will be on the 1944 to 1988 period, with some of the post-ERA landmark decisions to be considered in Chapters Four and Five.

As noted earlier, under EA44, s 76 LEAs were required to give effect to parental wishes concerning their children's education only in so far as such compliance would be 'compatible with the provision of efficient instruction and training and the avoidance of unreasonable public expenditure'. The early landmark cases in this area served primarily to reconfirm the scope of LEA discretion in this regard. *Watt*, concerning whether an LEA was obliged to meet the cost of educating a child in accordance with parental wishes at a private Catholic boarding school, in the absence of any suitable denominational public sector provision, established clearly that the LEA had discretion to have regard to matters beyond those set out in s 76, and that 'it cannot ... be said that a county council is at fault simply because it does not see fit to comply with the parent's wishes'. Subsequently, the court in *Cumings*, again concerning the provision of denominational education, followed this approach, showing, in Harris's terms (Harris, 1993, p 131) that 'in such cases LEAs had virtually unfettered discretion'.

Prior to reform in 1980, no formal avenue of local appeal was required by statute in relation to allocation of school places by a LEA, though, as Birkinshaw (1995, p 114) notes, most LEAs did have ad hoc, and sometimes ill-defined non-statutory appeals procedures in place. But a rather indirect, and somewhat drastic, device of challenge was available via the statutory provisions for the most persistent and determined of parents. If dissatisfied with the place allocated to their child, a parent could refuse to send their child to the school specified by the LEA, in response to which the authority would be likely to issue a School

Attendance Order requiring that the parent ensure that the child attended school. At this point, the LEA was required to accede to the parent's choice of school unless, under EA44, s 37(4), 'the proposed change of school is unreasonable or inexpedient in the interests of the child'. If the LEA was still unwilling to comply with the parental preference, it was open to the parent to challenge the decision on grounds of reasonableness, under s 68, or it was open to the relevant Minister, on reference from the parent, to 'give such direction ... as he thinks fit' under s 37. Clearly, this curious route of challenge involved a dramatic escalation of an individual complaint about allocation of a school place. Though this avenue did serve to increase the chances of parents obtaining a place for their child at their preferred school, the stakes could scarcely be higher than withdrawing a child from school in order to trigger the mechanism of challenge, and though the overall number of challenges increased somewhat in the 1970s, Stillman (1990, p 91) reports that it remained relatively low in relation to the overall number of school places allocated, and the proportionate success rate very low. Such cases did, however, attract a high publicity profile and served as a potential source of embarrassment for both local and central government.

Stillman (1990) identifies how this embarrassment, leading to a perception of a demand for greater parental choice, combined with the onset of a demographic trend towards falling school rolls and hence potential spare capacity in schools, to persuade the Labour government in 1977 of the case for reform. While seeking to preserve the LEAs planning capability via establishing operating capacities for their schools, the government had adopted plans for local appeal mechanisms in relation to admissions, with the exclusion, or at least marginalisation, of the Secretary of State's role in the process. Before these plans were transferred into legislation, the Conservatives won the 1979 General Election and started to place their stamp upon schooling as in so many other aspects of public service delivery in England. The parental choice provisions included in the Conservatives' 1980 Education Act (EA80) built upon the contents of Labour's proposals, which had been halted by the general election, though were somewhat more radical. While support for parental choice was increasingly presented as a good in itself within Conservative rhetoric and policies, and as a force which would serve as a source of pressure to drive up standards in schools (a theme which was to become ever more prominent through the 1980s and then beyond), the realities of demographic trends and pressures on public expenditure resulted in legislation which served as a compromise. While recognising 'the symbolic value of supporting a stronger role for parents in school admissions' (Adler et al, 1989, p 39), those in power 'concluded that the importance of reducing educational expenditure and strengthening the ability of LEAs to manage falling school rolls would have to limit the operation of parental choice' (Adler et al, 1989, p 39). Harris (1993, p 133) quotes the then Secretary of State for Education as stating that 'no choice can ever be absolute', and that 'The balance will have to be made between the choice of a parent and the demands on the local education authorities'.

As one of the present authors has argued elsewhere as regards the relevant provisions of EA80, s 6, 'In explicitly requiring LEAs to allow parents to express a preference, and requiring the LEA to admit the child to the chosen school, the 1980 Act *superficially* gives the appearance of reversing the balance of power' (Feintuck, 1994, p 13, emphasis added). The superficiality of the provisions arises from the substantial exceptions available to LEAs under s 6(3), and in particular s 6(3)(a) whereby parental preference could be overridden if 'compliance with the preference would prejudice the provision of efficient education or the efficient use of resources'. The scope of this exception is substantial, and certainly much broader than that in the comparable 1981 legislation relevant to Scotland (see Adler et al, 1989). In particular, as Stillman (1990, p 93) notes, the discretion given to LEAs under this provision does not distinguish between an individual school and schools as a whole in the locale, allowing LEAs lawfully to interpret the provision to pursue planning agendas designed to protect an individual school, a group or cluster of institutions, or the totality of school provision in their area.

The sense of compromise, or, more negatively 'fudge', incorporated in EA80 is readily apparent. In Maclure's terms, parents' wishes 'were to be taken into account, but not treated as sovereign', but, while apparently prioritising parental rights, in so far as it served to clarify the legal position, the Act could be viewed 'in reality as a way of curbing them more effectively' (Maclure, 1988, p 31). While the net effect of the EA80 provisions was therefore that 'parental preference' rather than 'parental choice' remained the reality, the Act did offer some support for parents via a requirement to publish admissions arrangements and policies, and the statutory requirement to establish local appeals committees.

Section 7 of EA80 required all admissions authorities, LEAs and governing bodies of Voluntary Aided schools, to establish a formal route of appeal for parents, and one certainly more conventional than the pre-existing device of challenge under EA44. The constitution of appeal committees was set out in the requirements of Schedule 2 to the Act, with guidance on practice and procedure drawn up by LEAs in conjunction with, and under the supervision of, the Council on Tribunals. In practice, Appeal Committees were to scrutinise admission decisions in relation to the parental preference, expressed under EA80, s 6, and the arrangements for admissions published by the admissions authority, under s 7. While other relevant matters were to be taken into account, the limitations contained in the terms of s 6(3), as previously discussed, were pivotal. In terms of the conduct of an appeal process, it was possible for parents to complain of maladministration to the Commissioner for Local Administration (the local government ombudsman). Beyond this, the scope for parental complaint to the Secretary of State, seeking the exercise of ministerial power under EA44, ss 68 and/or 99 remained in place. And, given that general principles and rules relevant to the conduct of tribunals (and public bodies more generally), relating to 'natural justice', a fair hearing and indeed 'reasonableness') were applied to Appeal Committees, alleged breach of such requirements could lead a particularly persistent (and wealthy or well-supported) parent to pursue challenge via judicial review. In reality, successful challenges via seeking ministerial intervention or judicial review were relatively rare, certainly in relation to the very large number of school admission decisions taken each year, with Harris (1990, p 159) noting that 'Between 1977 and 1984, only three or four interventions in respect of school allocations were made under s.68'.

Case law did develop, defining and refining the provisions of EA80, but the net effect, as Ruff reports, was that while the 1980 Act was interpreted by some as giving parents the right to choose a school, the reality remained that 'the right was not to choose a school, but the more limited right to express a preference for a school' (Ruff, 2002, p 153 and chapter 3 therein more generally). While the statutory provisions of EA80 established a framework within which admissions decisions had to be taken, they did not represent the totality of factors, which LEAs could take into account when allocating school places. Though EA80 required LEAs to publish their policies on admissions across the area, and individual governing bodies to publish theirs in relation to a specific school, nothing in the Act denied the ability of LEAs to have a policy and apply criteria within it. As the court confirmed, in *R v Greenwich LBC Shadow Education Committee ex p John Ball Primary School* ('*Greenwich*') (1990) LGR 589, decided post-ERA but still applying the EA80 provisions, local admissions policies adopted in relation to admissions may go beyond the factors referred to in s 6, and indeed that 'sibling priority and the proximity rule', relevant in the particular case but also common examples of criteria applied by LEAs, 'are sound and lawful policies whether or not they promote efficient education'.

In a similar vein, in *Choudhury v Governors of Bishop Challoner Roman Catholic Comprehensive School* [1992] 3 All ER 277 the House of Lords found that it was lawful for governors of an oversubscribed school to apply an admissions policy which prioritised children of a particular religious faith. Such policies can remain lawful within legislation on sexual and racial discrimination.

Thus, attempts by parents disappointed at having failed to obtain a place at an oversubscribed school to challenge the lawfulness of policies properly adopted and published by LEAs or governing bodies might often seem doomed to failure. That said the actions and decisions of an LEA, like any other public body, remain subject to the general oversight of the courts via its judicial review function. In general terms, as expressed by the court in *Council of Civil Service Unions v Minister for the Civil Service* ('*GCHQ*') [1985] AC 374, a public body's actions must not be illegal, irrational, procedurally improper, or disproportionate. More or less sophisticated tests have been developed by the British courts in relation to all these heads of review in response to cases involving the exercise of discretion by public bodies, including LEAs and governing bodies of state schools. Of particular potential significance here are cases involving the unlawful 'fettering of discretion' by public bodies, which would be relevant if an LEA was to apply a policy rigidly or dogmatically, and without consideration of exceptions to it (see Bradley and Ewing, 2011, pp 677–8). Equally of importance is the very broad requirement of reasonableness (encapsulated within 'rationality' in the *GCHQ* formula) deriving from the dictum of Lord Greene in *Associated Provincial Picture Houses v Wednesbury Corporation* (1948) 1 KB 223 and often interpreted in such a way as to grant extreme latitude to public bodies, with only the most egregious of decisions falling foul of this requirement.

Harris (2007, p 240) makes some key points in relation to the outcome of one of the judicial review decisions referred to earlier, *Cumings*. He notes how, in the Court of Appeal, in giving the leading judgment, Lord Denning found that 'the LEA was entitled to have regard 'not only to the wishes of the parents of one particular child, but also the wishes of parents of other children and groups of children', and that in this case 'the LEA was having regard to the *generality* of parents who sent their children to Roman Catholic primary schools or other schools' (original emphasis). As Harris notes: 'Lord Denning seemed to believe that the admissions policy was consistent with parental wishes, although not necessarily with those of every single parent, which in his view was not required' (Harris, 2007, p 240). There is an echo here of a position expressed by Dale that state schools 'do not exist ... primarily to serve the needs of any particular cohort of clients but of the community as a whole' (Dale, 1989, p 41). Though Denning's judgement in *Cumings* is bold and far from uncontroversial, and runs markedly counter to the position adopted earlier by the court in *Wood v Ealing LBC* [1967] Ch 364 (see Harris, 2007, p 241), it does provide some judicial support for the proposition 'that section 76 had a collectivist as well as individualist orientation' (Harris, 2007, p 240). Harris draws from this the interesting, and wholly reasonable, if somewhat provocative, conclusion, that 'As the admissions policy was considered acceptable to the generality of parents, the court's decision had the effect of adding legitimacy to a piece of local decision-making by a democratically elected council exercising a discretion conferred by Parliament' (Harris, 2007, p 240).

If, on occasion, some members of the judiciary were prepared to interpret legislation in ways that served to bolster the constitutional position of LEAs and to reflect or give some priority to collective interests in relation to school admission decisions and policies, this was far from a consistent trend, and such views became far less dominant in the 1980s. Harris (2007, p 243) notes a general trend towards increased consumerist expectations relating to state functions, though, in the context of school admissions, the precise relationship between this and any increased expectations arising from EA80 remains unclear. What is abundantly clear, however, is that LEAs, as part of local government, came under ferocious attack in this decade from the New Right and their supporters in the media. The attacks came on a number of fronts, and in combination served to undermine the sense of legitimacy for local government activity in the role of lead partner in schooling policy, which it had played since 1944.

Within the school system, and parental 'choice' in particular, the ideological agenda of the Conservative government would eventually be manifested in ERA. As Stillman (1990, p 94) observes, in response to pressures from central government for economy and efficiency, National Audit Office (NAO, 1986) figures indicate that local authorities took out of commission more than 250,000 school places between 1979 and 1985, with the government seeking a reduction of 430,000 more between 1987 and 1990. While this era was one of falling school rolls 'even with the reduction in children, the reduction in places will inevitably have reduced the amount of choice available' (Stillman, 1990, p 94). Stillman points towards the inherent conflict between government agendas of choice and economy in this context, but demonstrates also how the consequence was the availability of two sticks with which LEAs could then be beaten by central government, given that they were found to have 'neither given parents enough choice nor made enough savings' (Stillman, 1990, p 94)

In addition to provisions previously discussed, EA80 had also introduced the Assisted Places Scheme (APS), with a stated intention of allowing limited, means-tested state funding for access to private schools for children of families who would not otherwise be able to afford it. The scheme is described by Harris (2007, p 245) as 'a very much watered-down version of the voucher concept that had attracted support from right-leaning think tanks such as the Institute of Economic Affairs in the 1960s and 1970s'. 'Watered-down', says Harris (2007, p 248), because 'In the UK, the long tradition of state involvement and the potential political costs of de-nationalising schools limited the potential for privatisation of education to the extent that the voucher idea contemplated'. David Willetts (1997, p 42), in a pre-election document enthusiastically claimed that 'There was a burst of activity in education policy when we introduced the APS in 1980 to enable children from low-income households to enjoy the benefits of an independent education'. It was possible to challenge this claim, with research indicating that, in reality, the APS had the consequence of preserving social hierarchy with research demonstrating that 'the scheme did not in fact, achieve very much for those for whom it was supposedly intended, and that the majority of children who took "assisted places" came from homes with "educationally advantaged" parents' (Chitty, 2009, p 49). Similarly, Jenkins' (2007, p 118) assessment was that 'In the event, most were offspring of distressed middle-class parents and the subsidy merely rescued many lesser public schools from closure'.

Central government incursions during the 1980s into what had previously been the realm of LEAs were not, however, confined to financial matters. Harris (2007, p 95) summarises the range of other interventions, and captures the flavour of the times, as follows:

> The Conservative Government elected in 1979 railed against the uniformity of the comprehensive school system that had developed incrementally during the previous two decades and the increasing political interference in children's education by left-leaning councils and teachers. The Conservative's education reforms sought to wrest control of schools from LEAs, reducing LEA representation, guaranteeing parental representation on school governing bodies and placing governors in charge of their schools and their curriculum policies, human resources and finances.

Indeed there was an ideological assault on LEAs, which were condemned as profligate with public finances, inefficient, hidebound with restrictive practices and doctrinaire in their approach to education.

Wide-ranging justifications, both education-specific and more general, were offered for reducing the power and influence of LEAs. Surveying, even briefly, the range of lines of attack illustrates the rhetoric, and its implementation, of a very different worldview to that which had prevailed in schooling in the previous 40 years. Charting the 10 Education Acts relevant to England and Wales passed by Conservative governments between 1979 and 1988, Tomlinson (2005, p 29-30) summarises the position effectively:

> Influential civil servants in the Department for Education and Science and idiosyncratic secretaries of state for education were able to centralize and consolidate influence over the curriculum, examination and teaching methods and notions of teaching as a profession staffed by responsible and reflexive practitioners came under attack. … The relationship between central and local authorities, school structures and governance, funding and resourcing, curriculum, pedagogy and assessment, modes of inspection, teacher autonomy and training, early years and post-16, ancillary services, relationships with parents, higher education and vocational training, were all to be subject to scrutiny, criticism and legislation.

While 1988 is often viewed as the critical tipping point in the reform of the 1944 settlement of schooling, it is clear that the policy direction was firmly established in the decade preceding that Act. That said, the charge of 'producer domination' of the school system which can be found to underlie many of the Conservative Party's initiatives and policies in the 1980s can also be traced to Labour Prime Minister James Callaghan's Ruskin College speech in 1976, calling for a 'Great Debate' on education, in which he required of teachers that they 'must satisfy the parents and industry that what you are doing meets their requirements and the needs of their children'. With the challenge coming from a Labour Prime Minister, pursued with vigour by post-1979 Conservative administrations, 'There was a recognisable consensus of opinion against the educational establishment. This stretched across political and social divisions to accuse the functionaries of the system of subordinating the needs of children to their own interests and convenience' (Maclure, 1988, p x). This level of distrust by politicians of both major parties of those at the heart of the education system, and the emphasis on responsiveness to the wishes of individual parents and the needs of the industrial economy represents a quantum shift from the approach embodied in the 1944 settlement.

3.3 The constitutional nature of educational change, 1979–88

Writing in 2012, it is remarkable how distant the schooling system that prevailed from 1944 to 1988 can seem. The network established under EA44, of partnerships between powerful LEAs, respected teaching professionals, and central government taking a limited role of oversight, seems truly to come from another age. Even before ERA, the 1980s saw the first substantial steps taken towards the dismantling of this edifice and its replacement with one oriented towards responsiveness to national economic needs and the wishes of individual parents, delivered by a series of quasi-autonomous schools competing with each other for resources, with their performance measured against narrow indicators designed primarily to inform the process of parental choice.

Setting aside for the moment the broader, partisan political context in which education reform takes place, the central accusation levelled against the LEA-centred 1944 settlement by its later critics was that of unresponsiveness to parental wishes, manifested especially, though not exclusively, in relation to decision-making on admissions. Despite the discourse concerning 'parent power', of course there was little attempt to involve parents in deliberative processes to design the features of a new system. Rather, the reforms from ERA onwards were developed and imposed by central government based on assumptions or assertions that these were what parents wanted.

As discussed previously, the basic position, whether under EA44 or EA80, was accurately described by Maclure (1988, p 31) as one in which 'parents' wishes were to be taken into account, but not treated as sovereign'. This situation was the one chosen by the legislators, and embodied in the Acts, and incorporated a clear resolution of the tension or dynamic between local school structures being the result of choices exercised by individual parents, or one in which a local system of schools is developed in accordance with planning priorities determined by a local authority, in pursuit of collective objectives, and subject (in theory at least) to democratic oversight. Even debate about the precise location of education decision making, whether it was local or central government, became marginalised as the emphasis in political debate shifted to the use of market forces to deliver society's needs. The basic position underlying the 1944 settlement, that education policy, of which admissions is a part, seems a legitimate locus for public decision making, especially if viewed as 'education for the common good', became embattled and marginalised.

The nature and range of assaults on the position of the LEA in this settlement, charted earlier in this chapter, has highlighted persistent doubts over the claim that the democratic accountability of LEAs was sufficient to establish legitimacy in this process. In addition, as noted in Chapter Two, the reality was that policy related to schooling became increasingly subject to direct influence from the highest political level, in Downing Street, rather than remaining within the domain of the Department for Education; a trend which, it will be suggested in Chapter Four, has continued to the present. This increasingly partisan approach to questions regarding schooling, in parallel with a broader shift towards prioritising market forces across social fields, formed the basis for a fundamental challenge to the LEA's post-1944 position as the central body in organising and co-ordinating the education system. Interventions such as those requiring LEAs to stop providing free milk to schoolchildren over the age of seven, even where LEAs remained willing to fund it (Byrne, 1994, p 381), were based on financial control of local government, as part of a broader central government economic agenda of constraining public expenditure, rather than any educational or social objectives. Increasingly, accountability of local government became focused upon mechanisms of restraint and audit, with local authority decision making scrutinised in terms of economy, efficiency and effectiveness rather than with a focus on any contribution to social welfare. The risk with such forms of scrutiny is that judgements will likely be made based on information obtained by valuing readily measurable outputs, rather than by measuring what is identified as being of value within an education system. Summarising the situation, Jones et al (2007, p 566) state:

> [C]entral government concerns (justified or otherwise) about the efficiency of local government service provision and about variations in standards within and across councils and across the county, coupled with central government regulation of local authorities and large-scale public apathy when it comes to local elections, raise questions about the continued existence of, and need for, independent local government.

Certainly, participation rates in local elections were small, and getting smaller; in local elections in England in 1994 only 44% voted and a new low was reached in the May 1999 elections when just 30% voted (see Rallings and Thrasher, 1994). Direct engagement in local politics appeared to be increasingly undertaken by an active political class rather than at grass-roots community level. It would be wrong to elide accountability and participation for, as Gray notes: 'Where [participation] differs from accountability can be found in the point that accountability is essentially an internal mechanism, concerned with how the state machinery is organised, while participation is essentially an external mechanism, concerned with the wider relationship of the state with the general public' (Gray, 1994, p 43). But the 'revolution' pursued by the Thatcher administrations, contributing to what Marquand (2004) describes as the decline of the public domain, sought to cut through the niceties of such distinctions. As Gray observes:

> The emphasis fell on accountability to the local electorate, responsiveness to clients, competition, and contracting-out to the private sector, greater efficiency and better management. The underlying theme of this revolutionary process contained a shift in emphasis from *democratic* accountability to *economic* accountability: a concern with the public as economic actors rather than as 'citizens'. (Gray, 1994, p 65, original emphasis)

The shift to a consumerist perspective in relation to 'public' services such as education implied a concomitant and far-reaching emphasis on the individual service user (or, in the case of schooling, their representatives as parents) rather than the collective. This process did not reach its zenith until ERA, discussed in the next chapter, but the values to be given statutory form in ERA were developed within the Conservative Party while in opposition prior to 1979, and then in government. While never challenging overtly the fundamental assumption of the necessity and desirability of universality of schooling as a basic expectation of the welfare state under EA44, the policies which were developed, prioritising mechanisms of individual choice over those of collective planning, in some ways found a ready home in the field of education. For, beyond the vision of education for the common good apparently embodied in the 1944 settlement and to which schools contribute, it is important to note that schools also, in their credentialing function, simultaneously serve to differentiate between pupils. As a result, ambitious parents will always be attracted to schools which, by whatever measure, appear most likely to serve the interests of their child in terms of measurable success in examination results as a gateway to improved future life-chances. In such a situation, some mechanism has to be in place to determine fair school admissions processes, and given the significance of such decisions, it is necessary that decision-making processes in this area be subject to effective mechanisms of accountability. If in the period from 1944 to 1988 identifiable weaknesses in this regard existed in relation to LEAs this would constitute a matter of legitimate concern, though whether the correct response was to disempower LEAs rather than to strengthen the mechanisms of accountability to which they were subject is clearly debatable. The 'New Right' critics of the status quo, who engineered the emphasis on choice and economic accountability, were pursuing a political choice to go down this route rather than pursuing an alternative of subjecting LEAs to more effective accountability via options within pre-existing democratic and constitutional paradigms.

It has to be accepted that some of the criticisms of LEAs will have had foundation. In particular, there is no problem with making the concession to their critics that they were sometimes found to be unresponsive to the wishes of individual parents in respect of choice of school. Any such lack of responsiveness derived from the operation by LEAs of a framework of decision making within a structure established by parliament via statute, subject to electoral scrutiny, incorporating (post-1980) local appeal structures, and overseen by the judicial system. Thus, the key indicators of constitutional accountability were all in place in relation to LEAs; even if parents' wishes were not always met, and teachers and LEAs did not always do what central government wanted, they operated within the system established by parliament, and subject to constitutional and legal norms and mechanisms of accountability. The outcomes of the system resulted from a consciously determined political settlement of the schooling system. It was a system designed to permit planning, prioritisation and management of a local system of schools by a democratically (and legally) accountable local authority. By the 1970s and 1980s, 30 or 40 years after this settlement, unsurprisingly, the model, which had incorporated internal tensions between the parties to the settlement, began to weaken, or the legitimacy of it did. The net effects of the developments up to 1988 considered in this chapter are summarised by Meredith:

> One of the fundamental policies and objects of the Education Act 1944 – the creation of a carefully calculated strategic planning balance of power between the central

> department and LEAs – will have been overturned, to be
> replaced by a system which is lacking in institutional balance,
> seriously defective in terms of the procedural regime under
> which it operates, lacking in openness and accessibility, and,
> above all, lacking in accountability. (Meredith, 1995, p 243)

As will be considered in the next chapter, a political choice was made and given effect in ERA, and subsequent legislation, that the public and collective oriented values of the 1944 settlement were not the values that should be prioritised. A *political* choice was made to give priority to a different set of values. This does not mean that the pre-existing system was defective in democratic or constitutional terms; though probably not perfect, it broadly met basic democratic and constitutional expectations, and was designed with such checks and balances at its heart, and there was no pressing democratic, constitutional or legal reason why LEAs could not have been reformed in such a way as to strengthen the accountability of their operation within the premises of a public- or collectively-oriented education system. It means merely that education was to be reshaped according to a different political world-view, which prioritised the individual and the market over the collective and the state. Whether the post-1988 system fares better or worse against democratic and constitutional norms can only be assessed after close scrutiny of it, a task which is undertaken in the next two chapters.

FOUR

Admissions in a quasi-market system: policy development 1988 to 2012

4.1 Introduction

In this chapter and the next, accounts are given from two different perspectives of the introduction of choice as the organising principle for school admissions. This chapter will examine the political steps, and the legislative and regulatory approaches taken by central government to secure the necessary pre-conditions for establishing choice as the key policy for school admissions: the creation of a quasi-market through school diversity, greater freedom to control admissions at school level, and the limiting of local government powers. This account will be presented in three phases: the phase of policy initiation that started with the Thatcher governments and found its greatest expression in the 1988 Education Reform Act (ERA); the period of continuity and expansion as the market 'baton' was passed to the New Labour reformers in government in the period from 1997 to 2010; and, at the time of writing, the current phase of policy acceleration under the Coalition government. In Chapter Five, the focus will be on the outcomes of school admissions processes within the quasi-market: how parents and pupils have experienced, and how schools and local authorities have reacted to, the realities of choice in admissions, and the responses of the relevant legal and administrative processes when parental preference has come into conflict with school admissions practice.

The move away from the planning mode of school admissions was marked by the Thatcher government's emphasis on the use of market and business models to respond to 'inefficiencies' in the delivery of public services; in essence, how to transfer 'the logic, model and visions of a private company' (Ball, 2008, p 7) to the organisation and distribution of school places. Since 1988, school admissions have been increasingly based upon a quasi-market system predicated on choice, though, as will be demonstrated in this chapter and the next, there is plentiful evidence indicating that the 'choice' is not always, as had been originally promised, that of parental choice of school but rather of school choice of pupil.

From the Conservative government's perspective, the most significant impediment to progressing this agenda was the power of the local authorities in determining the running of schools. In the general context of explaining public service reform, Loughlin (2003, p 521) identifies 'a disintegration of the constitutional tradition of local government'. This disintegration became more pronounced when the Conservatives returned to power in 1979, offering a reform agenda which was:

> Based on the need to shift the boundaries between public and private, to promote market processes over planning techniques, and to assert the principle of consumer sovereignty, the consequences for local government seemed evident. The collectivist delivery arrangements of local services came to be seen as an impediment to the government's objective of extending the sphere of market relations. (Loughlin, 2003, p 541)

For Loughlin, the intention of the government in this period was to remove systematically the traditional welfare state redistributive function of the local authorities and to 'convert collectively organised redistributive services into trading services (or quasi-trading services) and then to subject these trading services – together with local public goods provided by local authorities to market testing' (Loughlin, 2003, p 547). Of course, in an entirely 'pure' market place, the state would have few functions, other than attention to ensuring certainty via legal formalities and process as envisaged in classical interpretations of the liberal state, but in a quasi-market place the state still needed to maintain a significant level of regulation and control (see Le Grand, 1991; Glennerster, 1991; Le Grand and Bartlett, 1993; Sayer, 1995, quoted in Ball, 2008, p 45). In the context of education, as Walford (2000, p 145) notes, 'it was a "quasi-market" rather than a free market, because the state retained many powers over schools and gave itself several new ones'. In a quasi-market in schooling, the issue of admissions moves to centre stage, as not all offerings are of similar quality and not all purchasers are equally skilled in the arts of achieving an offer from the right school for their child. In a 'pure' market place, for instance, in the buying of a product or service, availability of funds may often be the sole determinant to access. In the market place for school places, other assets and behaviours come into play: the leveraging of economic and social capital, the ability to network and influence, or the readiness to complain. Of course, it is right to accept that some parents also deployed such 'assets' during the local authority-based 'planning' period discussed in the previous chapter; however, there might be thought to be a qualitative difference between such behaviour being merely incidental to previous admissions processes as compared to forming an inevitable and fundamental aspect of a quasi-market approach.

4.2 A paradigm shift: legislating for choice and diversity

While the measures introduced in ERA are often presented as a key turning point in the administration of schooling in England, it should be clear from the previous chapter that many of the themes that would be amplified and extended in ERA had been established in the 10 years or so preceding the Act's passage. Even so, it is difficult to overstate the landmark significance of ERA in changing the orientation of the statutory framework for schooling. As Maclure (1988, p ix) suggests, ERA 'altered the basic power structure of the education system', but here the focus will remain on ERA's impact upon practices and decisions relating to admissions to schools, avoiding any attempt to summarise the extensive academic coverage of what is an enormous, wide-ranging, and in some ways contradictory Act.

The reforms contained in ERA introduced into the administration of schooling in England and Wales a series of quasi-market forces replacing a model, which previously, as discussed in Chapter Three, under the settlement established by the 1944 Education Act (EA44) had been based largely upon decision making by local education authorities (LEAs) as a branch of local government. Thus, the basis for claims of legitimacy in decision making relating to schools shifted fundamentally, from being premised on accountability via the democratic expectations attaching to local authorities, to a model of accountability via the exercise of individual (parental) choices within a competitive market framework. The Conservative governments from 1979 to 1997 'in seeking to apply market theories and enhance choice claimed that these would encourage schools to perform better and be more responsive to their consumers, leading to educational practice that better meets consumer needs and preferences' (Woods et al, 1998, p 1). That said, ERA was not exclusively concerned with the diffusion of power to a diverse range of individual schools or 'consumers' within this competitive market framework. Most conspicuously, the introduction for the first time of a national curriculum and associated testing arrangements may be viewed as a strongly centralising measure reflecting a drive towards a standardisation of educational product, even if the suppliers of that product were supposed to have greater financial autonomy. In Tomlinson's analysis, in contrast with EA44, ERA:

> was about individual entrepreneurism and competitiveness, achieved through bringing education into the marketplace by consumer choice. It was not concerned with principles of equity and a fully comprehensive state system. It was also, paradoxically, about increasing the influence of the central state on education by reducing local powers and taking control of what was to be taught in schools. (Tomlinson, 2005, p 51)

This paradox becomes much more explicable when viewed through the lens of Gamble's thesis developed in *The free economy and the strong state* (1994). The removal or rendering impotent of intermediate locations of public power, between the market and central government, is fundamental to the approach identified in Gamble's work, and, as Ball observes, 'In many ways the Conservatives' twin-track approach to reform, centralisation and devolution, coalesced around the weakening, and dismantling of LEA influence' (Ball, 2008, p 78), and indeed in the case of the ILEA, *bête noire* of the Conservative Party and the associated right-wing press, resulted in it being disbanded .

The consequential problems faced by LEAs in practice post-ERA due to their diminished influence amounted to an apparently inescapable spiral of decline, described vividly by the Audit Commission:

> The dispersal of LEA powers encourages central government to take more powers to itself and to use these powers more actively; which in turn limits the scope and incentives for LEAs to act of their own volition; which in turn encourages central government to assume more powers of direction and co-ordination; which in turn reduces the LEA role still further. (Audit Commission, 1996, quoted by Woods et al, 1998, p 203)

Given the extensive literature available discussing the content and consequences of ERA noted in earlier chapters (see for example, Maclure, 1988; Flude and Hammer, 1990; Simon, 1991, chapter 11; Chitty, 2009, chapter 4), it is only necessary here to give the briefest outline of the measures that the Act contained in pursuit of this twin-track agenda. The local competitive market between schools was to be developed via a degree of financial autonomy under the provisions on Local Management of Schools (LMS). In addition, the Open Enrolment (OE) provisions had the apparent intention of increasing parental choice, while funding following pupils provided incentives for schools actively to seek to attract pupils. Meanwhile, for schools looking to achieve a greater degree of autonomy, freed entirely from LEA influence, the opportunity was provided to 'opt out' by seeking Grant Maintained (GM) status. At the same time, the legislation opened up the possibility of development of new schools in the form of City Technology Colleges (CTCs), also independent of the local authority though this time carrying the additional feature of private sponsorship. Although this latter scheme did not result in the anticipated creation of a large number of schools, with a total of only 15 by 1993 (Chitty, 2009, p 102), it did serve as the blueprint (and the legislative foundation) for New Labour's later introduction of the City Academies.

From a constitutional perspective, the passage of ERA through parliament heralded a new and assertive style of decision making by the Executive with many criticisms emanating from the LEAs, the teaching profession and their associations, concerning the lack of time for consultation, coinciding as it did with the summer holidays, and government's refusal to publish the record of the consultation response (Haviland, 1988). The contrast to the three-year consultation and drafting process in preparation for EA44 could not have been more striking. ERA represented, from a constitutional perspective, the transfer of public power from the local authorities to those in charge of individual schools, and as such could be viewed as a substantial privatisation of public decision making. From a democratic or constitutional perspective, such a step would be problematic in the absence of adequate mechanisms being put in place to ensure accountability in the exercise of public powers within the new locations of authority, both in schools by headteachers and governing bodies and in the centralised bureaucracy associated with the curriculum, testing and inspection of schools.

In addition, in as far as the post-ERA structures did empower parents of schoolchildren, it is necessary to think carefully about the capacity in which they act or are treated within these structures. There is, as Ranson (1990, p 14) makes clear, a world of difference, and in constitutional expectations, between being treated as a consumer and as a citizen. While the expectations of a consumer might be relatively tightly defined, and will be expressed exclusively in terms of individual claims or entitlements, those of a citizen, as noted in Chapter One, are likely to be significantly more extensive. Given the notion of citizenship as a collective entity, this must necessarily be viewed and expressed in the more complex context of common interests and the mix of factors and values, which imply both claims and duties for citizens. In Ranson's terms, 'A consumer expresses self-interest registered privately and with uncertain (and often malign) public consequences. A citizen, however, has a concern for the well-being of others as well as the health of society, and both should become the subject of public debate in order to constitute a public choice' (Ranson, 1990, p 15).

A parallel position, though put in slightly different terms, is adopted by Woods et al (1998), extending beyond parents, as parents or as consumers, and beyond the children themselves: 'More widely still, there are other stakeholders – the wider community – who have a legitimate interest in the quality and impact of schools'. Woods et al suggest criteria that could constitute a 'public interest' approach to the administration and delivery of education. While acknowledging the difficulties of this term, they highlight some principles which underlie their discussion in this context: 'fairness, social integration, a concern with raising educational quality and standards, the importance of participation and responsiveness in a democratic society ... [and] ... clarity in policy aims, ... [and] ... aspiring to serve all families equally well and not disadvantaging particular groups or social classes' (Woods et al, 1998, p 199). While recognising fully concerns regarding the difficulty of 'public interest' as a concept (see Feintuck, 2004), it is possible to accept as reasonably uncontroversial their statement of what the contents of such a construct might be in the context of schooling. Interestingly, their list of 'public interest' values are wholly consistent with the factors which might be included in any approach to schooling which prioritises values of citizenship (as opposed to those of consumers) and from such a perspective these values are very much the standards against which it would be proper to judge any system of administration of education, whether within a quasi-market framework or the model of administration centred on LEAs from 1944 to 1988.

Legislation passed in the early 1990s, notably the enormous 1993 Education Act (EA93), built directly on the foundations laid by ERA, and introduced measures designed to encourage more schools to opt-out of LEA control, further marginalising LEAs and indeed putting in place a mechanism to transfer responsibility for admissions to the Funding Agency for Schools (established under the Act) in areas where 75% of schools in an area had acquired GM status. The Conservatives' 1992 White Paper, which prepared the ground for EA93, made clear that 'The Government believes that school autonomy and parental choice – combined with the National Curriculum – are the keys to achieving higher standards in all schools' (DfE, 1992, p 15). The claimed link between parental choice and school standards could not be clearer, while the title of the White Paper, *Choice and Diversity: a new framework for schools*, highlighted the particular extension of, or variation on, the ERA theme that would be pursued during the Major administrations. Echoing the 'Citizen's Charter' initiative, and sharing the thin version of 'citizenship' ('citizen as consumer') on which that was based, parents would exercise choice driven by information in the league tables, while 'schools would increasingly compete for pupils by offering various specialisations' (Chitty, 2009, p 55). The inevitability of parents being drawn towards those schools appearing from league tables to be the most successful was addressed in the White Paper in a manner that might appear remarkably sanguine. Noting that 'Diversity entails a range of choices available to parents', and that 'Parents can choose the school they believe best suited to the particular interests and aptitude of their children' (DfE, 1992, p 10, para 1.49), the White Paper did acknowledge the likelihood of oversubscription:

> The fact that a school is strong in a particular field may increase the demand to attend, but it does not necessarily follow that selective entry criteria have to be imposed by the school. The selection that takes place is parent-driven. The principle of open access remains. As demand to attend increases, so the school may require extra resources to cope with the range of talent available. (DfE, 1992, para 1.47)

Though some financial incentives were offered to encourage schools to pursue a degree of specialisation, the likelihood of ready and immediate funding for infinite expansion of popular schools was always unrealistic from the perspective of public finances. Meanwhile the questionable desirability of ever-larger schools was not addressed, nor the reality that with ever increasing size would likely come detrimental changes to the feel, ethos, success and popularity of such schools, potentially resulting in over-capacity as and when parental demand shifted. The outcomes of parental choice were simply the results of market forces (more properly 'quasi-market forces') and, within Conservative philosophy of the period were to be accepted and indeed encouraged, rather than challenged. The reality of oversubscription is that 'choice of school' by parent tropes readily into 'selection of pupil by the school'; the only remaining question is how that selection is undertaken, whether by formal entry test or by application of other admissions criteria. The essence of the agenda established in the 1992 White Paper, which built directly upon the foundations laid by ERA, was summarised from a critical perspective as 'encouraging selection under a rhetoric of diversity' (Tomlinson, 2005, p 48).

4.3 New Labour: continuity and extension

The first change of party of government since 1979 came in 1997. Anyone expecting or hoping for radical change to the direction of schooling policy on the coming to power of 'New Labour' was quickly to be disappointed. A sense of what was to come occurred earlier in 1994 when Tony Blair, a few days after his election as leader, removed Ann Taylor, the shadow education secretary, and replaced her with the moderniser David Blunkett. Blunkett's biographer, Stephen Pollard (2005, p 204), considered that Taylor was seen as 'representative of a tradition in which Labour's education policy was in thrall to the teaching unions and the educational establishment, of which the NUT was by far the most antediluvian example'. In assessing Blunkett's approach to his new responsibilities as shadow education secretary, Pollard (2005, p 205) thought he had 'a clear choice: adopt a knee-jerk hostility to Conservative reforms simply because they had been introduced by the Conservatives; or build on them. He chose the latter'. Pollard summed up the *realpolitik* of Blair and Blunkett's strategy for education:

> So what if grant-maintained schools were not regarded as socialistically pure? They comprised fewer than 1,000 of the total of 24,000 schools. And why waste so much political energy on the 160 remaining grammar schools? Politically, too, it was suicidal; many of the grant-maintained schools were (quite deliberately) in Conservative-held marginal seats – the very constituencies Labour needed to win. (Pollard, 2005, p 206)

For Chitty (2009, p 61), 'By the time of the 1997 General Election, it was clear that New Labour was committed to pursuing many of the Conservative's more divisive education policies, with education being allowed to continue as a market commodity driven by consumer demands'. With an emphasis on 'standards rather than structures' and on improving resources available for early-years schooling and ensuring a much better degree of access to information technology in all schools, New Labour had developed an approach designed to render their image more palatable in order to attract middle-class voters (Gould, 1998). Early proposals to reform the content and structure of league tables, in an attempt to illustrate 'value-added' by schools rather than simply absolute standards achieved, and a commitment to establish national guidelines on admissions set by the Secretary of State (which will be returned to later in this chapter) were all attractive reforms for those concerned with the outcomes of the provisions of ERA and subsequent legislation affecting schools. The divisive effects of opting-out and the development of CTCs were to be addressed to a degree by a levelling out of funding and the re-labelling of all state schools within one of three categories: 'community schools' (essentially those schools remaining under LEA control), 'voluntary schools' (a re-working of the idea of voluntary aided and controlled schools), and 'foundation schools' (a replacement model for the GM schools). Notwithstanding the rhetoric, it will be apparent that the reforms promised and delivered in New Labour's first years in power did nothing to challenge the hegemony of quasi-market forces in schooling established under the Conservatives. The continuities in direction were striking. The pre-existing emphasis on the central claim of parental choice went unchallenged, with diversity of schooling re-emphasised as a means of meeting the demands of parents.

New Labour's coming to power, and preparations for it, inevitably also re-awakened an issue which had haunted the party throughout the post-War period, and especially through the 1960s and 1970s – the question of grammar schools. Even before the 1997 General Election campaign, it had become clear that the New Labour leadership would not seek to establish a national policy in relation to such schools, and would intend to leave the matter to be settled at a local level, though given the disabled state in which LEAs found themselves by this stage, it took some imagination to see many LEAs in reality having the strength to grasp this nettle. Certainly, as Chitty reports (2009, pp 60–1), overt selection by test for the country's remaining grammar schools remained a source of significant friction and division within the Labour Party in the period around the General Election of 1997, though arguably it was the strong suspicion of covert selection, borne by critics of admissions arrangements under the ERA settlement, that generally drew greater attention.

Without changing the overall direction of education policy in any significant way, the very substantial 1998 School Standards and Framework Act (SSFA) was presented by New Labour as a major reform. Of particular significance for the present study are the provisions of ss 84–89 which established reformed admissions arrangements, with the Secretary of State required to issue a Code of Practice and responsible for the organisation of new admissions authorities, appeals panels and adjudicators, and LEAs required to coordinate the expression of preference by parents, again confirming the relegation of LEAs from principal deliverer of local education to that of, at most, facilitator. These moves were seen by West et al (2004, p 348) as 'an attempt to alleviate problems created by the development of a largely unregulated market, as regards school admissions', and might be thought to bear on what Whitty (2002, p 135) called 'the balance between consumer rights and citizen rights' in this context.

In an interview with one of the authors in 2010, Fiona Millar recollected the atmosphere at the time and considered that there was a lack of detailed awareness at the top of the Labour government about the level of social segregation prevailing in schools:

> "I always think a lot of it was based on the fact that Tony Blair wanted to create a lot of schools like the London Oratory, which was where his children went and he knew it was a grant maintained school which became a foundation school. So, he had this idea that if he gave schools freedom they would all be morphed immediately into The Oratory. He saw a lot of faith schools that were like that but the problem was that he didn't recognise that The Oratory was a highly selective school. The faith schools he was looking at were successful and very good schools but they also had very favourable intakes because they were using their freedoms to create themselves a much more favourable intake." (Stevens, interview transcript, April 2010, previously unpublished section)

Further clarity over the future direction of education policy was achieved via the government's 2001 Green Paper *Building on success: raising standards and promoting diversity* (DfEE, 2001). As Tomlinson (2005, p 121-2) notes, 'The Green Paper criticized comprehensive schools for apparently not developing a "distinctive character and mission", despite the largest ever study of comprehensive schools demonstrating that the schools were responding to their localities and developing a distinctive ethos'. Immediately following their return to power in the June 2001 election, New Labour presented a White Paper, described by Tomlinson (2005, p 122) as a re-write of the Green Paper, with a strong emphasis on diversity, but a diverse system in which 'schools differ markedly from each other in the particular contribution they choose to make but are equally excellent in giving their students a broad curriculum'. The lengthy 2002 Education Act (EA02) that followed required *inter alia* each LEA to establish a School Admissions Forum, while the Secretary of State was granted powers to permit greater autonomy to innovate for schools viewed as successful, and also to close schools seen as under-performing. Certainly, the 2001 White Paper affirmed greater diversity and specialisation as the core organising features within secondary schooling. In addition to pursuing an expansion of schools supported by faith groups or other private sponsors, the specialist schools were to be supplemented by advanced specialist schools expected to be still more innovative, and Beacon Schools with a mission to establish and spread good practice among other schools within their area.

These measures further cemented the use of markets in education and, indeed, even a change of the party of government at this stage would have been unlikely to bring about substantial policy alteration in this regard, given how Chitty (2009, p 81) points to a high degree of overlap between the two main parties' stated education policies by 2004, which both featured centrally the twin pillars of choice and diversity. Some distinction was still possible, in particular as regards Conservative policy moving increasingly towards state funding for new schools to be run by faith groups, parents and private companies (the development of Free Schools post-2010 is discussed later in this chapter) which, in Chitty's terms (Chitty, 2009, p 83), 'would finally break the link between state funding and state provision' of schooling. It was clear that, as Thatcher had claimed of so much of her social and economic policy agenda, in relation to schooling, there would be 'no turning back' from the direction set in ERA, and indeed the policy was now beginning to be extended to its logical conclusion.

The direction of policy intent would be reconfirmed in the White Paper *Higher standards, better schools for all: more choice for parents and pupils* (DfES, 2005) leading to the 2006 Education and Inspections Act (EIA06). In addition to further extending the new Academies programme, any existing secondary school could establish its own Trust or link to an existing one, in conjunction with business, faith groups, charities, parent or community groups, or universities. Chitty (2009, p 86) observes that the White Paper referred to how 'the local authority must move from being a provider of education to being its local commissioner and the champion of parent choice', with all new schools to be self-governing foundation schools. The government's intention to move towards greater independence caused consternation and Blair was forced to make concessions including strengthening the Admissions Code to include the banning of selection interviews (other than for boarders). Despite this, the general direction of the legislation remained unchanged and led to a backbench rebellion as it passed through its parliamentary stages (see Shaw, 2007, pp 70–73). In an interview with one of the authors in 2010, Fiona Millar, in her capacity as Chair of Comprehensive Future, considered that Blair had overreached himself and exaggerated his intentions:

> "Well, I suppose the White Paper appeared to be a step too far for a lot of people, I think. It really was a step too far because the spin, and the introduction, talked about making every school an independent state school. Actually, that wasn't quite the intention. I mean it was a massive error of propaganda on the part of the government to spin it in that way because the trust schools were not independent state schools, they were always going to be maintained state schools. …
>
> But then they created the impression that every school would become an independent state school and I think the Labour backbenchers just stood up and said: Enough is enough – it will end up with chaos, which is what the Tories are proposing: lots of tiny little independent entities operating as little islands on their own with no community 'glue' binding them together and so I think that's why you got the alternative White Paper group with a hundred or so Labour MPs and that got whittled down and 30-something rebelled, didn't they? They had to rely on Tory support to get the Bill through." (Millar, quoted in Stevens, 2011, p 174)

Although, as a direct consequence of the negotiations over EIA06, the Schools Adjudicator was to take on a somewhat more pro-active role in overseeing the Admissions Code than had been initially envisaged, the fundamental risk highlighted by many critics remained that identified by Chitty: 'Informal selection could still be practised and would undoubtedly continue because of the intense competition between schools for the most "motivated" pupils, the weak and vulnerable inevitably suffering in the process' (Chitty, 2009, p 88).

The replacement of Tony Blair as Prime Minister by Gordon Brown and the appointment of Ed Balls as Secretary of State for the newly created Department for Children, Schools and Families (DCSF) saw a detectable reorientation of priorities and a lessening in the policy dominance of choice and diversity in schools. Instead, Brown and

Balls renewed attempts to address school failure through the National Challenge programme resulting in a reduction of 'failing' schools from 600 in 2007 to 237 in 2009. Seldon and Lodge (2010, p 420) considered that it was Balls who was always the keener to move away from the Blairite agenda, whereas 'Brown wished to keep in with the Blairites and right-wing press, who wanted to keep to the standards agenda'. No matter the differences between Brown and Balls, Seldon and Lodge quoted an interviewee close to the Department who considered that 'choice, diversity, Academies and empowering parents were all down played or mothballed'. When it came to the Academies, Seldon and Lodge (2010, p 420) considered that Balls reoriented their placement more in line with the original criteria. Vernon Coaker MP reinforced this opinion in an interview with one of the authors of this book in March 2011. As Minister of State for Schools and Learners in the DCSF between 2009 and 2010, he thought that the emphasis on Academies as a solution for underperforming schools in deprived areas only came back into serious focus during the Ed Balls period. In Vernon Coaker's view, this was the only viable route if the policy was to reflect the political and social aims of the Labour Party:

> "So, all the way through the New Labour period we freed up the system a bit within a comprehensive education system but how do we do that in a way that drives change, drives attainment and drives improvement without letting the market rip in a way which may benefit some but does so at the disadvantage of others?
>
> [....] How do you reconcile that with the Labour Party's political and social objectives of equality of opportunity? Which is then when you come particularly to look at underperformance and using the Academies to drive [out] that underperformance and linking that with social deprivation and trying to raise attainment in some of the most difficult and challenging areas.
>
> [...] When Ed Balls comes in, in 2007, then a real sense that we've got the Academies programme and we will now put an emphasis on ensuring that the Academies are put into the poorest areas and the weakest performing schools and we use that to drive change." (Vernon Coaker MP, quoted in Stevens, 2011, p 141)

The Brown–Balls period between 2007 and 2010 signalled a rare interlude when the emphasis of policy relating to schools shifted somewhat away from the priorities of choice and diversity but, as will be seen, these policies were by then so firmly entrenched at a systemic level that it was simple, as the Coalition government has demonstrated, to resume the Blairite agenda at an accelerated pace when the political will to do so re-emerged after the 2010 General Election.

One of the continuities across the whole period of the Labour government was a commitment to better regulate school admissions. The first Code of Practice for School Admissions was introduced in 1999, for the first time raising the status of central government's directions to local authorities, headteachers and governing bodies including those schools that were their own admissions authorities from 'guidance' to 'mandatory requirement'. A rather weak form of wording in the 1999 Code (DfEE, 1999) and the updated version in 2003 (DfES, 2003) requiring those in charge of admissions to 'have regard to' the Code was strengthened in 2007 (DfES, 2007) to 'act in accordance with' the mandatory aspects of the Code. While concerns could legitimately be raised regarding the use of secondary powers (subject to less scrutiny than primary legislation) to address such important policy objectives, it is difficult to argue against any attempt to pursue the problem targeted by this particular measure; increasing evidence (Taylor et al, 2001; Gorard et al, 2003; West et al, 2003, 2004; Coldron et al, 2008) including research commissioned by the DfES (Coldron et al, 2002) indicated that a significant minority of schools, and in particular those which were their own admissions authorities, had been abusing both the letter and the spirit of the Code.

The Labour government's final attempt at codification of the guidance on admissions came in the form of the 2009 School Admissions Code and the parallel School Admissions Appeal Code. The overall orientation and objectives of the 2009 Code were set out by reference to 'the Government's aim to create a schools system shaped by parents which delivers excellence and equity, developing the talents and potential of every child, regardless of their background; a system where all parents feel they have the same opportunities to apply for the schools they want for their child' (para 1.3). The emphasis on parental role and influence alongside the reference to 'the talents and potential of every child' could be viewed as a curious juxtaposition of the post- ERA individualist language of choice and a harking back to the language of the 1944 settlement.

An intention was spelt out in para 2.4 in terms of 'achieving good practice in setting oversubscription criteria for admissions authorities to help them ensure that their admission arrangements are fair to all children and their families, and promote social equity rather than working against it'. In pursuit of this agenda, the Code restated existing provisions requiring the admission of children with statements of special educational needs who have a school named in their statement, and giving the highest priority in oversubscription criteria for children in care. It also explicitly ruled out the use of interviews (for either parents or children) to determine the extent to which an application met oversubscription criteria (avoiding the use of subjective criteria, perhaps based on social class) and stated that 'it is important that schools ... policies, for example on school uniform, do not inadvertently discourage applications from poorer families'. Beyond these specific groups or examples, while not aiming to set out an exhaustive or comprehensive list of criteria, the Code, in an attempt to achieve a transparent system, prohibited 'unfair' oversubscription criteria. The list of 'unfair' criteria that an admissions authority was not permitted to use was extensive, running to some 15 criteria and variations. Of these, perhaps the most important prohibition for present purposes was that of giving priority based on 'Parents' willingness to give practical support to the ethos of the school', including 'asking parents to commit themselves or their child to taking part in activities outside of normal school hours', and/or 'asking parents to support the school financially or in any other practical way'. The Code went on to prohibit priority being given 'according to the occupational, financial or marital status of parents' or 'according to the educational achievement or background of their parents', and, while permitting consideration of religious activities for designated faith schools with this as one of their published criteria (though faith-based oversubscription criteria were addressed separately within the Code), outlawed giving priority according to children's, or their parents', 'particular interests, specialist knowledge or hobbies'. It is clear that, as with the measure prohibiting interviewing applicant children and parents to assess the extent to which criteria have been met, such measures were targeted at avoiding the tendency noted by some critics for popular and successful schools to attract pupils 'in their own image' by reference to culture or nebulous concepts like 'ethos'.

At one level, clarification of acceptable criteria and the express statement of the prohibition of some of the more subjective or 'softer' criteria should be welcomed and such steps might be expected to go some way towards avoiding the crudest mechanisms of covert selection against subjective criteria, such as those noted earlier in relation to early GM schools and CTCs, which may serve the interests of the school and those pupils selected, but may do a disservice to those children rejected and/or wider expectations of equality of treatment across the community. But such prohibitions do not in and of themselves address underlying social differences in ability or likelihood to engage to maximum effectiveness in the processes for obtaining places at oversubscribed schools. That said, in fairness to any attempts or desires on the part of New Labour to address inequalities in this context, para 1 of the Code refers directly to the fact that 'Attainment gaps between children of different social backgrounds are not closing fast enough and too many of the children facing the greatest disadvantages are also attending the poorest performing schools', and later states that 'A fair system is one that provides parents with clear information about admissions and supports those parents who find it hardest to understand the system'. Despite such concerns being stated explicitly, doubts may exist over whether the substantive content of the Code could be expected to address such matters in any meaningful manner, and it remains possible that more direct interventions, perhaps along the lines of the 'pupil premium' introduced by the 2010 Coalition, if properly managed and overseen, might be more effective in this regard.

While the introduction and the further strengthening of the School Admissions Code undertaken during the Labour period in office was welcomed by the teaching unions, the wider educational academic establishment, interest groups supporting state education and the Parliamentary Labour Party, the Code in itself was no guarantee that 'fairness' would occur on the ground. Following extensive research analysing the nature of the adherence, or otherwise, of various types of schools to the successive Codes of Practice during the New Labour period, Noden and West (2009, p 41), building on Le Grand's distinction between 'procedural' and 'substantive' fairness in public policy (Le Grand, 1982), concluded that, despite increased improvements in, and policing of, the School Admissions Code, it could not on its own deliver fair admissions decisions. Three reasons were presented for this conclusion: that 'substantively fair outcomes cannot be achieved simply through procedurally fair mechanisms'; that 'one unintended consequence of operating an increasingly more demanding compliance regime is that more schools may inadvertently fall foul of changes in admissions rules'; and, that 'fairness may be diminished and local arrangements undermined without any individual admission authority breaking the School Admissions Code'. Research by Noden and West (2009, p 36) into the effectiveness of the changes introduced through the 2006 Education and Inspections Act and the 2007 School Admissions Code noted that while they 'had been effective in reducing the use of criteria that may advantage some groups of pupils over others ... further issues relating to the admissions process ... suggest legislative changes are needed if some groups of pupils are not to be discriminated against'. The researchers noted above recommended that local authorities should have greater control of school admissions, including over those schools acting as their own admissions authorities. In particular, it was recommended that it was the overall coordination of oversubscription criteria that was a crucial prerequisite to fair admissions. In the next section, the Coalition government's activity in relation to school admissions policy will be outlined, and it will be apparent that key changes introduced by the 2011 Education Act (EA11) and the 2012 School Admissions Code (DfE, 2012a) suggest little likelihood of movement towards implementing such recommendations.

4.4 The Coalition: policy acceleration, 2010–12

The first change of party of government since 1997, and only the second since 1979, came about following the 2010 General Election, when a government was formed by the coalition of Conservatives led by David Cameron, and Liberal Democrats under Nick Clegg. The political intentions for schools policy were quickly made clear. *The Guardian* (19 July 2010) reported that Michael Gove, the Coalition government's Secretary of State for Education, considered that he was a 'born-again Blairite' and 'wanted to build on plans by [the] former prime minister … to give Academy freedoms to every school'. Gove sought to address the political drift in education policy post-Blair and 'restore freedoms removed from Academies under Gordon Brown'. In a television interview, Gove suggested that there had been a definite split within the Labour Party over its education policy and that he was sympathetic to Blair's emphasis on freedom for schools: 'the problem that we've had over the past 13 years is too much bureaucratic control. People attack me for increasing the Academy programme, doing what Tony Blair wanted to do and what Ed [Balls] and his team managed to prevent in the last five years' (BBC1, *The Andrew Marr Show*, 21 November 2010).

On 25 May 2010, in the Queen's Speech, outlining the new government's programme of legislation, it was announced that 'Legislation will be introduced to enable more schools to achieve Academy status and give them greater freedom over the curriculum'. The ensuing Academies Bill was passed rapidly through Parliament in 77 days using fast-track powers normally reserved for national emergencies. For the Labour Party, now in opposition, Gove's intentions concerning the future direction of the English school system were plain, and Ed Balls, in his then capacity as shadow Secretary of State for Education, in the debates conducted during the second reading of the Academies Bill, outlined his fears of the consequences:

> "The policy is not an extension or even radical reshaping; it is a complete perversion of the Academies programme. ... It is not a progressive policy for education in the 21st century, but a return to the old grant-maintained school system of the 1990s. It will not break the link between poverty and deprivation, but entrench that unfairness even further, with extra resources and support going not to those who need it most, but those who are already ahead. My very real fear is that that will lead to not only chaos and confusion, but deep unfairness and a return to a two-tier education policy as the Secretary of State clears local authorities out of the way and then encourages a chaotic free market in school places." (*Hansard*, 2 June 2010, column 477)

Vernon Coaker MP, then Labour's shadow Minister for Education, in summarising the Labour Party's opposition to the Academies Bill during the second reading and in particular the invitation for 'excellent' schools to become Academies, summarised his view of the likely effects if this policy was adopted:

> "The Bill will visit huge injustice upon those children and young people who most need our help, and it will cause confusion, worry and division for children and parents everywhere. By elevating market mores above the core principles of co-operation, accountability, democracy and equality, it will turn our education system into a dismal experiment in educational Darwinism. It will be the survival of the fittest and the demise of the rest. ...
>
> Education is a public good, not a private commodity. The common good is served not when parents and children engage with schools as consumers pursuing relative advantage, but when they act as citizens and partners who understand their crucial role as co-creators of learning and educational success." (*Hansard*, 19 July 2010, column 125)

Building on the 1996 Education Act, s 482, as amended by EA02, s 65, the 2010 Academies Act (AA10) allows maintained schools (primary and special, as well as secondary) to apply to become Academies with an automatic 'fast-track' route provided for schools rated 'outstanding' by Ofsted. It empowers the Secretary of State to require schools eligible for intervention to convert into Academies and designates Academy trusts as having 'exempt charity status'. This status exempts Academies from the requirement to register with the Charity Commission and the associated need to present an annual summary of accounts. Instead, they were to report to the Young People's Learning Agency. This Agency was later abolished under EA11, s 66 and its functions are assumed by the new Education Funding Agency from 1 April 2012. At the same time, any schools transferring to Academy status which previously selected pupils will be allowed to continue to do so. By the end of August 2010, the National Audit Office (NAO) reported a total of 203 Academies already open (under previous provisions), with a rapid expansion of the sector envisaged. Given this prospect, the NAO report observes tersely, 'Academies' greater independence brings risks to governance and accountability which will need to be managed as the Programme expands' (NAO, 2010, Summary, para 17). A further extension of the programme was announced in November 2010 – all schools rated 'good' or 'satisfactory' were to be allowed to apply for Academy status, though the latter would need to form a partnership with a school identified as 'outstanding' .

Many of the governing bodies and headteachers deciding to opt for Academy status admitted that the main attraction was the access to the 10% extra funding kept back by local authorities for services for all local schools. Mike Baker (*The Guardian*, 19 April 2011) reported on a poll conducted by the Association of School and College Leaders indicating that '72% [of their membership] said they believed it would help them financially. Only 24% were motivated by dissatisfaction with their local authority'. Baker's conclusion was that: 'soon a tipping point will be reached and even the most reluctant will feel unable to resist the tide. Once several large secondary schools have converted, taking their share of central budgets, a local authority will be unable to support those schools that remain ...', with the likely consequence ultimately being the departure from local authority influence of all, or a vast majority of secondary schools.

Featuring in AA10 as a further expansion of choice and diversity policies, was the provision for the development of 'Free Schools', sharing many of the liberties enjoyed by Academies including freedom from local authority influence, freedom relating to curriculum, freedom to establish pay and conditions for staff, and to vary term dates and length of school day. On 18 June 2010, Gove announced the proposals in a letter to Chief Executives and Directors of Children's Services, informing them that: 'These schools aim to tackle educational inequality and give greater powers to parents and pupils to choose a good school. Under the plans it will be easier for groups to set up new schools in areas where there is parental demand as part of our shared objectives to improve parental choice and quality'. Inevitably, critics of the Free Schools proposal were able to point to the same concerns regarding accountability and privatisation of power relevant to Academies. Meanwhile, though Gove was reported as presenting the Free Schools policy as being likely to 'help close the achievement gap between rich and poor' (*BBC News*, 18 June 2010), there were signs of unhappiness from the Liberal Democrat Coalition partners. At their annual conference in Liverpool in September 2010, some party members put forward and 'overwhelmingly' carried a motion that Free Schools risked 'increasing social divisiveness and inequity in a system that is already unfair'; that it would 'worsen educational outcomes for the majority of children' and 'further complicate admissions procedures' (*BBC News*, 20 September 2010).

The DfE's Equality Assessment document (DfE, 2010a, point 82) relating to the Free Schools provisions in AA10, dismissed a 2003 study suggesting that Free Schools in Sweden had increased social segregation as 'anecdotal'. A study by Susanne Wiborg (2010) from the Institute of Education, however, presents evidence that social segregation had indeed increased. In examining a number of studies (including Bunar, 2008 and 2009 and the Swedish National Agency for Education (Skolverket), 2006) conducted on Swedish Free Schools over the past 17 years, Wiborg found that on the level of their positive impact on pupil achievement, the evidence was inconclusive with a slight indication that middle-class pupils fared better but pupils from deprived backgrounds less well and that social segregation overall had increased. Despite these deficiencies, Wiborg makes the important point that, unlike the English situation, Free Schools in Sweden exist within a framework of accountability shared between national and local tiers of government, resulting in the following phenomenon:

> The peculiarity of Swedish school choice is thus that, on the one hand it is deregulated with vouchers and competition between schools, and, on the other hand, it has firmly remained under central and local municipality responsibility through powerful instruments of control, financial resources, national curriculum and inspection. (Wiborg, 2010, p 13)

Wiborg's argument is that Free Schools were introduced in Sweden on the periphery of a system of comprehensive schooling firmly based on social democratic values and that, 'even in the context of this very egalitarian environment', some social segregation had occurred. She suggests that policy makers in England have not built their school reforms on the same underlying values and that, 'in the context of a more divided system, similar reforms in England may have more damaging effects on inequality and school segregation' (Wiborg, 2010, p 19).

The often mentioned 'attainment gap' between pupils originating from relatively affluent and relatively poor backgrounds is an ever-present theme in any debate regarding equity and equality in schooling and allocation of school places. As well as changes initiated by AA10, the Coalition government was quick to adopt the 'pupil premium', a policy initiative that had been promised in both the manifestos of the Coalition partners, as a cash incentive to encourage schools to seek actively to recruit children from poorer backgrounds, to be identified by eligibility for free school meals. Introduced in April 2011, the pupil premium is set at £488 per pupil for 2011–12 and will increase to £600 per pupil in 2012–13; in addition, children from families serving in the armed forces will receive £200 rising to £250 in the same period. The DfE had determined that it would be for individual schools to decide how to spend the pupil premium 'as they see fit' but after representations from the House of Lords, indicated that 'new measures will be included in performance tables to capture the achievement of those deprived pupils covered by the pupil premium'. Additionally, from September 2012, schools will be required to publish information online about the use they have made of their pupil premium funds ('Pupil Premium – what you need to know', DfE, 2012g). In a detailed study of alternative ways of delivering the pupil premium, the Institute of Fiscal Studies (2010) has expressed some doubts about how much of a difference the level of payment set will make to the problem of social segregation and warned of possible unintended consequences. It remains to be seen how effective the reporting system now established will be for the needs of policy makers and researchers in providing relevant information, and how comparative data (excepting the performance tables) can be presented when school websites are reporting on progress in their own highly individual ways. It will also be interesting to see what, if any, enforcement mechanisms or penalties will be applied to schools that are deemed less than wise in their expenditure decisions.

The pupil premium proposal certainly has a markedly different flavour to most reforms of education in recent times. In effect a form of social engineering, positively discriminating in favour of disadvantaged groups, it seeks directly to re-shape the outcomes of the operation of the quasi-market in education, and to influence the exercise of schools' autonomy in admissions arrangements. It constitutes an implicit recognition that apparent parental choice, diversity of provision, and autonomy for schools will not necessarily deliver all of the socially desirable outcomes associated with schooling. It demonstrates an acknowledgement that a role remains for government interventions which structure how admissions are determined, in pursuit of what might be called 'public interest' objectives associated with citizenship rather than consumerism, and collective rather than individual interests, which extend beyond, and on occasion can be thought legitimately to trump, the operation of market forces (see Feintuck, 2004). Though not without problems in terms of implementation and monitoring, it is a rare example in recent years, when education reform has been characterised generally by pursuit of individual interests by parents and schools, of a proposal which refers back to an era in which public, and publicly accountable, intervention has been taken in direct pursuit of public and stated objectives.

4.5 Governance by contract

The arrival of Academies represented a landmark in the running of state education in England. While the Conservative's 'independent' state schools – the GM schools and the CTCs – inspired the Academies model, the legal structure was significantly different. GM schools, the predominant model, had been founded on detailed statutory provisions, with any variation in practice when compared to maintained schools incorporated into legislation, but Academies were to be run through contracts, known as 'funding agreements' between the Secretary of State and the Academy Trust (nominated by the Academy's sponsor). In this context, it is important to be clear that the use of 'contract' here refers to a specific legal form of agreement, with specific legal meaning and consequences, very different from the so-called 'political contract' noted in Chapter Two by way of referring to the arrangements under EA44.

As public lawyer David Wolfe indicates, Academies, in law, are treated as independent schools, though he makes clear: 'That is not to say that independent schools are uncontrolled, but the legal control (and thus the rights of parents/pupils) is very different and much more limited' (Wolfe, 2011, pp 21–2). Wolfe, when interviewed by one of the authors in May 2010, expanded on the legal significance of the contractual relationship and the resultant high level of freedom and room for manoeuvre available to the Academies when compared to the experience of maintained schools:

"There is a stark contrast between the rest of the education system where there is a lot of law, a lot of statutory materials, a lot of regulation, a lot of guidance and the Academies ... where there is really almost nothing. ... The Academies model is very open ... only a single provision in an Act of Parliament and everything else done through contract." (Stevens, 2011, pp 78 and 79)

Based on his experience of judicial review work and other legal action, Wolfe believed that the quality of funding agreements had improved, after starting in a less than satisfactory manner. He considered that, with the arrival of Ed Balls, the more recent funding agreements drawn up by the DCSF were 'probably as good as it gets given that this was being done by contract'. But for Wolfe, a contract, even a well-drawn up contract, had distinct limitations in terms of the rights that parents and pupils should expect to have from state-provided schooling:

"[T]he contract is between the Secretary of State and the academy sponsor. The child, the parent is not a party to that contract. On ordinary basic legal provisions, you can't enforce a contract to which you are not a party. ... Sometimes you can enforce a contract to which you are not a party but it is quite rare. ... This is stuff that has never really been tested in court and it actually goes back to your constitutional question, there is a much bigger issue about the state operating through private contracts. ... There is a systemic constitutional issue around control of privatised, outsourced services and this will only become more important in the next parliamentary period." (Stevens, 2011, p 81)

Freedland (1994) identified the emergence of this issue at the time when the Thatcher government started to move some public functions to the private sector, and considered that it raised 'major concerns about the capacity of our system of public law to deal adequately with the new demands placed upon it by this process of contractualisation' and that:

The doctrine of privity of contract ensures that the consumer has no direct contractual relationship with the service procurer. It would not be wholly surprising to find that, by extension of that reasoning, there were many situations in which the citizen as consumer had no sufficient interest to seek judicial review of the actions or policies of the government department [that] had procured the service in question. In one sense, the implications of privity of contract go deeper still. By insisting on the exclusiveness of the bi-partite contract, the doctrine of privity of contract both practically and symbolically singles out the interest of the individual as consumer from the larger group interest, of which it forms a part, as well as from the general public interest. (Freedland, 1994, pp 86 and 88)

Freedland (1994, pp 102 and 104) noted that government departments made great play that those entering into such service contracts would remain fully accountable but he thought their definition of accountability was narrowly defined and dominated by matters of financial efficiency and targets. What he thought was lacking was 'a legal framework which recognises or is truly capable of regulating either the process of contractualisation or the new kinds of relationships which it creates'. Other public lawyers have noted the constitutional ramifications. For example, Auby (2007, p 49) asked: 'In so far as government contracts sometimes become an instrument for implementing policy, how is it possible to accept that they make their way out of the reach of statutory provisions and parliamentary permission?' (see also Harden, 1992).

In the parliamentary debates surrounding AA10, MPs and Peers gained further insight into the legal differences between Academies and maintained schools, the implications of which had attracted little curiosity when the Academies were first introduced. As Wolfe explained in interview:

> "It started off ... as a single section of legislation in an Act, with very limited detail and very limited constraints, to do something that I think was probably originally intended – I suspect, if you had been a ... bystander ... you would have said, 'What are you voting for here?' They would have said, 'This is a pilot exercise, this is a new model that is being tried, we are giving the state this extra power to try this new model and we'll just see what happens.' I don't think they would have expected for it to then develop with no more scrutiny into the vast edifice it has become ..." (Stevens, 2011, p 78)

Some further clarification was achieved in discussions regarding the Academies and the then current School Admissions Code of Practice (DCSF, 2009a) when, following questions put forward in debate, Lord Hill, Parliamentary Under Secretary of State for Schools, confirmed that 'Academies are required to adopt practices and arrangements that are consistent with, or in accordance with, the Code and the School Admission Appeals Code through their funding agreements', and elaborated on the arrangements for admissions pertaining in Academies, in a written response:

> [There was] a need for different provisions in respect of objections on admissions arrangements [and that] these different approaches are necessary because of the contractual nature of our relationship with Academies – the Schools Adjudicator and Local Government Ombudsman are not parties to the contract and so could not, for example, make binding changes to the admission arrangements by varying it, but they do mirror closely the procedures for maintained schools. (DfE, 2010b)

Lack of clarity over the precise status of Academies was confirmed in debate when Baroness Williams noted that s 87 of the 2010 Equality Act exempted Academies from its provisions because they were 'independent' schools. Lord Hill's written explanation sent to Baroness Williams is instructive:

> The only provision in Part 6 [of the 2010 Equality Act] that does not apply to independent schools (including Academies) is section 87, which extends the powers of the Secretary of State to give direction to schools under sections 496 and 497 of the Education Act 1996. This is because those powers are not exercisable in relation to Academies. *The Secretary of State's relationship with Academies is largely governed by the Academy's funding agreement.* [italics added] Generally, it is not common for the Secretary of State to give directions under s.496 and 497 of the Education Act, and we would not expect those powers to be used under the Equality Act as a matter of routine. (DfE, 2010c)

Following these matters being raised, Lord Hill confirmed that Academies would be placed on the consolidated lists of public bodies under 'Schedule 19' of the 2010 Equality Act. On 15 June 2010, following the second debate, Lord Hill, in a letter to colleagues in the House of Lords who spoke in the debate, spelled out some broad principles about the conduct of Academies. The first of these was that there would be 'no change to, or weakening of the requirement that all state funded schools including Academies must comply with the School Admissions Code'. In February 2012, the new School Admissions Code stated: 'Academies are required by their funding agreements to comply with the Code and the law relating to admissions, though the Secretary of State has the power to vary this requirement where there is a demonstrable need' (DfE, 2012a, p 3). Though the parliamentary process may be thought to have achieved a satisfactory outcome, on the narrow point of ensuring that Academies will be subject to the School Admissions Code, the broader concerns identified by Wolfe (2011) regarding what Harden (1992) terms 'government by contract' remain.

4.6 The 2011 Education Act and the 2012 School Admissions Code

EA11 commenced its legislative journey on 27 January 2011, preceded by the publication in November 2010 of the White Paper *The importance of teaching* (DfE, 2010d), and with a more conventional timetable for parliamentary scrutiny and debate when compared to AA10. In the second reading debate, Andy Burnham, at that time shadow Secretary of State for Education, described the Education Bill as "an audacious request" involving the addition of a further 50 powers to the Secretary of State and, while he broadly supported some elements of the Bill (such as proposals relating to early years provision and school discipline, subject to further assurances about the powers to search pupils), Labour would oppose the Bill because it represented "too big a gamble with the life chances of our children, and because … it takes power from pupils, parents, professionals and the public, leaving them with fewer protections in a less publicly accountable education system" (*Hansard*, columns 180 and 181, 8 February 2012).

Of particular note in the context of the present study was the DfE's two-pronged strategy to alter admissions policies and practices through EA11 and also through the introduction of a revised School Admissions Code. Building on Ball's (2008) identification of a phenomenon of 'policy ratchetting', it might be suggested that a form of 'simultaneous policy ratchetting' took place where the combination of changes introduced by the Bill and the Code resulted in a radical alteration of power relationships between central government, the schools adjudicator and local authorities.

In combination, EA11, s 34 and the 2012 School Admissions Code bring about a number of significant departures from the 2009 Code. The 2012 Code allows 'popular' schools to expand without seeking permission from their local authorities, and while previous codes required schools to gain permission for expansion of the school roll over a certain number (in the 2009 Code, it was 22), the new Code seems to accept implicitly that expansion in some schools might cause problems elsewhere in the local system of provision. In addition, apart from brief statements that school places 'should be allocated and offered … in an open and fair way', that admissions practices needed to be 'fair, clear and objective' (DfE, 2012a, p 6) and that Appeals Panels were serving a judicial function and must be 'transparent, accessible, independent and impartial and operate according to principles of natural justice' (DfE, 2012a, p 7), the 2012 Code substantially removes contextual statements (so typical in the Labour period) based on collective, social values. This omission may have been due to Gove's view, with some apparent justification, that the previous Code was too long and complicated, having 138 pages (now reduced to 61) and containing 600 mandatory requirements but, nevertheless, the practical language and tone stands in marked contrast to the 2009 Code and its predecessors. Further, although Academies and Free Schools were 'required by their funding agreements' to comply with the new Code, the Secretary of State was given 'the power to vary this requirement if there is a demonstrable need' (DfE, 2012a, p 2). Given that, at the time of writing, nearly half of all secondary schools are now Academies, this power presents a substantial opportunity for central government involvement with admissions practices.

Perhaps of more significance for present purposes are two further departures from the previous regulatory regime. The first of these, arising from EA11, s 36, allows, for the first time, 'any body or person to refer to the adjudicator an objection concerning the admissions arrangements of any state-funded school', but s 34(4) simultaneously repeals the power of the school adjudicator to direct schools to modify their admissions arrangements if found to be in contravention of the Code. In justifying the government's position, Nick Gibb, Minister for Schools, stated that:

> "It [the section] removes the adjudicator's power to directly modify arrangements as part of his decision in relation to objections received from parents and other persons. We believe that this is the right step. It should be for schools to implement such decisions, leaving them to decide how and

what to change to comply with the adjudicator's binding decision. We should trust schools to set their own admissions arrangements and to respond appropriately to any decision made by the adjudicator." (HOC, 2011a, p 777)

Politicians placing their trust in schools may seem to be a positive value. In terms of democratic accountability, however, the feasibility of ensuring that the increasing number of schools that act as their own admissions authorities all abide by the Code under such liberal governance must be questioned. In terms of overall effectiveness, this restriction of the OSA's powers presents a significant potential barrier to its overall authority.

The second very significant change to the structure for the local admissions 'system' is brought about by EA11, s 34(2)(a), which removes the requirement under SSFA, s 85(a) on England's local authorities to establish a School Admissions Forum for their area. In the Public Bill Committee's sitting on 29 March 2011, Kevin Brennan MP (Labour), in putting forward an amendment (later withdrawn) to preserve the School Admissions Forums, argued that:

> "Such a move is unwise at a time when the numbers of schools that set their own criteria is increasing. In a few years' time, we could have more than 20,000 schools setting their own admissions criteria. Now is not the time to remove an effective local mechanism working in favour of fair admissions [...] The government have provided no evidence of the need to make the proposed change [...] Parents regardless of where they live are entitled to have an effective, independent monitoring body in each local authority to ensure fair admissions criteria and processes as laid down in the School Admissions Code, and to ensure they are operated by all admission authorities." (HOC, 2011a, pp 770–1)

In response, the Minister for Schools sought to reassure those MPs who had concerns about the removal of the requirement to run School Admissions Forums that the Bill sought to remove a duty but 'does not ban or abolish them' and that they could be adopted 'if that is the right local solution' (HOC, 2011a, pp 773–4).

In their attempts to scrutinise the proposed changes in admissions policy and practice proposed by the 2011 Education Bill and the re-drafting of the School Admissions Code, parliamentarians became frustrated by a number of delays in publishing the final draft of the Code and perceived 'gaps' in the rigour of relevant paperwork attached to the Bill. Several MPs and Peers questioned ministerial representatives from the DfE about the problem of the delays in publishing the final draft code while debates were still progressing on the matter in the House of Commons. For example, Julie Hilling MP (Labour) stated that it was 'outrageous that we are looking to make wholesale changes to legislation without seeing what will replace it' (HOC, 2011a, p 773). In a reply to another Opposition question regarding whether an equalities impact assessment had been conducted in respect of the proposal to remove the obligation for local authorities to establish School Admissions Forums, the Minister for Schools responded that such an exercise had been conducted for the White Paper as a whole. Though stating that 'in a more autonomous school system' it was vital that local authorities should act as the 'guardians of social justice', this document makes no reference to the role of School Admissions Forums and the likely impact on inequality levels if they were no longer mandatory. It did, however, make reference to England having one of 'the most stratified and segregated school systems in the world', highlighting the presence of public schools as the cause of this rather than further social inequalities present within the state school sector (see this argument expounded by Jenkins et al, 2006).

Outside parliament, a queue of concerned teaching organisations and campaign groups formed to protest against the proposed changes to the School Admissions Code. In written submissions to the Public Bill Committee on the matter of the 2011 Education Bill, the Campaign for State Education stated that 'the proposed changes to admissions ... (would) bring about unfairness and social division in the admissions process' and that it 'deplores, in the strongest possible terms, the weakening of the power of the Schools Adjudicator'; the NASUWT's submission argued that, 'These changes will have a profoundly negative impact on the process of ensuring and securing fair admissions' and Comprehensive Future wanted clause 34 'largely removed' because 'evidence is strong that schools that are their own admissions authorities do not take the proportion of children on free school meals represented in their community' and they also wondered why 'the government has provided no explanation of why the changes are needed'.

Overall the changes to school admissions policy instituted by EA11 and the 2012 Code have increased the power and reach of the Secretary of State, the DfE and individual schools in making decisions relating to admissions while simultaneously reducing the influence of both the Office of the Schools Adjudicator and the local authorities. The significant risk that such moves will potentially disadvantage some pupils and parents is readily apparent. Whatever a government's political orientation, prior experience and existing evidence would indicate that a liberalisation and diversification of the school system, accompanied by a weakening of local structures of control, presents a number of possible risks to what most parents and pupils would identify as a fair and transparent admissions system. With the increase of individually run admissions authorities, why the rowing back of the influence of the Schools Adjudicator and the potential denial of a local means of complaint for parents? None of the documentation in the White Paper of the draft Bill supplied any reasoning for these proposed changes.

At the time of writing it still remains to be seen what the effects of relevant parts of EA11 and the 2012 School Admissions Code will be on admissions practices in England's schools. But concerns must exist over the intended and unintended consequences of some aspects of the legislation and the Code as they interact with the rapid expansion of the Academies programme and the introduction of Free Schools and the consequent increase in school-controlled admissions authorities. As will be suggested by the consideration of the realities of admissions practices in England since the introduction of quasi-market forces, discussed in the next chapter, it is hard to escape a conclusion that there is a substantial likelihood that social segregation in schooling will increase.

4.7 Conclusion

In contrast with the relative stability in the statutory framework for the 30 years following EA44, commentators often note the quantity and pace of education reform from the 1980s onwards. Chitty (2009, p 85) observes that the 2005 White Paper 'heralded the fortieth Education Act since 1980', while Tomlinson (2005, pp 119–20) charts an almost unbelievably dense list of Acts, reports, ministerial changes and other events relevant to schooling from 2000–05. Yet the changes to legislation and ministerial personnel can serve to blind observers to the very real continuities in themes established by ERA in 1988 and pursued, with only minor variations, by all governments since, with the rhetoric of the reforms consistently focussing on standards via choice and diversity, and, sometimes more explicitly than at others, seeking to remove what was presented as the 'dead-hand' of LEA power. Meanwhile, opponents and critics of the reforms have consistently emphasised concerns regarding privatisation of power in education, accountability in the exercise of such power, and equity of treatment as between relatively advantaged and disadvantaged pupils.

With rare exceptions, including the Coalition's 'pupil premium' proposal which appeared to be targeted at some version of substantive fairness, the reforms from 1988 onwards charted in this chapter demonstrate a focus on the now very familiar themes of 'choice and diversity' in schooling. The principal focus of such reforms has been on the development of mechanisms which best serve and enable the operation of a quasi-market, and though there has been much talk among policy-makers and politicians of standards in education, the narrow approach to standards in terms of valuing the measurable can also properly be viewed as instrumental in facilitating apparent differentiation and choice between schools in pursuit of rendering more effective the operation of market forces. While substantive equity and equality remain vital elements of the legitimating rhetoric of a modern democracy such as Britain, procedural fairness is also central to such expectations. If, as the evidence suggests (see, for example, Noden and West, 2009), the admissions processes now in place for schools are open to local interpretation by individual schools and admissions authorities, we should have concerns about whether expectations of substantive or procedural fairness are likely to be met, especially if those exercising power at individual schools are not subject to rigorous mechanisms of accountability in relation to their exercise of public power.

This chapter has traced central government's involvement in, and indeed active domination of, the policy development and associated legislation and regulation that has transformed England's approach to school admissions to a quasi-market system. In the next chapter, the extent to which 'choice' is a practical reality in this context and how the allocation of school places is regulated in practice via legal and administrative processes will be considered.

FIVE

The realities of choice and accountability in the quasi-market

5.1 Introducing the practical realities of choice

The harshest critics of admissions arrangements within the quasi-market for schooling offer much, often blunt, comment. When it is reported in the quality media that 'An insidious mix of selection by ability, faith and postcode is wreaking havoc on the entire schools system' (Fiona Millar, *The Guardian*, 12 April 2010), or that 'School leaders are calling on politicians to end what they call "the misleading rhetoric" of school choice – which they say cannot be delivered' (BBC, 2008), we have cause to consider seriously whether the outcomes of the system are consistent with democratic and constitutional expectations, and indeed the extent to which choice of school is a reality rather than an aspiration or empty promise.

The oversubscribed school is the precise point at which the rhetoric of parental choice meets the stark reality of limited places in popular schools, and in this context the power to choose seems to shift from parents to those managing the admissions process. Operating within a quasi-market context, there will be strong pressures on, or temptations for, those exercising the power of selection (in 'non-selective' schools) to prioritise choosing those pupils who will best serve the interests of the individual school, rather than any broader social priorities, a phenomenon implicitly recognised and addressed by policies such as the 'pupil premium' (see Chapter Four) and 'fair banding' (see Chapter Six) espoused by the 2010 Coalition. Though schools are required to state publicly their admissions criteria, in situations of oversubscription there is the possibility of the occurrence of what Chitty (1992, pp 96–7) identifies as informal selection, or what we might term 'covert selection', where published policies on admissions are not followed or factors or practices additional to published criteria are adopted, by schools claiming not to be 'selective'. As Whitty (2002, p 130) suggests, 'The covert forms of selection ... may ... produce greater inequalities, as socially advantaged parents learn to decipher the "real" admissions criteria'. From constitutional and democratic perspectives, equity and accountability in the exercise of such power of selection will be imperative. It might also be expected that such practices would on occasion be found to be unlawful. In the time since the 1988 Education Reform Act (ERA), reviewed in this chapter, came into force, the legal requirements, guidance, practices and routes of appeal have all changed significantly. While a wholly chronological narrative will not be pursued here, broadly, three different stages are apparent, reflecting changes in emphasis if not substantial changes of direction: the immediate post-ERA period to 1997, the New Labour reforms, and the early period of the Coalition government's policies.

5.2 The admission questions post-1988

In Chapter Three, it was noted that 'parental choice' of school in the 1980s could, in reality, be much more accurately represented as a right to express a preference. Substantial potential existed for such preferences not being met, and the appeals and judicial processes, though strengthened by the 1980 Education Act (EA80), remained somewhat deferential to the planning, and hence admissions, powers of local education authorities (LEAs). In essence, LEAs enjoyed powers to manipulate schools' admissions numbers in pursuit of systemic planning objectives, and could effectively override parental preference in pursuit of economy or efficiency.

Central to the marketisation of schooling under ERA were the Open Enrolment (OE) provisions of ss 26–32. Maclure (1988, p 26) observes that 'The main aim behind these provisions was to increase significantly the power of parents *as consumers*' (emphasis added). Though fitting the rhetoric of consumerism, and the objective of breaking perceived 'producer domination' of the schooling system, the OE provisions of ERA did not go as far as might be expected. Their principal effect was to ensure that LEAs or diocesan authorities, in pursuit of planning objectives, were not able to place artificial caps on admissions below the maximum physical capacity of the school in response to local demographic trends, long- or short-term. More specifically, standard numbers for admissions to schools were fixed at the (unusually high) 1979 level, with LEAs expressly forbidden from setting a number below this figure, and the ability to override parental preference based on 'prejudice to efficient education and/or efficient use of resources' under s 6(3) EA80 expressly removed by s 26(9) unless the standard number (or any higher level set) had been reached. Any reduction of the admissions figure below the standard number required the approval of the Secretary of State, who, under s 28(7) could effectively only approve such a reduction based on an actual physical reduction in the capacity of the school buildings. The statutory terms were sufficiently explicit that any Secretary of State who sought to incorporate a wider range of reasons into a decision to approve a reduction in numbers 'would court an action for judicial review' (Maclure, 1988, p 32).

The apparent intention of these provisions was clearly to maximise the number of school places from which parents could 'choose', as a fundamental element of the implementation of a quasi-market in schooling. The use by LEAs of 'planned admission levels' below the physical capacity of a school, to ensure the viability of a number of schools within a local system, 'based on a notion of the common good' (Clough et al, 1989, p 32) had, according to the DES, 'inhibited and delayed the necessary rationalisation of schools and at the same time acted as a barrier to the exercise of effective parental choice' (Clough et al, 1989, p 32). Writing in 1989, Clough et al (1989, p 33) report LEAs claiming that prior to OE under ERA, parental choice was already being met in approximately 95% of cases, and quote one CEO as reporting that, after appeals, only 0.3% of parents had been 'forced to an unacceptable school'. Harris (1990, p 166) expresses, quite reasonably, a degree of scepticism about the suggestion that such a high proportion of children went to their parents' first choice school (especially considering the restriction on possible choices relating to geography and feeder requirements, built in before the 'menu' of choice is determined), but he acknowledges also that school choice legislation had in reality only made a marginal difference to parental satisfaction rates in relation to school places. Though recognising the potential for distortion by reference to parents expressing preferences with more or less strategic thinking as to likelihood of preferences being met, the Institute for Public Policy Research (IPPR, 2007, p 6) reported that in the year 2000, as regards secondary school places, '85 per cent of parents were offered a place for their child at their favourite school' though 'In London, where there are more schools to choose from, the percentage getting an offer from their favourite school drops to just 68 per cent'.

Whether any particular percentage of parents failing to obtain a place for their child at their first choice school is acceptable is a matter of judgement, though as should already be apparent, there is no viable system that can guarantee first choices will be met in all cases. Whether the shift to OE was necessary or appropriate, given the challenge it posed to the management of a local system of schools, and its 'destabilising effect on local schools provision' (Harris, 1990, p 160) is clearly debatable. While its logic is very clear, in market terms at least, early critics pointed to a range of perceived problems flowing from OE, summarised by Clough et al:

> [P]opular schools will become either larger or more selective in their intakes, leaving the others (and the children in them) to their fate. In general terms, the loss of pupils to the 'popular' schools will clearly have a damaging effect on other schools, both in terms of resources (especially in the context of local financial management) and in terms of morale. It is likely to encourage the re-introduction of covert selective admission to those 'popular' schools, which would further erode the comprehensive ideal and the principles of education for all. ... Furthermore, the open market orientation of the proposals could exacerbate divisions that already exist in society by favouring those with the cultural resources to make informed choices ... (Clough et al, 1989, p 33)

From the government's perspective, parental choice was to be informed by league tables, with a school's ranking based on its pupils' performances in national tests, though evidence suggests that 'softer' factors, and in particular the wishes of the child, are often central to the preference stated. Walford (1996, p 57) points towards a range of research indicating that some parents tend to place a higher premium on 'process criteria' such as the likely happiness of their child, rather than 'product criteria' such as examination results. He adds that research also indicates that many parents also attach great significance to their child's expressed preferences in this regard, with a clear suggestion of variation across social class in relation to this potentially crucial decision. The core factors identified by Woods et al (1998, p 124 et seq) are academic standards, proximity or ease of travel, and the child's happiness at the school. Some identifiable patterns do emerge related to social class, with middle-class parents, when compared with their working-class counterparts, tending to place more emphasis on non-core factors such as the school's atmosphere, and the behaviour of its pupils outside the school, while working-class parents placed a higher priority on the child's friendship groups attending the same preferred school. Walford (1996, p 58) also finds this social-class dimension to how choice is exercised confirmed by Ball's (1993, p 4) conclusion that one of the major effects of the quasi-market reforms of education has been 'the reproduction of relative class (and ethnic) advantages and disadvantages'.

For working-class parents in Woods et al's (1998) study, proximity and/or convenience of home-school travel proved a significant non-core factor. Meanwhile Burgess et al (2006, p 13) draw an unambiguous conclusion that 'Affluent families whose nearest secondary school is of poor quality are much more likely to "bus" their children out to schools further away than are poor families'. In addition, given the willingness of parents seeking places at desirable schools to move into a neighbourhood which would maximise the likelihood of their child obtaining entry to the school, a direct relationship between financial means (to buy houses in the relevant area) and access to desirable schools becomes immediately apparent. Despite perceived benefits in terms of traffic congestion and environmental pollution, any attempt to move to a near or totally neighbourhood-based admissions system would simply increase class differences as a result of affluent parents being able to buy housing near to the most attractive schools: Burgess et al (2006, p 15) find the policy 'likely to be the most exclusionary system, with access to good schools highly dependant on income'. By way of contrast with this picture of certain groups being able to exercise choice positively and effectively, it is worth noting Woods et al's (1998, p 120 et seq) indication that, because of a range of factors (including availability of places, admission arrangements and transport practicalities), many parents feel that in reality their meaningful choice of school is strictly limited. Confirming socio-economic class inequalities in relation to choice, the IPPR (2007, p 17), drawing on Burgess et al (2006), notes that 'only 44 per cent of pupils eligible for free school meals have a "good" school within their nearest three schools compared to 61 per cent of pupils not eligible for free school meals'.

While LEAs were generally subjected to extreme pressure to achieve economies via removal of surplus places in the school system, any meaningful degree of parental choice implies the necessity of spare capacity at attractive schools: 'Without over-capacity in schools, parents will quickly find that their choices are severely curtailed, and that it is the schools that choose which children to accept rather than the parents and children choosing a school' (Walford, 1996, p 59). Any satisfaction rate, based on the exercise of very limited choice would scarcely meet the rhetoric of parental choice, and indeed even proponents of market mechanisms in schooling, such as the Social Market Foundation (SMF) acknowledge the need to address 'the inability of some parents to exercise free choice' (SMF, 2005, p 69) and hence the need they state for 'increasing the number of good school places' (SMF, 2005, p 13).

It is also clear that many parents will place a high premium on education for their child in what Burgess et al (2006, p 15) refer to as 'an exclusive peer group', or a school with an intake with a high degree of racial, cultural or religious homogeneity consonant with their family background; certainly, state support for schools founded on religious faith, and permitted expressly to use observance of that faith as a high priority admissions criteria, seems almost inevitably to further an agenda of segregation. In concluding a later study, Burgess et al identify 'school socio-economic composition' as one of 'the main characteristics that parents care about' (Burgess et al, 2009, p 32) and point towards the possibility that 'It may be that what families want is for their child to go to a school with other children "like" their own. This could mean many things, but it might mean "like" in terms of socio-economic status. [...] This would obviously encourage greater social stratification in schools' (Burgess et al, 2009, p 32). Of course, teachers might be expected to be more aware than most of the significance of education, and the importance of the school children attend. As such, giving the children of teachers a high priority in the selection criteria at their school, could serve as a significant mechanism in attracting teachers to work at an oversubscribed school.

There is a further interesting congeries of issues here. Promises of choice and diversity may be latched onto most strongly by middle-class parents, and though they are likely to be able to 'play the admissions game' most effectively, any disappointments in respect of preferences not being met, despite being probably relatively low in number, are likely to be pursued articulately and persistently, and to attract significant profile and nuisance value for admissions authorities and politicians. Meanwhile abundant research indicated that the quasi-market introduced into schooling by ERA had not served well those students starting with relative disadvantage of whatever kind. For example, in 1996, Walford found that, in relation to the new tranche of well-funded City Technology Colleges (CTCs), such schools 'took great care to ensure that [they were] taking children with a wide ability range, but the whole entry procedure means that selection is based on the degree of motivation of parents and children instead. Children and families where there is a low level of interest in education simply do not apply' (Walford, 1996, p 53). Walford also points towards evidence that by the mid-1990s some 30% of Grant Maintained (GM) schools, while still claiming the label 'comprehensive schools', were found to be 'using covert selection', with one having 'introduced a selection examination' (Walford, 1996, p 55). Such an outcome was hardly surprising. In 1994 it was already possible to assert with confidence that the criteria adopted by some of the first wave of GM schools, 'such as the ability of potential pupils and parents to play a full role in the whole life of the school or by reference to the maintenance of the ethos of a school, can easily take the form of racial or cultural exclusivity', and that emphasis on 'the right children and the right parents' appears to offer significant potential for a school, if oversubscribed, to recruit 'in its own image' (Feintuck, 1994, p 119).

Given the conclusion reached by Woods et al (1998, p 214) that 'some families have more limited cultural resources than others and are less well placed to make "satisfactory" decisions in relation to schooling', it might be considered that forms of 'positive action' might be desirable in terms of addressing such issues, should a government find them to be of concern. Such concerns are acknowledged by the SMF (2005, p 11) in terms of 'supporting less privileged families in choosing a school', and since the 2006 Education and Inspections Act, local authorities were required to provide 'Choice Advisers', drawing on funding provided by central government (IPPR, 2007, p 8) to 'provide support to those parents who most need help in navigating the secondary schools admissions process' (DCSF, 2009a, Appendix 5). Later, the contract with the service provider for the Choice Advice Support and Quality Assurance Network was discontinued by the Coalition government on 31 March 2011 with the DfE indicating that 'it would not be letting another contract nor replicating the service' (DfE, 2011b).

Though the issues relating to CTCs and GM schools were new phenomena in the 1990s, diversity of type of school inevitably produces questions about establishing and preserving types of schools with a distinctive orientation. As with the 1944 Education Act (EA44), where (as discussed in Chapter Three) the claims of religious groups were significant in shaping the legislative framework, those involved with drafting ERA were conscious of and responded to significant pressure to ensure that the provisions did not have the consequence of limiting their control over admission to the school by reference to religious faith, allowing them to preserve the distinctive ethos of such schools (Maclure, 1988, pp 33–4).

But the overarching, simple reality remains that identified by many commentators: once a school becomes popular to the point of oversubscription, it is the school which ultimately exercises a power of choice. Though required to adhere to their own specified and published admissions criteria, the fear of covert selection incorporating other factors was already of substantial concern in the years immediately following ERA. Such concerns arose especially in the context of the newly established CTCs and 'opted out' GM schools. Some such schools openly sought to go beyond any covert policies of selection. As Walford reports, by the mid–1990s some GM schools had already applied successfully for a change of character to become fully academically selective grammar schools, while others had been granted permission to select up to half of their intake (Walford, 1996, p 55). But it is perhaps 'covert' selection that remains the more problematic issue, from a perspective of equity and accountability at least.

With a specific brief to have an intake across a wide ability range from a specific locale, CTCs, like GM schools also had a tendency to be popular, oversubscribed, and hence in a position to engage in selection by one means or another. In relation to one CTC, researchers observed how a child whose parent had applied to the school took a simple non-verbal reasoning test, which was then used to ensure a range of abilities is selected in accordance with the stated requirement. Potential pupils were also interviewed along with a parent:

> [H]eads and teachers in the nearby LEA schools claimed that the CTC was selecting those very parents who have the most interest in their children's education, and those children who are most keen and enthusiastic. They argued that the CTC was selecting children who, while they might not be particularly academically able, had special skills and interests in sport, art, drama or other activities. These children were seen as invigorating the atmosphere of the school, providing models for other children, and being rewarding for the teachers to teach. Heads and teachers in nearby schools thus saw their schools as having been impoverished by the CTC's selection of these well-motivated pupils. (Walford, 1996, p 53)

Beyond questions surrounding the 'soft' criteria applied by GM schools and CTCs, operating outside the LEA system, in selecting their intake, further concerns arose regarding how adjustments could subsequently be made to the school population. In 1992, it was reported that one LEA had asked the Secretary of State to investigate allegations amounting to claims that the school had engaged in a 'campaign to shed problem pupils and those under-achieving' (Feintuck, 1994, p 120; see also Chitty 1992, pp 96–7). This seems to be consistent with a trend identified by Walford: 'the growth of "adverse selection" where "mistakes" in initial selection procedures are increasingly rectified through temporary or permanent exclusions' (Walford, 1996, p 55) or what West et al (2004, p 347) refer to in terms of schools that 'select in' and 'select out'. A report by the Children's Commissioner (2012) considering the use of exclusions by schools, sometimes on an 'unofficial' basis, appears to confirm such practices and indeed indicates a casual abuse of power by those managing some schools, with adverse effects in particular for already disadvantaged groups of children including those with special educational needs (SEN), Travellers, and those of African-Caribbean origins. Whether particular types of schools are more prone to such behaviour needs to be monitored on an ongoing basis (see Sutton Trust, 2008). Tomlinson (2005, pp 127–9) reports similar concerns relating to the first wave of Academies.

Even after political pressure within the Labour Party contributed to the government putting in place in 1999, and on a statutory footing, a School Admissions Code of Practice, Gorard et al (2003, p 186) point out: 'What choice policies may do is change the rules by which segregation takes place, but without markedly increasing or eliminating levels of segregation that are largely shaped by structural factors'. This nuanced view of the position is persuasive, seeming to be a realistic and plausible account of the outcomes of the choice mechanisms first introduced by ERA. There should be no surprise here, given that, at that time, addressing inequalities within or via education was scarcely at the heart of the Thatcher administration. Rather the political agenda was concerned with a remodelling of the state and society in pursuit of the removal of perceived producer domination as an obstacle to consumerist interests. Chitty (2009, p 91) also highlights much later a significant number of complaints in 2008 regarding non-compliance by admissions authorities with the then new Admissions Code, of which a 'disproportionate number were faith or foundation schools'. Within an environment where funding follows pupils, and schools are ranked by reference to performance in public examinations, there is a strong incentive for schools to use any influence over admissions arrangements that they may have to attract those pupils most likely to contribute to enhancing the future reputation of the school via measurable academic success. Allen et al (2010b, p 23) refer to studies which have moved beyond suspicion or anecdote to show that 'schools that are their own admission authority are more likely to have admissions criteria that enable schools to be unfairly selective in their intakes', confirming a need for effective regulation of such powers. It seems clear that those schools acting as their own 'admissions authority', operating outside traditional local authority structures, will need particular scrutiny to ensure that the market pressures do not drive them down routes of questionable legality or legitimacy, leading the IPPR (2007, p 18) to conclude that no school should administer its own admissions or be its own admissions authority. Just as schools might seek to 'stretch' admission arrangements to attract the most desirable pupils, so there are also clear incentives for parents to be tempted to use dishonest means (for example, falsifying their residential address to meet criteria relating to proximity or catchment area) to obtain places at the most desirable schools, a phenomenon regularly reported in the general and specialist media, and one which the Office of the Schools Adjudicator (2009a) has reported as being significant and growing.

Though originating in the 1993 Education Act, successive governments encouraged widespread specialisation within secondary schools as one measure to enhance diversity and choice, and hence drive up educational standards. Commenting on the proposals for specialist status which were incorporated into the 1998 School Standards and Framework Act (SSFA), Chitty, among others, presents a highly sceptical view of the specialist schools agenda in terms of equality: 'It was argued by many that the Government's concept of specialist schools would simply create (or exacerbate) an unbalanced academic and social mix in inner-city schools. In a class-divided and highly competitive society ... specialisms could never be equal: they would rapidly be ranked in a hierarchy of status' (Chitty, 2009, p 69). Confirming Gerwirtz et al's (1995) suggestion that specialisms can act as a mechanism which benefits 'high academic ability and middle-class children', and that, 'In particular, the development of specialisms such as dance or music indirectly discriminates against working class children' (Walford, 1996, p 59), Chitty goes on to point towards criticisms of the policy made by a former Director of the Institute of Education:

> Except in music and perhaps art, it does not seem possible to diagnose specific aptitudes for most school curriculum subjects. Instead, what seems to emerge from such testing is a general ability to learn, which is often, but not always, associated with the various advantages of coming from a middle-class home. How can headteachers know if the 'aptitude' of a ten-year-old in German shows anything more than the parents' ability to pay for language lessons? (Peter Mortimore, quoted in Chitty, 2009, p 70)

Quite beyond the questions of social segregation or stratification raised by covert selection or by specialisation, the processes just discussed, relating to admissions and also exclusions, raise immediate and pressing questions regarding accountability in the exercise of power by those managing schools. School admissions authorities do not have unfettered discretion in relation to the decisions they take, but, in theory at least, must abide by criteria set out in their published admissions policy or, if not, can be subject to challenge.

5.3 The law, the courts and parental preference

While the statutory framework for schooling has changed repeatedly and frequently since ERA, the legal issues around admissions have in some respects remained remarkably constant. Historically, the courts had confirmed clearly that LEAs were entitled to have admissions policies, which did not necessarily result in all parental wishes being met. Writing in 1993, Harris helpfully summarised the position as follows:

> Even before the 1980 Act it was quite legitimate for an LEA to have an admissions policy and to apply it in the exercise of its discretion on the allocation of school places. The 1980 Act provides that 'the policy followed in deciding admissions' must be published by LEAs and governors. Naturally such policies must not be applied too rigidly, for the legitimate exercise of discretion requires consideration of exceptional cases. Any policy which is applied must not only be reasonable in the broad *Wednesbury* sense of being a policy which a reasonable LEA would apply, it must also be consistent with the LEA's statutory obligations [including sex and race discrimination under specific legislation]. They would also include the obligations in Section 6 itself, for example the duty in Section 6(5) to give equal preference to persons living in another district. The 1980 Act does not specify criteria which should be applied or taken into account when prioritising applications; it only provides (in Section 6(3)) grounds on which preference may be denied.
>
> But that is not to say that the circumstances in which parental preference may be denied under Section 6(3) provide the only basis on which the policy may operate. LEAs may generally incorporate within their allocation policy a range of factors, including geographical proximity to the school or the presence of siblings at the school. (Harris, 1993, pp 135–6)

As Harris observed, guidance from the DES immediately following the introduction of OE under ERA stated that, subject to general anti-discrimination legislation, LEAs and governors were free to apply 'any reasonable criteria they wish for deciding which pupils should have priority of admission' (Harris, 1993, p 138). By 1993, however, in pursuit of the 'choice and diversity' agenda, central government guidance on admissions was becoming slightly more detailed. Harris (1993, p 138) points towards the DfE's 1992 Draft Circular's advice on 'oversubscription criteria' as preferring 'objective criteria' (such as sibling or family connections, home to school distance, catchment areas, feeder arrangements with primary schools, and ability or aptitude in overtly selective schools) while accepting more cautiously criteria involving 'an element of judgement' (such as medical or social grounds, contribution to the life of the school or pastoral benefit, desire for single sex benefit or religious affiliation, though of course such factors could legitimately be given priority in published admissions criteria). Subject to general anti-discrimination legislation and, in particular, post-1998 the provisions of the Human Rights Act (HRA), these criteria, in varying combinations and priorities, covered the vast majority of criteria applied in taking admissions decisions for oversubscribed schools. The Draft Circular also identified some criteria as unacceptable, including those intended to seek to exclude students with identified SEN, or potentially disruptive pupils, and, of interest in light of the discussion to follow in the next chapter, it outlawed the use of drawing of lots, stating that 'drawing lots clearly cannot be described as exercising a discretion' (Harris, 1993, p 139). The likely net effect of this guidance was summarised contemporaneously as follows:

> This guidance is unlikely to have much impact on most existing admissions policies ... Indeed, it seems that the principal goal is to improve the clarity of admissions procedures for the benefit of parents, admissions authorities and appeal bodies. Most LEAs and governing bodies already operate policies, which generally conform to the guidance, and the prospects of parents securing the school of their choice will not change. (Harris, 1993, p 140)

In terms of legal protection of parental choice under the 1980 Act and ERA, a series of cases sought to define and refine the precise nature of the task to be undertaken by LEAs in determining how admissions authorities must take into account parental preference as opposed to any 'prejudice to efficient education or use of resources' (under s 6(3)(a)) (see Harris, 1993, pp 145–8; and Ruff, 2002, pp 201–4). The most prominent case law on school admissions in this era centred on two issues: cross-border admissions between LEA areas, and parental preferences in relation to racial and/or religious make up of the school their child was to attend.

The position on cross-border admissions received high-profile consideration in the case of *R v Shadow Education Committee of the Greenwich London Borough Council ex p The Governors of John Ball Primary School ('Greenwich')* (1989) 88 LGR 589, resulting in a decision which Ruff (2002, p 200) describes as 'famous, if not notorious, in education law'. The *Greenwich* ruling is based on the Court of Appeal's construction of s 6(5) of EA80, and the principle established here was, in effect, subsequently reconfirmed in s 86(8) SSFA. The judgment's meaning and extent was amplified in subsequent cases (notably *R v Bromley LBC ex p C and others* [1992] 1 FLR 174, discussed in some detail by Harris (1993, pp 152–4), and *R v Rotherham MBC, ex p LT* [2000] ELR 76) but the essence of the *Greenwich* ruling was set out straightforwardly in the DfEE's 1999 School Admissions Code (para 5.4):'The 1989 Greenwich judgment established that LEA maintained schools may not give priority to children simply because of the fact that they live in the authority's administrative area. Applications for the authority's schools by parents living outside the LEA area must be considered equally'. The DfEE described the judgment as being a 'sensible recognition' of the realities of cross-boundary movement of pupils, and indeed, a government minister in debate had expressly highlighted the expectation of increased applications from outside the LEA area (see Harris, 1993, p 150). Especially in metropolitan London, more than one LEA's schools will likely be within reasonable travelling distance of many children, and the problems for LEAs resulting from this position are obvious.

A further, and often noted, expression of middle-class advantage can be manifested much less subtly in cases where admissions authorities give a high priority in their admissions criteria to policies of catchment areas or geographical proximity. Even with some of the obstacles to cross-border movement ironed out post-*Greenwich*, it is worth emphasising that simple geography will often be crucial in determining choice, with practicalities of home–school transport being a central factor, and the range of viable options between which a 'choice' can be made thus likely to be substantially greater in urban rather than rural settings. In essence, LEAs found themselves under a duty to plan local schooling to meet the needs of their authority's population, but post-*Greenwich* faced the problem of needing'to respond to consumer demand from a wide geographical area' (Harris, 1993, p 153) extending beyond the individual authority's boundaries. While such matters had historically generally been resolved via co-operation and reciprocity between neighbouring LEAs, the process became substantially more complex in situations where individual schools, such as GM schools, acted in effect as their own individual admissions authority, rendering such solutions more difficult. In 1999, a response to this fragmentation of LEA leadership in organising local admissions arrangements came in the form of the establishment of Local Admissions Forums, designed to 'help to develop a real consensus at a local level' (see Ruff, 2002, p 173), subsequently given legislative standing under the 2002 Education Act, though, perhaps significantly, removed as a requirement by s 34 of the 2011 Education Act. The resulting admissions arrangements adopted could be objected to by any LEA or other admissions authority, and in relation to pre-existing selection arrangements by a group of ten or more parents, via complaint to an Adjudicator, established under the SSFA, who was required to publish a reasoned decision as to whether or not to uphold the objection.

As noted earlier, one of the 'objective' admissions criteria noted with approval by the DfES was the use of geographical catchment areas. Ruff (2002, pp 203–5) notes that although catchment areas should not in general be designed so as to follow and reconfirm authority boundaries, case law subsequent to *Greenwich* has confirmed that catchment areas can lawfully have the effect of giving priority to a resident within an LEA area over one residing outside the area, where such priority arises purely incidentally, rather than by design or intention, from the manner in which a catchment has been designated. Despite such a permissive approach, it is also clear that courts will seek to give effect to clearly specified mandatory requirements imposed on admissions authorities. Thus, in *R (on the application of Governing Body of Drayton Manor High School) v Schools Adjudicator* ('*Drayton Manor*') [2008] EWHC 3119, at para 17), the court found that an admissions criterion applied in that case failed to comply with the School Admissions Code then in force as it did not,

> ... actively promote equity and indirectly discriminates against economically less advantaged families unable to afford housing in the areas benefiting from it. It has the effect of excluding a significant proportion of children living close to the school and for whom the school should be a real option, if that is their parents' preference, in order to promote community cohesion and to enable them to benefit from this excellent school.

While the willingness of courts on occasion to give effect to such requirements seems a positive development, awareness must be retained of the ability of government, as discussed in Chapter Four in relation to the case of the 2010 Coalition government, to introduce revised versions of the Code which do not impose such rigorous or specific requirements as regards social equity.

Almost inevitably, any greater clarity achieved by piecemeal development of a body of case law on school admissions failed to keep pace with the ever-increasing expectations of school choice sold to parents by politicians. Flowing from this reality came an increased emphasis on the parental right of appeal of decisions via administrative means, and scrutiny of the actions and effectiveness of the appeal panels. Parents remaining dissatisfied with the outcome of appeal committee decisions have had a range of possible avenues of further complaint. An application to the courts for judicial review is one such. An alternative is complaint to the Commissioner for Local Administration (Local Government Ombudsman) though Wolfe (2011) notes that this route of complaint is not now available in relation to maintained schools by virtue of EA11, s 45. A third option is to ask the Secretary of State to review an appeal committee's decision. While the last of these options pursues a political route to overturning a decision, the CLA route is focused only on a claim of 'maladministration' by the public authority (largely avoiding review of the merits of a claim), while in a judicial review action the courts will again be avoiding merits review but rather will be working within a jurisdiction permitting them to scrutinise the decision taken against standards of, in shorthand form (as discussed in Chapter One), illegality, irrationality, procedural impropriety or proportionality. The powers and practices of appeal panels have been further defined and refined on an *ad hoc* basis in cases coming before the courts on this basis.

On the key ground often employed by admissions authorities, the refusal of a place at an oversubscribed school based on the requirement that admission would prejudice economic or efficient education (SSFA, s 86(3)(a)), the courts had established a two-stage process summarised in the following terms by Lord Justice Woolf in *R v Commissioner for Local Administration, ex p Croydon LBC* [1989] 1 All ER 1033:

> [I]t is indeed a two stage exercise on which they embark: the first being to decide what is really a question of fact, is there or would there be prejudice to the efficient education etc. if this child were admitted, and the second, the question of discretion, balancing between the degree of prejudice

and the extent of applicability of the parental factors [or preference].

… Unless an appeal committee comes to the conclusion that compliance with the parents' preference would prejudice the provision of efficient education or the efficient use of resources, the local education authority remains under a duty to comply with the expressed preference and if they fail to do so they are in breach of duty. Accordingly, an appeal will automatically be allowed if an appeal committee do not consider that to give effect to the preference would result in such prejudice. If, however, an appeal committee comes to the conclusion that efficiency would be prejudiced by complying with the preference, then the appeal committee will have to proceed to the second stage and decide how to exercise its discretion, by weighing up the advantages which would be achieved by complying with the preference as against the prejudice this would cause.

In a sense, all of the routes of challenge imply consideration of the reasons for arriving at an admissions decision, and cases such as *R (on the application of Omotosho) v Harris Academy, Crystal Palace* [2011] All ER (D) 161 confirm the willingness of courts to quash decisions where reasons given are inadequate. At an even more general level, cases such as *R (on the application of Ahmad) v Waltham Forest LBC* [2007] EWHC 957 confirm that bodies such as admissions appeal panels must operate within the broad parameters of the judicial understanding of reasonableness. Such cases do serve to clarify the manner in which local authorities must take decisions, and the scope of appeal committee powers. Likewise, the 2009 Code of Practice on admission appeals (DCSF, 2009a) sought to clarify good practice on matters such as how appeals from multiple parents should be dealt with. Meanwhile the Schools Adjudicator 'has a key role in ensuring a fair admissions system by enforcing statutory requirements' (para 4.1). Required to consider any admissions arrangements referred to them by a local authority, appeals panel or Secretary of State, the Adjudicator is also empowered to 'consider the admission arrangements for that school as a whole, not just the specific subject of the objection, and the effect of these in the context of all the admission arrangements in the area' (para 4.3). Though the IPPR (2007, p 8) correctly identify the role as essentially reactive, the Schools Adjudicator had a brief extending to a systemic examination of admissions arrangements rather than simply responding to the facts of a particular case; a potentially useful development given the fragmentation of admissions arrangements as part of the agenda of breaking up the historic power and influence of LEAs over school admissions. However, as mentioned in the previous chapter, the Coalition government's 2012 Admissions Code (DfE, 2012a) has placed some limitations on the role of the Office of the Schools Adjudicator (OSA).

Inevitably, such guidance, procedures and additional bodies do not form the last word on complaints about admissions arrangements, with persistent parents continually seeking to challenge specific aspects of admissions policies and appeal committee practices (see Harris, 1993 and 2007; Ruff, 2002). One notable landmark was *R v Sheffield City Council, ex p H* [1999] ELR 511, in which a majority of the Court of Appeal found that the appeal committee could properly consider not only the merits of an appeal by an individual aggrieved parent in relation to the policy set by the LEA, but could also in the course of an appeal by a parent consider the LEA's admissions policy, somewhat more broadly reviewing its legality in relation to the terms of the statutory provisions on admissions, and, by extension, as illustrated in the *Drayton Manor* case, in relation to the terms of the mandatory School Admissions Code. The *Sheffield* case is interesting not only for its majority finding, but also for an impressive, and in many ways persuasive, dissenting judgment from Lord Justice Laws, seeking to confine the scope of appeal committee decision making to matters of fact in relation to particular cases, rather than matters of lawfulness in relation to LEA policy. Such a view might be thought to be more consistent with a conventional judicial view of the appropriate scope of the powers of a body such as an admissions appeal committee.

The wording adopted in SSFA, Schedule 24, para 12 seemed to indicate a role for appeal panels very much akin to the judicial review function undertaken by the courts in relation to public authorities. Considered by the Court of Appeal in *R v Richmond upon Thames LBC and Education Appeal Committee, ex p JC* [2001] ELR 21, Lord Justice Kennedy interpreted this to mean that '... it allows the appeal committee to have regard to powerful evidence of a highly significant change of circumstances which for one reason or another could not have been placed before the original admissions authority, and thus to do justice, without undermining the purposes of the legislation as a whole'. Serving to seek to avoid appeal committees becoming engaged in full re-hearing of cases previously determined by admissions authorities, while allowing them to ensure that the intention of the statute is given effect to, like the matters considered in the *Sheffield* case, this might seem primarily of interest to scholars of public law. They may seem to be focused on somewhat esoteric matters relating to the powers of local public bodies and their relationship with the courts. But the legal cases concerning the scope of appeal committee powers and their practices are not just of academic or legal interest. Rather, they form the basis on which disputes relating to school admissions are ultimately settled, and form the key mechanism by which the intention of statutory clauses which set the framework for such powers are clarified and defined. They act not only to resolve the individual dispute being heard, but also serve to establish future practice by admissions authorities and appeal committees. As Tweedie (1986) indicated clearly, decisions as regards individual cases in social programmes such as schooling will potentially have cumulative and systemic effects extending beyond the individual case. They serve to establish authoritatively the extent of lawful power and its exercise within the existing statutory and constitutional schema, and serve as the last word (absent fresh legislation) on the extent to which parental preference for a school will be met in practice. What the courts do not generally do, and in accordance with their constitutional position should not do, is overtly to rewrite the law in such a way as to change national or local policy on school admissions so as to subvert the intention underlying the statutory framework in force at any time. Thus, though judgments may have consequences extending beyond the instant case, the courts' creativity in this respect is, and constitutionally should be, strictly limited. Though it may not feel satisfactory to individual parents aggrieved at having their child denied a place at their preferred school, the reality is that they should not expect the courts to produce outcomes which cut across the policies enshrined by parliament in legislation. Though legal processes will have some role in interpreting and applying education law, it might be thought preferable that the policy intentions on school admissions should ultimately be the outcome of political rather than legal decision making.

The scope of legal provisions with a potential impact on school admissions has increased significantly over the last 35 years. Anti-discrimination legislation, starting with the 1975 Sex Discrimination Act (SDA) and the 1976 Race Relations Act (RRA) imposed duties on school admissions authorities not to discriminate on grounds of sex, colour, race, nationality or ethnic or national origins. In a similar vein, issues arise in relation to the parental preference for an education in accordance with their religious belief, with the 2006 Equality Act imposing 'equivalent non-discrimination duties to those concerning race and sex' (Harris, 2007, p 164), though as the 2009 School Admissions Code made clear (DCSF, 2009a, para 2.46) 'those schools designated by the Secretary of State as having a religious character (faith schools) are exempt and are permitted to use faith-based oversubscription criteria in order to give higher priority in admissions to children who are members of, or who practise, their faith or denomination'. Thus, secular expectations of equality of treatment remained substantially compromised by granting recognition to and priority for religious beliefs within the processes of admissions to oversubscribed schools within the state-funded education system.

As Harris observes (2007, p 147), the result of SDA was a series of cases confirming a default position of an expectation of equal numbers of places in a locality for boys and girls within single-sex schools, a preference which some parents hold strongly (see Ruff, 2002, pp 161–6; and Harris, 2007, chapter 4). Meanwhile much of the school-related case law on race has revolved around responses by schools and LEAs to issues involving manner of dress with cultural or religious associations or significance, and/or the wearing of religious symbols by pupils in school (see Harris, 2007, pp 154–62; Knights, 2005). In addition, high profile cases arose in the context of schooling concerning what appear to be 'racially motivated school choices' (Harris, 1993, p 141). Parental preference based on a particular desired outcome in relation to the racial make up of the school that their child will attend clearly serves to bring to the fore potential conflict between two principles which are said to inform education policy, what Harris describes as 'individual parental choice and racial harmony via a multi-cultural approach to educational provision' (Harris, 2007, p 145). By way of contrast with the United States, where segregation in schooling formed the context for a landmark legal ruling in support of equal rights (*Brown v Board of Education* 347 US 483 (1954)), Harris concludes in relation to *R v Cleveland County Council ex p Commission for Racial Equality* ([1994] ELR 44), that 'where choice of school is concerned the clear purpose of the RRA 1976 in promoting equal treatment and discouraging racial discrimination may be negated' (Harris, 2007, p 144). Again, it may seem that interpretation by the courts of the legal provisions will not serve to re-prioritise educational policy preferences, but will serve essentially to confirm the political policy choices made in drafting the legislation. Even the advent of the 1998 Human Rights Act (HRA), effectively incorporating into UK law the provisions of the ECHR, might be thought to have relatively little impact here. Harris summarises the position and issues succinctly:

> [R]ecognition of parental rights of choice over school selection can lead to forms of segregation through 'white flight', as in the case of the Dewsbury parents in 1988, or as

a result of the Asian parents in some areas gravitating towards particular schools, leading to schools with a high proportion of Asian pupils, while the Cleveland case indicated that the mandatory nature of the duty to comply with parental preference where a community school has places may serve to reinforce this process. While segregation of pupils on the basis of race or ethnicity is a form of unlawful discrimination, the law does not prevent de facto segregation from occurring through parental choice. In effect therefore, LEAs and schools are unable to avoid reinforcement of the discriminatory behaviour of some parents. For many parents, however, this is not simply an issue of choice but an issue of access to a social institution that safeguards their cultural integrity. (Harris, 2007, p 154)

As Forsey et al's study of *The globalisation of school choice* (2008) illustrates, evidence on school choice from other jurisdictions indicates that the tendency to produce or to further segregation in schooling is by no means unique to the UK. For example, Oplatka, writing in the Israeli context, argues that the findings there 'tend to align with some major conjectures in the criticism of school choice policy, especially in that school choice is held responsible for increasing ethnic, racial and religious segregation and not minimizing it, as some advocates of this reform maintained' (Oplatka, 2008, p 126).

While the law might address matters of unequal treatment based on race, gender or religion and the like, a still broader range of factors has to be considered in relation to admission to school and access to the education provided. The language medium used for education will be a priority for many (for example in parts of the UK where Welsh, or Scots Gaelic might be options), and access to suitable schooling for children in communities with an itinerant life-style – 'Travellers' – (see generally, Sandland, 2008), remains perennially problematic. As Harris observes,

[F]or the human rights position to be that the state's duty is little more than to provide educational facilities and do nothing more to facilitate access to them seems absurd. The notion of universal provision surely implies its practical availability and that its denial, other than on sound academic grounds, must be prevented if at all possible. While ... it is for the state to make policy decisions about the allocation of resources, a situation that helps to prevent the right to

> education from being absolute, one would assume that
> a guarantee of support for access is necessarily implied.
> (Harris, 2007, p 142)

While it remains clear that though 'choice' of school within the state education system is clearly not an absolute right, the basis for organising schools between which choice can be exercised implies clearly the need for management of a system of schools. But the judicial system will not respond to such systemic needs unless a legislative framework is established which permits or requires it to do so. Neither can the judicial system be expected to address perceived problems relating to the likelihood of access to a preferred publicly funded school being exercised on a profoundly advantaged basis by those parents with the financial ability available to move into the relevant area, and/or simply with the social capital to know how to play the admissions system to best effect. Neither general human rights law nor education-specific provisions have anything to say about such inequalities. Nor, of course, does the law speak to the raw financial power exercised by affluent parents in buying education for their children at sometimes very prestigious and apparently successful schools within the private sector; Mark Goodwin (2009, p 273) suggests that 'exit' to the private sector was an option pursued by a significant number of parents dissatisfied with the allocation process incorporating an element of lottery introduced in Brighton and Hove in 2007, discussed further in Chapter Six.

Thus, the legal position on school admission processes remains one of a limited and conditional reconciliation of a series of what are often contradictory social claims and political objectives. In this context, the judicial process does not seem to contain sufficient internal logic or independent force to effect substantial change on the statutory framework established by the political forces which dominate the legislative process. Though this is essentially constitutionally proper, recognition of this reality is important if over-inflated or unrealistic hopes or expectations of the legal system are to be avoided. The policy direction of education, and of crucial aspects of it such as admissions to schools, will be established in the political context, and in interpreting these choices as expressed in legislative form, the judicial system can at most be expected to produce narrow and marginal variations to the overall policy direction established by legislation.

5.4 Is there any choice about choice?

The dominant paradigm for education reform in England has been since 1988 that of the quasi-market. Though certainly not unique to the national context, we find here a particularly striking example of how 'educational discourse has shifted to embrace the ideology of competition and market forces' (Forsey et al, 2008, p 14, quoting Boulton and Coldron). It may seem that there is now little choice about admission to schools being based upon some notion of choice.

But it is clear that the market is not the only perspective from which school admissions can legitimately be viewed or judged. Noted from the very start of this book has been the diverse range of functions which education is associated with, ranging through human development, to servicing economic needs, and credentialing in such a way as to differentiate between those emerging from the education system. A state-funded school system might also be expected to form an essential element in cementing social solidarity via shared knowledge, values and experience. Clearly, not all such factors relate exclusively to individual preference or choice, or even, in the case of the broader social functions, relate exclusively to individual need or claim. As such, it is proper to acknowledge a wide range of values associated with schooling, and hence admission to schools, and to scrutinise the admissions process from a range of perspectives extending beyond parental choice.

If it was to be assumed that all parents are equally motivated and equipped to pursue the best available state education for their child, and if an equally diverse range of schools is available for all parents to choose from, and if the available mechanisms of stating a preference of school successfully ensure that all parents are equally informed as to available choices, it might be expected that all schools would have an intake reflecting a broad spread of social and cultural backgrounds. Yet it remains manifestly the case that this outcome has not been the end product of the choice agenda in schooling pursued since 1988. As Burgess et al find:

> The present system, which can be characterised as a mixture of neighbourhood schooling (where pupils simply attend their local school) and choice-based schooling, leads to the sorting of pupils. Pupils are not evenly spread across a group of schools in terms of their key stage test scores, their eligibility for free school meals, or their ethnicity. This sorting is higher where there is more choice. The interplay of the decisions of schools, parents and LEAs produces an

outcome in which there is clustering together of pupils scoring well in the key stage tests, and a clustering of pupils from poorer backgrounds. This is unlikely to be to the advantage of the latter pupils. (Burgess et al, 2006, p 14)

Evidence that choice mechanisms have any positive impact on social integration is hard to find: 'What choice policies may do is change the rules by which segregation takes place, but without markedly increasing or eliminating levels of segregation that are largely shaped by structural factors' (Gorard et al, 2003, p 186, quoted in Walford, 1996, p 103). The evidence indicating that policies of choice in schooling have served only to reproduce social hierarchy and segregation is summarised succinctly by IPPR (2007, p 9), drawing on Burgess et al's 2004 work: 'overall schools tended to be more segregated than the pupil's neighbourhood in terms of ability ... and ... that where there is more choice available (measured by the number of nearby schools), school segregation is higher'. It is worth restating Walford's simple but telling observation: 'Put crudely, if there is a hierarchy of schools, someone has to attend those at the bottom of the hierarchy if others are selected for those schools at the top' (Walford, 2008, p 104). While artificial limits on school numbers are prohibited, for whatever reason, or combination of diverse reasons, the most popular schools will be oversubscribed absent unlimited expansion of such institutions, which, if permitted, would inevitably change their very nature. There are no easy solutions from any perspective, and we should be sceptical of any suggestion or claim that any policy options can readily resolve this situation.

While it is clear that debate can be informed legitimately by a wide range of perspectives which extend beyond the particularly dominant perspective of choice as embodied in the quasi-market reforms of English education, it can be difficult to resist the charms of choice: 'The *idea* of choice offers alluring promises of equality, freedom, democracy and pleasure that traverses political and social boundaries. It reflects and evokes deep desires for autonomy, control and self-expression' (Forsey et al, 2008, p 9, original emphasis). As such, opposition to choice *per se* is a difficult case to make, in schooling as elsewhere. Yet rarely do critics of the quasi-market in education direct their antagonism towards choice in and of itself. Rather, opposition tends to focus on the outcomes and consequences of having choice centre stage in this context, and claims that there are negative consequences outweighing any perceived benefits that might accrue from the exercise of individual choice. It is at this point that dialogue between competing positions becomes near impossible, because opponents of choice in schooling tend to focus on what they view as threats posed by choice of school to a set of values relating to equity of treatment, social integration, and the collective purposes of education in a democratic context, while proponents of choice via markets tend to emphasise the value of individual choice as a human good in itself, and also present it as a lever suitable for pushing up educational standards in an economically efficient manner.

There is apparently little scope for dialogue between two such different discourses, and a real risk that 'discussion' between the competing positions will in reality amount to nothing more than attacks from firmly entrenched positions. In this context, Mark Goodwin attempts to establish that 'choice need not be seen as a threat to the equity and quality of service provision and that there are good reasons for those who identify with progressive politics to support greater choice in public services' (Goodwin, 2009, p 270). His stated agenda therefore becomes one of considering choice in the context of schooling 'in isolation from any neoliberal ideological baggage' (Goodwin, 2009, p 270).

In pursuit of this difficult task, Goodwin seeks to unpack the arguments deployed in favour of choice: arguments from 'liberty', 'equity' and 'economy'. In relation to liberty, he finds that rather than forming a simple extension of a libertarian philosophy, choice in schooling can be presented instead as an aspect of 'governance-driven choice strategies' – seeming to imply that the exercise of choice in this context is nothing more than a practical manifestation of the exercise of 'voice' within the political system. In relation to arguments about equity, along the lines that the exercise of choice in schooling produces socially regressive outcomes, he points towards possible arguments that any reproduction of segregation or stratification under choice systems does not produce demonstrably 'worse' outcomes than the predominant alternative of neighbourhood schooling. In relation to questions of economic efficiency, and standards being driven up by the mechanism of parental choice, he adopts an argument suggesting that the lack of evidence of progress in this regard results from the project's incompleteness: 'There are so many distortions and faulty mechanisms in the quasi-market for secondary schooling that it is not reasonable to anticipate a systematic improvement in standards resulting from competitive pressures' (Goodwin, 2009, p 276). In this context he goes on to address directly some of the problems typically pointed towards by 'progressive' critics of school choice:

> The undesirable effects associated with school diversity, such as schools using their discretion over admissions to 'improve'

intake, are the result of incomplete marketisation, which allows over-subscribed schools to choose pupils rather than the reverse, thus disrupting the market mechanism. The problem of schools choosing pupils might be addressed by greater flexibility of school places and less imposition of a centrally controlled school model such as academies [... and ...] by developing a funding mechanism that is more responsive to changes in school composition. (Goodwin, 2009, p 277)

Notwithstanding Mark Goodwin's stated objective of separating choice of school from the neo-liberal ideology with which it is invariably associated, the hackles of many critics of the quasi-market in schooling will doubtless have well and truly risen by this stage! The picture Goodwin points towards seems to be one of ever-expanding super-schools with a high degree of autonomy over structures. Just as consumers often seem to shop at supermarkets while bemoaning the decline of small specialist high-street outlets, it would seem likely that the attractions of such ever-larger schools would likely wane in due course, but with any alternatives by then having been killed off.

Yet Goodwin also nods towards an alternative perspective 'that, in preference to choice, the best strategy for educational governance involves creating more opportunities for the general public to be involved in the deliberative processes of local government (and therefore in governance of education)' (Goodwin, 2009, p 277). While he properly raises problems in this regard, in relation to a high degree of apathy to such engagement in the traditional mechanisms of local politics, it is worth emphasising also that any such deliberative processes imply a substantial role for local authorities in education; a position which has been consistently diminished and marginalised over more than 20 years of education reform, and might prove rather difficult to reinvigorate.

Goodwin points towards the need to avoid dogmatic opposition to choice, and indeed for supporters of choice not to over-estimate the ability of choice to change the school system. Yet ultimately 'progressive' critics of choice may still have grounds to take issue with the position he adopts. It seems that, ultimately, the 'extension of democratic rights' he envisages seems to be focused almost exclusively on, or privileging, a particular sub-set of rights, related to individualism and consumerism, while the broader democratic value set embodied in our constitutional settlement, associated with citizenship, can be said to incorporate properly a much broader set of values. More specifically, it seems that the primary form of 'voice' envisaged by

Goodwin, the exercise of choice, again fails to capture a constitutional and democratic expectation that citizens, or their representatives, should have some input into formulation choice over policy options, requiring legitimate public institutions beyond the market, while 'voice' in the simple form of choice can be wholly detached from this expectation, relating exclusively to a consumerist vision of the individual. The only institution determining the nature and range of choices available in this situation is the market, while it might properly be argued that policy formulation within a service such as education, publicly funded and serving public agendas, should be shaped and overseen by institutions which are accountable via deliberative political processes. To simply hand over decision-making power over the future shape of schooling to the market, or to randomness (as discussed in Chapter Six), is to deny and avoid the democratic expectation that decision making in such a crucial area will be capable of being challenged and held to account in accordance with constitutional and democratic norms and is to pre-determine that the outcomes and distributions resulting from such allocation processes are outcomes which are desirable. It is to deny significance to those systemic factors extending beyond the outcomes of decisions pertaining to individuals. Instead of institutions incorporating the full set of values associated with citizenship, including collective interests, the institution of the market reflects and builds upon only the values of the individual consumer.

This privileging of choice over alternative drivers for administering school admissions is premised both on the neo-liberal vision (of libertarian origin) of choice as a good in itself, but also on a belief that the exercise of market forces in the form of parental choice will drive up educational standards in schools. Leaving aside for the moment questions over what exactly is meant or understood by 'standards', as Harris observes:

> [R]ights of choice are likely to be enjoyed unequally across society and to create social barriers through the de facto segregation that tends to result from their exercise ... [and] ... Given the absence of clear evidence that competition has a marked impact in terms of raising school standards within the state sector we are left merely with the libertarian argument for choice. (Harris, 2007, p 315)

Thus it is worth standing back a little and viewing the idea of choice as a good in itself. If, for the purposes of argument, it is accepted that choice is a good in itself, presumably any legitimate perspective must view it as only one of a number of 'goods' potentially relating to education. These could be listed in many different ways, but the list of criteria Woods et al (1998) set out as aspects of 'the public interest' in schooling, noted in Chapter Four, is again helpful here. The values or principles they list include fairness, social integration, a concern with raising educational quality and standards, the importance of participation and responsiveness in a democratic society, and clarity in policy aims. Overall, they refer to a vision of 'the schooling system, as a public service, aspiring to serve all families equally well and not disadvantaging particular groups or social classes' (Woods et al, 1998, p 199). Though by no means an uncontroversial or exhaustive list, it is telling that this wide-ranging set of criteria does not include reference to 'choice'. This is possibly because choice is not viewed from within this perspective as a good in itself in relation to schooling; rather, it would appear to be one mechanism for determining how places will be allocated within a system oriented towards the kind of public interest objectives identified. On this view, in so far as choice enhances the delivery of such criteria, or at least does not obstruct their delivery, then it is to be, respectively, welcomed or not deprecated.

If choice is given a central position in relation to school admissions, this is as a result of a political belief in choice and markets as goods and ends in themselves rather than because of any inherent relationship to or support it offers for educational outcomes. The selection of choice as a primary driver for school admissions is a statement of political preference, and it is a preference for a particular procedure rather than identifiable educational objectives, which, as Woods et al suggest, need to be the subject of debate. The use of choice in school admissions may tend to lead to certain outcomes, but they should properly be judged in relation to standards or values which have been debated and determined within the political system, rather than being accepted as the inevitable and unchangeable outcomes of a particular process which has been chosen as an ideological preference. If the outcomes of the admissions process are not consonant with the set of values for the education system, there must be room for debate about whether choice is the best mechanism to serve as the driver for the allocation of school places – there must be room for choice about choice.

5.5 Some conclusions on admissions in the quasi-market

Based on the context established in the previous chapter, and the evidence discussed in this chapter regarding the outcomes of the exercise of the parental choice mechanisms in relation to school admissions in England post–1988, certain conclusions can be reached in relation to the sort of 'public interest' criteria set out by Woods et al (1998).

Though such factors were not central to the thinking of those who introduced the quasi-market in ERA, it seems clear from the material presented in the previous section that there is no evidence to suggest that, more than 20 years after ERA, parental choice mechanisms have increased social integration in schooling or facilitated the reduction of segregation or social stratification; indeed, quite the opposite seems to be the case. As regards educational standards, which were central to the rhetoric of proponents of the quasi-market, even those such as Mark Goodwin (2009) seeking to make a case for avoiding dogmatic objections to choice, or the SMF (2005) who actively support it in principle, cannot point to clear and substantial improvements arising from the exercise of choice though they may attribute this to the incompleteness of current market arrangements. There remain a small but significant number of parents who do not receive a place for their child at the school they have 'chosen'. Local authorities, founded on the basis of democratic structures, however imperfect, have, through reform measures taken by governments, become increasingly marginal to school admissions. A local system of schooling has been replaced by an increasingly atomised model with multiple admissions authorities requiring close scrutiny to ensure that expectations of accountability are met in these 'privatised' public institutions operating outside conventional lines of accountability. Evidence presented by the Children's Commissioner (2012) on apparent abuses of the power to exclude children can only add to concerns related to such a situation. Though driving up standards was central to the rhetoric associated with the introduction of quasi-market forces, there is scant evidence of any benefits to the education system as a whole emerging from over twenty years of development and redevelopment of mechanisms for parental choice. Meanwhile, where oversubscription occurs, parental choice remains mythical, with the ability of parents to state a preference, as prior to ERA, remaining the inevitable reality. Concerns about the power of selection being located in the hands of admissions authorities (often individual schools) remain, through structuring of such discretion via School Admissions Codes (though susceptible to ready reform by government Ministers), oversight from bodies such as the Schools Adjudicator, and the potential for occasional intervention by the courts, may all have potential to offer a degree of reassurance in this regard.

But we have also observed the limits of legal oversight. Mechanisms of review can at most be expected to ensure compliance with the legal framework within which school admissions are expected to take place – given the centrality of the concept of 'Supremacy of Parliament' within the British constitutional schema, the courts cannot be expected to shift the basis of the process beyond that established in the legislation. The courts can be expected to intervene to enforce procedural propriety, but they are unlikely ever to find grounds to intervene to develop substantive rights, such as having a place at a specific school, in the absence of specific foundations for such a decision in statute or precedent case law. The most that can realistically be expected from the courts is marginal variation, rather than major departure, from direction set by government in statute or under delegated powers.

Yet the courts should be expected to act as guardians of the constitution, and as discussed in Chapter One this implies protecting the values which inform that constitutional settlement, and, by virtue of the HRA, this now includes a broad jurisdiction to review the actions of public bodies in relation to their compatibility with a broad set of rights and expectations. While giving the courts substantial ability to intervene to protect specified rights, which decisions may have incidental consequences for school admission processes, nothing in British case law or statute establishes a right for a child to be educated at the school of a parent's choice. Any expectations to the contrary raised in parents by politicians or the media, in connection with HRA or education-specific legislation, are unfounded. As dispute resolution mechanisms tend to respond to individual cases and complaints rather than collective or systemic issues (as noted in Chapter One), if it is thought that affirmative action is necessary to equalise opportunity of access to the most desirable publicly funded schools, perhaps because some families lack the cultural or economic resources to allow them to 'play' the admissions game, this would require policy implementation or legislation in pursuit of such a policy; a task for government or parliament, not the judiciary. The recent introduction by the Coalition government of the 'pupil premium', with additional funding for schools attaching to pupils from within designated economically disadvantaged groups, would be an example of such an initiative, though, as noted in Chapter Four, more controls on, or monitoring of, how such additional funding is utilised might be thought necessary if its aims are to be achieved. But more general notions of equity remain underdeveloped and unenforceable.

It is important to avoid what Whitty (2002, p 135) terms 'golden age-ism' here. It is clear that the LEA-centred admissions model which preceded ERA could be considered far from perfect in terms of democratic accountability and responsiveness, and indeed in terms of outcome; not all parents were happy with the school allocation decisions made under it, and strong catchment area policies or proximity criteria resulting in 'selection by mortgage' may well have contributed substantially to reproducing social stratification in the school system. Yet, fundamentally, the local authority based approach ensured that policy decisions could be made, planning could be undertaken, and a system of schools developed; and, crucially, these activities were conducted on a reasoned basis which was subject to scrutiny by political processes and the courts in terms of the procedural propriety, legality and rationality of the decision-making process. When such decision making is left to quasi-market forces, with outcomes being the result of individual preferences expressed by parents translated into decisions taken by admissions authorities, there is little left to challenge or engage with in terms of the substance of decisions. 'The atomisation of educational decision-making' (Whitty, 2002, p 92) appears close to being the antithesis of planning or deliberation, and serves to emphasise the absence of 'contexts for determining appropriate institutional and curricular arrangements on behalf of the whole society'.

Clearly, strengthening the mechanisms of scrutiny and accountability in relation to decision making is desirable in terms of compliance with constitutional expectations attaching to such processes in the context of public services. Likewise, making adjustments to the processes relating to choice might ensure that they better meet the interests of individual 'consumers'. However, such measures will do nothing to incorporate the broader set of educational values associated with citizenship such as those listed by Woods et al in their identification of 'public interest' criteria. In Whitty's terms, 'If we want equity to remain on the educational agenda, we should certainly be looking to find new ways of making educational decision-making a part of democratic life and a legitimate public sphere' (Whitty, 2002, p 93) for there is nothing in quasi-market mechanisms which is designed or able to accommodate such values. It seems that if the constitutional and democratic expectations of accountability in the fulfilment of public service activities are to be met, and if the courts are to be able to engage effectively in protecting these interests, it will be necessary to articulate and specify these values with reasonable clarity within the political system and to give them legislative form. Given the hegemony of market-oriented thinking across the political mainstream in Britain and much of the rest of the developed world, such steps seem unlikely. It would seem therefore that, for better or for worse, market forces are likely to remain the dominant force in school admissions systems for the foreseeable future. As the material discussed in this chapter has suggested, in terms of both educational outcomes and social equity, there is little if any evidence to suggest that this is for the better, and much to suggest that it is for the worse.

SIX

Admissions by lottery

6.1 Introduction

The previous three chapters have charted how a system of school admissions premised, in theory at least, on parental choice came to supersede a system centred on admissions policies determined and managed by local education authorities (LEAs). The two different models appear to represent contrasting responses to the wide range of expectations, values and priorities underlying debate regarding school admissions. Competing for priority, in this context, are agenda items relating *inter alia* to equality, equity of treatment, national economic needs, local democratic expectations and individual choice. The LEA–centred and choice-based models discussed previously will inevitably give different priorities to these and other factors implicated in decision making about admissions. In general terms, while the LEA–centred model might be expected to emphasise collective and local democratic values, on occasion to the detriment of individual preference, the choice model (with choice exercised unevenly) may be likely to prioritise individual choice over collective planning agendas. As will be clear from previous discussion, neither approach can be considered wholly successful on its own terms and, inevitably, both will be subject to heavy criticism from alternative perspectives.

With little if any sign from any major political party of plans for any return to an admissions system centred on local authority powers, attention in recent years has inevitably focused on perceived failings in the parental choice model introduced from 1988 onwards, and on proposals for its reform. In this regard, criticisms come from two prominent and quite distinct perspectives. The first is from parents disappointed at their children not having been admitted to an oversubscribed school of their choice. As noted in previous chapters, though relatively small in numbers, complaints from disgruntled parents, especially perhaps those from affluent and articulate groups who may have bought a house in the proximity of a popular school only to find a place not available for their child as a result of oversubscription, are persistent and prominent in the popular media, even if coverage might be thought to overstate the degree of dissatisfaction. It should be unsurprising if the rhetoric of choice in schooling perpetuated since 1988 leads to genuine feelings of frustration and anger when choices are not met. The second is from commentators concerned with questions of equity and equality of opportunity who point towards the clear tendency, discussed in Chapter Five, of the parental choice system to reproduce social stratification and segregation. This latter angle of critique can also be related to an argument that the outcomes from the quasi–market mechanisms central to current school admissions practices neglect collective values as the structures incorporate only the values of the individual 'consumer' rather than the broader, democratic and collectively oriented values of the citizen which arguably should have a place in the system. From the first of these perspectives, the response is often that the complexities and uncertainties of the current system of 'choice' leaves disappointed parents feeling like the process is, in common parlance, little more than a lottery. From the second perspective, claims of 'a postcode lottery', by which the quality and choice of school depends on where children live may be presented or perceived as misleading, with the likelihood of success in being admitted to the most popular and successful schools being in reality 'closely correlated with parental income, class and ethnic background' (Peter Wilby, *TES*, 7 October 2005). If this is the case, then the reality of school admissions is far from the equal chance of success suggested by the term 'lottery'. The response to this, 'Forget postcodes, let's have a proper lottery', is not just a nice rhetorical flourish or a neat headline, but reflects an increasing interest in resort to random methods to allocate school places, and is likely to derive from dissatisfaction with the present system's perceived failure to address social stratification and segregation.

While 'real' lotteries have now been used to allocate places at oversubscribed schools in some areas over some time, in this chapter serious consideration will be given to whether such experiments might legitimately be used more widely. The intention here is not to advocate or deprecate the use of random methods in this context. Rather, the intention is to consider whether, in relation both to the range of substantive values at stake in admissions decisions and the background constitutional and legal norms, random methods might be considered any more or less legitimate than the approaches based on planning or choice considered earlier. In this sense, giving due consideration to the use of methods based on random selection may serve as a heuristic device: if approaches based on planning or choice are found not to deliver processes or outcomes preferable to those which random methods would deliver, their claims of legitimacy must be considered weak indeed.

Thus, the agenda pursued in this chapter is not one of campaigning for or against the adoption of random methods for allocating school places, but rather to scrutinise the extent to which the use of lotteries, to replace or supplement more conventional methods, would increase or decrease the legitimacy of decisions made in relation to school admissions. To make the authors' position clear at the outset of this discussion, the starting point adopted here is not in favour of lotteries. While the fundamental promise of lotteries may appear to be an attractive one of 'equal chance', Lawton (1977, p 8) refers back to Aristotle to make the point that 'injustice may result from treating unequals (sic) equally, as well as from treating equals unequally', and a clear preference must be stated for reasoned decisions which have regard both to concerns for equality in terms of citizenship and social justice, and also for decisions which accord with the expectations of rationality and accountability which underlie the constitutional and legal discourses on which legitimacy for public decisions is generally based. In this sense, alternatives to random selection, based on criteria such as need, merit, desert, and on adjudicative and deliberative methods (see Stone, 2011, pp 104–6), seem *prima facie* more attractive in relation to the allocation of an important social good such as schooling. But, given the questions raised regarding the 'fairness', rationality and accountability, and hence legitimacy, of decision making under planning- and choice-based admissions processes identified in previous chapters, it is proper to consider whether the alternative of random allocation fares any better or worse in respect of such criteria.

The attraction of random allocation of school places by lottery may originate from a critique of bureaucratic planning models and/or from a perception of failings in the choice model introduced post-1988. In Barbara Goodwin's terms:

> [T]he increasing interest in political and social lotteries may be attributable to discontent with existing democratic processes and to the realisation that there are many scarce social goods which should not be distributed through market mechanisms, such as university places or medical treatment. There is also a popular distrust of bureaucratic or elite processes of allocation, which often appear opaque or biased. (Goodwin, 2005, p 258)

Though currently most commonly used in practice as a tie-break mechanism, when all other listed criteria have failed to separate applicants, there are also moves towards utilising lotteries as a decision-making mechanism earlier in the process of allocating school places in England and in similar contexts in other countries (see Boyle, 2010, pp 31–51). Before any meaningful conclusions can be reached on the appropriateness or desirability of utilising random allocation of school places or extending the use of such methods, a range of issues need to be addressed. Clearly, its impact on parental choice or preference needs to be considered. Beyond this, however, lie a number of issues deriving from a very different perspective. The vision of democracy, and legitimacy deriving from accountability, which has informed discussion in this book is premised on the identification of values and policy choices via a process of rational discourse. Just as it might be suggested that market-based approaches to school admissions might deny or marginalise certain democratic values, so random methods of allocating school places might seem to fail to adhere to the constitutional, democratic and legal expectation of reasoned decision making and outcomes from such processes being amenable to reasoned debate, and whatever mechanisms or procedures are adopted, it seems reasonable to demand some justification for their adoption. Before turning to such broader arguments relating to justice and democracy, some examples of school admissions lotteries in practice, and responses to them will first be considered.

6.2 Admissions lotteries in practice

Discussion of the use of random methods for allocating school places began to develop some profile and momentum in the mid-2000s, when the 1988 Education Reform Act (ERA) open admissions policies, as amended, had been running for some 15 years. By this point some were beginning to argue that the ability of middle-class parents to best navigate the complex web of admissions systems, whether by purchasing property in the right area or other means (including, as noted in Chapter Five, on occasion, deception), had combined with pressures on oversubscribed schools to adopt systems that allowed them to 'select' the pupils most likely to contribute to the school's success in league tables, to result in social homogeneity in both the most popular (oversubscribed) schools and in the least attractive schools, reflecting underlying social stratification and segregation. The use of random methods for selection seemed one possible response to such issues by way of disrupting the potential for utilising social advantage through such means.

As unattractive as it might be, it is almost impossible to avoid entirely the flavour of 'class war' in this context. In 2005 the *TES* (7 October 2005) commented that 'according to estimates' house prices were 'at least 12 per cent more expensive if there is a popular school nearby – only the affluent can afford them'. A year earlier, it had reported how 'House prices inside popular schools' catchment areas have rocketed by up to £20,000'. While firm figures are hard to come by in this regard, Boyle (2010, p 69) also clearly identifies a house price premium in the vicinity of popular schools, though he estimates this as about £9,000 in London, which he notes looks 'reasonable' when compared with the average per-pupil spend on private education. Certainly this would seem a good financial decision for those parents able to make it, when compared with the cost of purchasing schooling in the private sector, which, as noted in Chapter Five, was reported as being an option chosen by some parents in Brighton and Hove dissatisfied with the lottery process used there. It is clear, however, that purchasing houses in expensive areas is not an option open to all parents, and also that policies seeking to diminish the advantages for the relatively wealthy would be controversial and difficult for any party in government: 'Planning admissions to ensure a social mix would enrage the parents of middle England who would find their children deliberately shut out of their preferred school in favour of those from the council estate down the road' (*TES*, 18 June 2004). By 2008, the *TES* (1 February 2008) was reporting that the *Mail on Sunday*, often thought to be one of the most prominent voices of the middle classes, was talking of the admissions lotteries then operating or planned in terms of being a 'twisted', 'cynical', 'frightening new experiment in social engineering'! Boyle draws on work by Gibbons and Machin (2006 and 2007) in the US and the UK to conclude that selection by lottery would not necessarily 'banish the house-price premium of a good local school', but that 'The lottery may be attractive to policy makers because it suggests it *might* break the link' (Boyle, 2010, p 69, original emphasis).

Certainly, prior to the arrival of the 2010 Coalition government at least, there seemed some substantial likelihood of the use of random allocation expanding further. A Local Government Association spokesperson was quoted in 2008 as suggesting that in the following year some 40% of local authorities would be using some form of lottery (*The Times*, 20 September 2008). However, the adoption of random allocation has not, as yet, become as wide-ranging a 'social experiment' as opponents might have feared. Though it was reported in 2009 that the number of schools utilising lotteries had risen six-fold since 2001, this was a rise from 1% of schools to 6% (*The Guardian*, 17 October 2009). More tellingly perhaps, lotteries were still generally being used as a tie-break mechanism, when all other criteria had proved indecisive, rather than as a primary mechanism for allocating places. In part, slow development of random systems for allocating places can be attributed to reluctance on the part of the politicians in power to embrace this approach. While noting that his government's School Admissions Code of Practice had set out that 'random allocation can be a legitimate way of determining a school place in tie-break situations', and that 'in some areas this is the fairest way of resolving a tiny minority of decisions', the then Secretary of State, Ed Balls, was also quoted in 2009 as follows:

> "I know the issue of lotteries is causing some concern to parents around the country.
> I have sympathy with the view that a lottery system can feel arbitrary, random and hard to explain to children in years 5 and 6 who don't know what's going to happen and don't know which children in their class they're going on to secondary school with.
> The code allows a role for random allocation, but I would be very concerned if it was happening other than as a last resort when other ways of allocating places have been exhausted." (BBC News, 1 March 2009)

As the Secretary of State noted, the School Admissions Code of Practice then current, which he had endorsed, did permit the use of random allocation:

> "Random allocation of school places can be good practice particularly for urban areas and secondary schools. However, it may not be suitable in rural areas. It may be used as the sole means of allocating places or alongside other oversubscription criteria, but only after criteria giving priority to children in care and the admission of children with a statement of special educational needs. Random allocation can widen access to schools for those unable to afford to buy houses near to favoured schools and create greater social equity." (DCSF, 2009a, para 2.33)

This limited endorsement of the utilisation of random methods in that version of the Code was followed up with requirements as regards transparency of operation and independent verification of the random allocation process (paras 2.34 and 2.35). It is clear therefore that government policy had shifted dramatically from the position held by the 1992 Conservative government under which, as stated in the 1992 Draft Circular, the DfE had included as an 'unacceptable criterion' the drawing of lots to allocate places, on the basis that 'drawing lots clearly cannot be described as exercising a discretion' (see Harris, 1993, p 139).

Random allocation of school places also received some passing attention from the House of Commons Education Committee (HOC, 2011c), but as a result of the concerns he had expressed about the use of random methods the Minister asked the Office of the Schools Adjudicator (OSA) to investigate and report on the use of random allocation. The somewhat thin report that emerged (OSA, 2009a) reaches fairly sanguine conclusions regarding what the investigation had revealed. At the most general level, the report finds that 'Although ... the use of random allocation is not uncommon, in practice it has had very little impact on the allocation of school places. This is because the vast majority of local authorities only use it as a tie-break to allocate the last remaining place[s]' (para 20), leading to an overall conclusion that there was no need to amend current legislation or the School Admissions Code of Practice. The picture revealed by the investigations summarised in the OSA's report suggests that approximately one in five local authorities used some form of random method in 2009 (30 of 150 respondents used it for primary schools, 29 of 150 for secondary schools). Of these only two used it as more than a tie-break in relation to secondary school places, where 'it is used by some single-sex schools to admit from a larger catchment area than they would otherwise do if the usual criterion of distance was used' (para 7). The report does detail some of the very narrow circumstances in which local authorities will utilise lottery as tie-break (para 10) and it is clear that such circumstances are strictly limited and will be unlikely to have much, if any impact on the overall pattern of admissions; even here, however, there will be 'winners' and 'losers' from the use of random methods, and we will need to return to this shortly.

The two local authorities that chose to use random allocation more widely than the norm, on which the OSA commented and which were the subject of much media attention, were Brighton and Hove, and Hertfordshire. In the former case, random allocation was included in the admission arrangements for all community secondary schools, but in conjunction with a catchment area policy; the policy is being reviewed in 2012. In the latter case, Hertfordshire, some 44% of the available places at the heavily oversubscribed single-sex secondary schools were allocated by random methods. Here, random allocation took place in relation to two groups of children: those outside the relevant school's 'priority area', and those 'in the priority area but for whom the school is not their nearest non-faith maintained school of the relevant gender and who do not satisfy other criteria (i.e. looked after children, medical or siblings)' (para 13). Reviewing the impact of the policy adopted in Brighton, Allen et al (2010a) reported that only very marginal changes had occurred in terms of socio-economic segregation. With admission patterns complicated by catchment areas being re-drawn, while they identified clear groups of 'winners' and 'losers' when compared with traditional non-random methods for allocating school places, because catchment areas were still applied as a prior criterion before the lottery, 'in reality there have been few spaces available at the most popular schools [to be allocated by lottery] once priority to those living within the catchment zone has been accounted for' (Allen et al, 2010a, p 17). Thus, neither Brighton and Hove nor Hertfordshire seem to represent radical attempts to introduce random methods. In both cases, the use of random methods is limited by other criteria, in particular by catchment or proximity criteria; they remain in essence tie-breaks, though applied to a wider range of cases than would generally be the case in other local authority areas.

Compared to the Labour Government's 2009 version, the Coalition government's 2012 School Admissions Code is much less positive about the use of random allocation. While the 2009 version had stated that the method 'can be particularly good practice for urban areas and secondary schools' and that it 'can be used as the sole means of allocating places or alongside other oversubscription criteria', in the 2012 version, the tone is prescriptive, stating that 'Local Authorities *must not* use random allocation as the principal oversubscription criteria for allocating places at all the schools in the area for which they are the admission authority' (original emphasis). The 2009 version of the Code also highlighted the link between random allocation and the need to 'create greater social equity' and help those families unable to buy houses near 'favoured schools', while the 2012 version makes no such link to social justice issues. Otherwise both versions of the Code require that random allocation procedures are independently verified and that 'looked after' children and 'previously looked after' children are prioritised.

Despite central government policy now seeking to steer admissions authorities away from random allocation, to a limited extent it has become embedded as part of the admissions scene, even if, subject to the limited exceptions just discussed, generally on the margins; and the arguments for and against its use remain, and demand consideration. As regards parental response to the introduction of some random allocation, the apoplectic and apocalyptic response from the *Mail on Sunday*, presumably claiming to speak on behalf of its readers, has already been noted, and to this could be added the somewhat more measured comment from *The Telegraph* (25 February 2011) under the headline 'School lotteries hitting the middle class' stating that 'Schools in more than a third of council areas are selecting low-ability students or using lotteries in an attempt to break the middle-class hold on the most sought-after places'. Despite this, Hertfordshire reported to the OSA that although they had found 'no significant level of concern ... officially raised, historically parents have struggled to fully understand the complexity of the single sex rules and the introduction of the random element has reduced the predictability of allocation outcomes' (OSA, 2009a, para 16). But it was the widespread adoption of random allocation in admission arrangements in Brighton and Hove's schools which attracted most media attention, and it is worth quoting at length the OSA's summary of reactions to the process:

> Brighton and Hove believes that its combination of catchment areas with a random allocation tie-break has improved the fairness of access to its community secondary schools. Under the previous system, where admission was based on distance, applicants to popular schools without the resources to buy or rent properties very close to the school had little likelihood of being allocated a place. The new system has improved the chances of securing a place for these families. The LA comments that at secondary school appeal hearings there has been little focus on the issue of random allocation, with far more attention being paid to school capacity issues. Their experience is that, overall, parents have accepted the change in a relatively short time. Inevitably though, there have been some complaints to appeal panels and the Admissions Team from those living very close to the more popular schools. (OSA, 2009a, para 15)

Despite Brighton and Hove's 'belief' that the process has increased fairness appearing to be challenged somewhat by the findings of Allen et al (2010a), this account does serve usefully to indicate some potential for such a policy to diminish somewhat the potential for 'selection by mortgage' which otherwise arises under straightforward catchment area or proximity rules, and suggests that it has not resulted in widespread parental dissatisfaction. That said, the cost of home–school transport might yet serve as a disincentive for less affluent parents to seek places at otherwise attractive schools beyond their immediate vicinity, while, as Boyle notes (2010, p 19), environmental concerns might also weigh in against proposals which would increase significantly the use of motor transport.

As regards parental opinion, the OSA confirmed that it had received very few complaints from parents mentioning random allocation as an issue (OSA, 2009a, para 19). In light of these findings, it might seem surprising that random methods have not been adopted more widely in England when it is well established in some other jurisdictions, for example, in cases of oversubscription in France, Belgium, New Zealand and Charter Schools in the US (Sutton Trust, 2010b, pp 22–3). The OSA's report does highlight a number of reasons why other local authorities (the majority) have been reluctant to adopt randomness. In addition to 'its high negative profile in the media' (para 18), 'They are concerned that it would act against the principle of local schools for local children, be inconsistent with the Government's green agenda in that it cannot be said to promote sustainable travel to school and that it would make it more difficult for parents to judge the likelihood of success when applying for school places' (para 24).

Given the relatively slight impact of the introduction of an element of randomness into the admissions processes in Brighton and Hove, it might be concluded that the muted response from parents seems appropriate. Beyond this, given the controversy attaching to the introduction of such schemes, it might also be concluded that if the effects of introducing a lottery in the formats used so far are so limited, the majority of local authorities might be thought to be behaving rationally or understandably in declining to adopt random methods in pursuit of any objectives of reducing stratification or segregation.

The implicit intention of introducing such methods seems to be to divorce allocation of school places from the pre-existing advantages of affluence which otherwise permits the wealthy to buy houses with in-built advantage in relation to school admission by virtue of their proximity to desirable schools – advantage cannot be bought within an equal chance lottery. As presently used, however, for example in Brighton and Hove, random allocation will only reduce the *certainty* of advantage accruing from wealth – buying a house in a certain area will not necessarily guarantee access to the most popular school if a random element is introduced. Where catchment areas or proximity remain as significant and prior criteria, the separation of advantage in school admissions from financial advantage will be far from complete. Where a random element is introduced late in the allocation process, after other criteria such as proximity have been applied, those with more financial or social capital will have persistent advantage which will be likely to play out before the random element comes into play; hence perhaps the minimal impact reported in relation to the Brighton and Hove example.

One conclusion which could be drawn from this is that there may still be value to be gained from random allocation in terms of equity agendas, but that, as yet, 'experiments' with such methods in England have not been taken far enough. An example of a much more radical proposal is found in the Social Market Foundation's Commission (SMF) 2004 report on school admissions.

The SMF's starting point is unambiguous, and is as clear a statement of the problems perceived by many commentators as can be found anywhere. The foreword to the report summarises the position as follows:

> School admissions in England and Wales do not sit well with equity and fairness. The Education Reform Act of 1988 attempted to weaken the middleclass hold on the best schools. And though it nominally established choice as the first principle in school admissions, in reality the preponderance of catchment areas and other proximity rules ensures that choice is meaningless for whole swathes of poor parents who want good schools but don't live in – and can't afford to move to – the right areas. The plethora of subtly different admissions authorities and admissions rules mean that the better-informed and more well connected parents can game the system to their advantage – and at others' expense. (SMF, 2004, p 6)

The prescription proposed in the Report in response to this situation is straightforward, if far from uncontroversial. It can be summarised simply, in terms of starting from a priority for parental choice of school (without reference to geography) followed by a national ballot for oversubscribed places where parental choice cannot be met due to lack of capacity, but with the addition of much greater flexibility over school expansion, contraction, opening and closing, to respond better to parental demand and hence minimise oversubscription issues (SMF, 2004, p 7). Maximum freedom of choice is the foremost priority, with random allocation being presented as the most appropriate mechanism for allocating places where it is not possible to meet the preferences of all parents.

In the context of school admissions, the SMF's proposals for tying together choice and random allocation methods in pursuit of an agenda apparently informed by social equity, might seem to represent an example of the approach pursued by Mark Goodwin (2009), discussed in the previous chapter, involving adopting choice mechanisms while claiming to separate them from the neo-liberal ideological baggage associated with choice and marketisation in public services. Indeed the SMF report seems to go further than this, explicitly linking choice and social justice in the context of school admissions.

It is immediately apparent, however, that crucial to the exercise of meaningful choice of schools beyond the immediate locale are the sheer practical obstacles to long-distance travel, and the ability of parents to provide or fund home-to-school transport – in the absence of provision of effective publicly funded transport, or financial support for less affluent parents in this regard, the real extent of choice will remain closely linked to wealth. Yet there remains also a more fundamental problem with the approach adopted in the SMF report. This derives from a position adopted which states 'Resolution of oversubscription by ballot *avoids attempting to rank the values* of school admissions' (SMF, 2004, p 8, emphasis added). But it is clear that utilisation of ballot mechanisms for dealing with oversubscription, rather than others such as, for example, proximity, will produce a specific set of outcomes. While it is not necessary here to explore the rules of probability attaching to random methods of distribution of a good, which are explored by Stone (Delannoi and Dowlen, 2010, chapter 8; Stone, 2011, pp 22–7), it is worth emphasising that, just as with planned or choice mechanisms adopted in relation to school admissions, so the patterns of outcomes relate to, indeed arise from, the mechanisms adopted; in a sense, particular outcomes are always engineered into the processes adopted, and to prefer one such process over another is, whether explicitly or implicitly, to prefer one set of outcomes and the values they reflect.

While recognising a range of 'Values in School Admissions' (SMF, 2004, p 8) which could serve as drivers for the admissions system, those writing the report feel 'unable to rank these values, and certainly to rank them in a way that would be deemed *fair* by all parties' (SMF, 2004, p 17, emphasis added), the Report's findings and prescription adopted are based on a clear and arguably reasonable range of justifications. These relate to choice being a good in itself (SMF, 2004, p 8); inequalities between parents in relation to financial and social capital; the desire to avoid schools effectively engaging in forms of selection, 'using pupil selection to improve their own outcomes at the expense of overall educational attainment'; and that advantages of 'favourable social justice implications' will flow from 'disadvantaged children attending better schools' (SMF, 2004, p 18). In adopting such reasoning, the SMF Report does *de facto* prioritise some 'Values in School Admissions' over others, such as academic selection or localism. The Report states that 'For these reasons, the Commission supports a system of increased choice and resolution of oversubscription by ballot, believing that it will not only produce desired outcomes, but it will also be a system that can be *seen to be fair* by parents' (SMF, 2004, p 18, original emphasis). While we might agree or disagree with the priority of some of the values more than others, in denying that the exercise is one of ranking and prioritising values, and instead falling back on a fuzzy and unspecified notion of 'fairness', the SMF's Report assumes that 'fairness' represents the appropriate and ultimate test of the legitimacy of a system of school admissions, and indeed assumes that its understanding of 'fairness' is universal and unchallengeable. At one level it is impossible to disagree with this kind of approach, as the concept of 'fairness', without explication, is extremely difficult to argue against – like similar terms such as 'the public interest', or indeed like motherhood and apple pie, it is difficult to argue against 'fairness', and hence it is often unhelpful in debate to use the term without substantial explanation. Individual understandings of 'fairness', in general, or in specific circumstances such as school admissions, are far from universal, indeed are likely to differ dramatically. And understanding what 'fairness' means in practice, both in procedural and substantive senses, seems to be essentially a democratic matter, to be determined within our constitutional scheme by the appropriate institutions, including where necessary the law.

6.3 Lotteries, justice and democracy

A rare judicial comment specifically on the use of a random method as a tie-break in the context of two oversubscribed schools in Lancashire is noted by Ruff (2002, pp 205–6) who is able to quote a High Court judge in the case of *R v Lancashire County Council, ex parte West* (27 July 1994):

> [P]arents confronted with option one (random selection) as opposed to option two (drawing lines on maps) might well choose the former rather than the latter.
>
> [I have] come to the conclusion that there was nothing unlawful in the system adopted, and followed for 12 years

> by the Local Education Authority. The Secretary of State
> does not like it very much. Of course I understand fully
> why the parents who are disappointed do not like it now.
> But I am wholly unable to see that it is unlawful. Indeed, I
> do not regard it as unfair in the circumstances. It could be
> much more unfair in some cases to draw lines on maps ...
> (Ruff, 2002, p 206)

For many parents, especially those who are losers in any lottery, random allocation may feel no fairer than any other system. Perhaps, as the then Secretary of State Ed Balls was quoted as saying in 2009, no system of admissions would ever "feel fully fair to parents if they can't get their child into their first choice school" (BBC, 1 March 2009). Just as those who make a 'choice' of school will be disappointed if their 'choice' ultimately is found to be only a preference which can be overridden by admissions criteria, so 'anger is understandable when they find they can only express a preference and then wait for the result of a random computer draw to decide' (*TES*, 1 February 2008). While it can be argued that a merit of random methods in allocation of school places is that 'Parents would continue to be disappointed, but at least they would understand why' (*TES*, 7 October 2005), 'understanding why' in this context appears to be based primarily on the transparency of the allocation process rather than any reasoning underlying admissions decisions – it is premised entirely on a concept of procedural fairness, rather than values claiming to represent substantive fairness. While another attraction may be seen to arise from it being 'Blind to social class and largely immune to parental influence' (*TES*, 7 October 2005), there might be expected to be other methods which could incorporate such concerns while remaining premised on rational decision making rather than simply handing over the process to some 'higher' force of chance.

Atherton (2006, p 6) starts an enquiry into modern forms of gambling by tracing its origins to biblical times, and identifies the modern lottery 'as the descendant of the practice of casting and drawing lots ... to divine the will of God'. In this context, 'the concept of pure chance could not exist at all. In a world ruled by an omnipotent and omniscient God, there was no room for chance to exist' (Atherton, 2006, p 6). While Stone (2011, pp 42–4) is able persuasively to distinguish secular lotteries from divination, a potential utility persists for those charged with making difficult decisions in deferring to a power beyond themselves; in the secular context, randomness. As Atherton notes, American conscripts were also selected for service in Vietnam via random method, suggesting that this might have been 'not so much to divine the will of God, as ... to ease the conscience of their commanders'. Likewise, referring to the use of lottery in medieval times in the context of trial by ordeal, Duxbury comments: 'Since the lottery would provide an outcome not dictated by human judgement, it was sometimes considered to be fairer than certain other medieval systems of trial' (Duxbury, 1999, p 18). Thus, resort to random methods may not only avoid human responsibility for difficult decisions, but might more specifically avoid moral or legal liability. However, even at this relatively early stage of his thoroughgoing inquiry into 'Random Justice', Duxbury emphasises that 'lotteries are not divorced from human judgement: people decide where lotteries should be used, what forms those lotteries should take and who falls into the pool of eligible candidates' (Duxbury, 1999, p 18). Decisions as to whether or how lotteries should be used to allocate benefits such as places at desirable schools, or dis-benefits such as military service, or in relation to civic tasks such as public office or jury service, are clearly based on a conscious policy choice that it is preferable to hand over certain tasks of allocation to chance, rather than to determine such allocations by reference to reasons. In this sense, one choice, presumably informed by reason, establishes the procedure by which other choices will be made without reference to it.

Whether we view the outcomes of lotteries as manifestations of divine will, or as expressions of mathematical chance, the potential for procedural purity in such processes have some obvious attractions. They have the clear potential to separate individual outcomes from any human decision as regards a specific case, which may be for pragmatic reasons akin to avoiding responsibility for a decision, or may be because a decision has been taken that the 'random' outcomes arising from mathematical chance (certain though odds will be, and hence predictable though such overall patterns will be over time) are desirable. In such circumstances, the distinction between overall policy and individual decisions becomes crucial – the choice of utilising random methods is a matter of policy choice, a choice that individual decisions will be taken by random methods and that the pattern of allocations which emerges is one which is desirable in policy terms.

Alternatively, random methods may be employed when all rational criteria deemed appropriate have apparently been exhausted – the lottery as tie-break. In reality, it is this latter context in which the majority of school allocation decisions by lottery are presently taken. Using a lottery in this context, effectively as a last resort seems, at one level, to be relatively uncontroversial. The use of random methods might seem eminently sensible in circumstances where two or more candidates appear wholly equal based on consideration of all available criteria. Resort to lottery in such circumstances might seem an entirely reasonable way of relieving the decision makers' pain from repeatedly banging their heads against a brick wall, or of avoiding them resorting to dubious or spurious reasons, or introducing new or extraneous factors, to attempt to justify what would ultimately be an essentially arbitrary choice.

Determining cases where decisions are finely balanced between the opposing arguments of two parties is the very essence of judicial decision making in adversarial court proceedings. Only cases that are at least reasonably finely balanced ever reach the courtroom – in other cases the relative strengths of the competing legal cases, and the inevitability or very great likelihood of one party triumphing will almost always lead to settlement, which avoids the delay and expense of trial in court. As such, it might be expected that there would be a substantial literature emerging from the judiciary, and commentators on judicial practices, regarding what, if anything, random methods can contribute in such circumstances, even if their views are likely to be confined to classical adversarial circumstances rather than questions of allocation of benefits such as places at desirable schools. It may therefore be somewhat surprising to find that relatively little comment has emerged from modern judges or legal scholars in common law jurisdictions regarding the use of random methods.

Duxbury's is one of very few works written from a legal perspective expressly focused on this issue. Much of Duxbury's argument is limited to the use of lottery as a tie-break, or as a heuristic to focus the decision maker's mind; in this latter connection, Duxbury talks of decision making 'in the shadow of a lottery', whereby if a decision is not reached by other means, random methods will be deployed. At the very least, Duxbury suggests, random methods should not be dismissed too readily. Though focused primarily on decision making in the context of the classic bipartite adversarial legal dispute rather than the allocation of social goods such as places at schools, Duxbury does touch in passing on examples such as the allocation of licences for broadcasting or oil drilling, and notes examples of admission to medical school being determined by lottery, weighted or otherwise (see also Goodwin, 2005, p 257), and the example of Lancashire schools referred to previously.

Duxbury (1999, p 13) observes the dichotomy noted previously regarding procedure and substance, and accepts that 'the outcome of a lottery rests on a process that bears no relevance to the issue in relation to which a decision is being reached'. This situation therefore stands in stark contrast to the usual expectation of reasoned decision making attaching to decisions taken by public bodies, including the judiciary. In general, 'The provision of reasons tends to render decision-makers accountable and to satisfy the expectation that disputants be subjected to an adjudicative system which exhibits procedural fairness' (Duxbury, 1999, p 4). Yet he also argues expressly that, 'in law, faith in reason is sometimes maintained at too high a cost' (Duxbury, 1999, p 175), and observing the fine distinctions sometimes drawn by judges to justify their 'reasoned' decisions, Duxbury talks of them pursuing 'pseudo-rationalism to excess' (Duxbury, 1999, p 139); he also points towards circumstances where there might be 'considerable support for the argument that a decision-making body ought generally to be providing not more but fewer reasons in an effort to deal with a greater number of cases (albeit in less detail)' (Duxbury, 1999, p 173). Such arguments ultimately seem to relate at least as much to efficiency as to justice.

Meanwhile, coming from a rather different perspective, rooted in political science, Barbara Goodwin adopts a more provocative position, suggesting that 'In the case of distributive lotteries ... their impartiality and foundational assumption of equality make them fair in process and just in the outcome *unless more compelling reasons can be advanced for non-random distribution*' (Goodwin, 2005, p 41, emphasis added). Thus, while Duxbury invites us not to dismiss random methods too easily, Goodwin in effect offers a scenario where random methods are presented as a possible default mechanism in the absence of clear and persuasive arguments for utilising alternative approaches. A challenge is therefore laid down by both authors for those preferring an alternative to random methods to make their case, and Goodwin's approach in this regard is close to the line of analysis adopted in the present work.

Both authors do offer clear steers as to how such cases might be established. Goodwin points towards a number of factors, ranging from consideration of human need, to personal merit and desert, to desire for avoidance of excessive risk or uncertainty, to support for human autonomy and control over their destiny, through to 'the processes of rational thought and deliberation to which we, as human beings, are committed' (Goodwin, 2005, p 56). In Duxbury's terms (1999, p 15) 'criteria such as merit, desert, competence and need' may all form the basis for using some method other than lottery. All of these may be factors on which we may be able to start building a case for the utilisation of a process of decision making other than randomness. Likewise, any meaningful conception of equality of citizenship (such as that set out in Chapter One), or equitable treatment of citizens implies access for all to the pre-requisite necessities for engaging in society as a citizen. Thus, while we might be content to leave the allocation of scarce *luxuries* to a form of lottery (see Goodwin, 2005, p 47), we might feel that the allocation of scarce *necessities*, such as places in the most desirable state-funded schools, are worthy of decision-making processes more demanding of rationalisation.

While being wary of being too easily seduced by the 'lure of reason' (Duxbury, 1999, p 114 *et seq*), and especially lawyers' never-ending quest for reasons to justify and legitimate decisions, to the extent that we live in a polity premised on rationality it seems appropriate to expect important social decisions to be susceptible to challenge, whether in political or legal discourse, by reference to their reasoning. As long as procedures are properly followed in random allocation processes, there is nothing to engage with in such discourse, and hence it might seem that where important decisions are being taken, regarding, for example, scarce necessities such as high quality schooling, there are persuasive arguments indicating that the burden of choosing to utilise random methods, contrary to Goodwin's provocative stance, should still fall on those seeking to deploy them. To do otherwise would be to offer support for a process of decision making susceptible to challenge only on procedural rather than substantive or normative grounds, which seems to cut across the fundamental expectations of our political, legal and constitutional schemas.

While it is possible to accept Duxbury's argument there may be situations in which the lawyer's never-ending quest for reasons, and hence grounds to challenge decisions, may at times seem overly demanding of decision makers, it can be argued powerfully that school admissions is an issue in relation to which the most demanding standards can properly be imposed. The allocation of school places is an area in which a one-off decision has long-term consequences both for individuals, and, when aggregated, for society as a whole. Goodwin considers a scenario relating to the allocation of roles within society, addressing a situation where roles may be assigned on a rotating basis, and observes that:

> [I]f the structure of society is partly or wholly determined in certain respects and necessarily entails inequalities (i.e. different roles with different intrinsic values and/or different rewards attached to them), and if people are *more* equal than the roles (i.e. roles and rewards are highly differentiated, people less so), *injustice will result from any once-and-for-all distribution.* (Goodwin, 2005, p 34, emphasis on last two lines added)

The scenario Goodwin outlines here seems highly relevant to allocation of school places, given the enormous impact quality of schooling will have on the life chances, and societal roles, of those receiving it. It is apparent that schooling is not a situation where rotation of places is an option; rather it can be viewed as a 'game' in which each player generally has only one chance to succeed, and the consequences of success or failure are frequently permanent, or at the very least deep-seated, long-lasting and extremely difficult to remedy subsequently. Given the enormous potential significance of schooling to subsequent life chances and to the expectations of effective citizenship so central to our view of democracy, and the ongoing differences (actual and/or perceived) in quality across the state school sector, it seems reasonable to expect decisions on allocation of places to be subjected to rigorous standards of decision making, and of accountability. The quest must therefore be for the maximum reasonably feasible level of accountability, in accordance with the democratic expectations attached to a public service such as education. In this context, it seems desirable both that procedural standards are transparently maintained, and, that normative expectations are established and adhered to in the decision-making process. While random methods may meet the first of these expectations, they do not engage at all with the latter. As such, the giving of reasoned decisions referenced to specified criteria seems a wholly reasonable expectation. When all established criteria have been utilised and have failed to separate candidates, then, as Duxbury suggests, recourse to lottery seems an appropriate way forward. But there must be a strong supposition in place that best efforts will have been made, via mechanisms consistent with our constitutional and democratic expectations of rationality in decision making, to determine in advance, and apply rigorously, criteria in accordance with which attempts at reason will be made, before resort is had to blind chance. Simply put, decisions regarding the 'scarce necessity' of high-quality state-funded schooling seem too important to be left to chance, other than as a last resort.

6.4 'A frightening new experiment in social engineering'?

As should be apparent from this chapter and the previous three, all admissions systems are planned, in the sense that in as far as outcomes can be predicted or observed, these outcomes are chosen (planned for) along with the system; this is as true of random methods as of LEA-centred or choice-based systems. In that sense, the outcomes of all admission systems considered can equally be described properly as 'social engineering', as the social outcomes are engineered into the system chosen. From this perspective, random methods are not inherently more or less 'frightening' than any other method, which might be adopted for allocating school places. The question remains, however, as to whether the utilisation of random methods is desirable, in terms of adding something of value to the admissions processes.

Some potential advantages of random allocation are readily apparent. Most obvious of these is the ability of lotteries to import a high degree of procedural purity into the admissions process. Provided only that lotteries are properly administered, and overseen so as to ensure proper practice, they provide a method of allocating places wholly separated from values or human factors, individual or collective, whether based on policy or prejudice, which administrative decision making usually incorporates. As such, once lawfully adopted, they are likely to be relatively free from the sorts of legal challenge which more conventional decision making can be subjected to. Though, given ongoing differences in the desirability of different schools, they do not promise equality of outcome for all participants, genuine equal chance lotteries do seem to promise at least an equal likelihood of any participant receiving the most (and least) desirable outcomes.

Related to this first possible advantage is Duxbury's point of avoiding the pursuit to excess of 'pseudo-rationalism' (Duxbury, 1999, p 139) as an aspect of the lawyer's never-ending quest for reasons, susceptible to challenge, with which to justify decisions. From such a perspective, random allocation, which Barbara Goodwin identifies as 'a-rational' (Goodwin, quoted in Delannoi and Dowlen 2010, p 106) might seem at least equally attractive. While Duxbury's observations are largely in the context of judicial decision making, and our context is primarily administrative in nature, his approach still seems to have some application. Cutting through potentially hair-splitting debates, random methods remove the decision entirely from the realm of human reasoning, and, in avoiding excessive or protracted argumentation about reasons or justifications for individual decisions, may render the decision-making process more efficient in procedural terms. Certainly, there appears to be strong justifications available for resort to lottery as a tie-break when all available established rational criteria have been exhausted.

There is an issue here which both Duxbury and Stone point towards, relating to the possibility, and possible desirability, of replacing a situation of indeterminacy with one of randomness. While there is an extensive literature on the theme of uncertainty and indeterminacy in other contexts, for example risk regulation in relation to the environment (see

Feintuck, 2005, and references therein), it is possible for the moment to work simply with Stone's identification of a context of indeterminacy as being a situation in which 'there are no legitimate reasons for distinguishing between ... claimants, and many illegitimate reasons'. In such a situation, Stone continues: 'To recognize a difference would therefore be to discriminate between them on the basis of something irrelevant to their claims. It would therefore constitute a rights violation' (Stone, 2011, pp 84–5). Such an approach, avoiding invalid supposed reasons, or the tenuous legal reasoning referred to by Duxbury, seems valuable in terms of offering assurance as to the impartiality of an allocation process which employs randomness (Stone, 2011, p 78); given that it will take into account only the strength of particular claims (which have been found to be equal) based on whatever prior criteria have been agreed while refusing to respond to criteria beyond these which might permit other preferences or criteria to be brought into the decision-making process. In such a situation, Stone argues persuasively, the 'sanitizing' effect (Stone, 2011, p 65) of the procedural purity of a lottery, in screening out extraneous factors, can be of substantial value and hence in situations of indeterminacy random allocation should not be considered 'second best' (Stone, 2011, p 87).

In taking reasons relating to individual cases out of the equation, the adoption of random methods may also promote a particular conception of fairness in relation to the process. For some, de-personalisation of the process via lottery and the procedural purity on which it is based, instead handing the decision over to 'blind chance', may feel fairer than the outcomes of processes which take into account, perhaps in complex and sometimes apparently opaque-seeming ways, a congeries of policy criteria and priorities. For those who are, or might be, disadvantaged by complex administrative arrangements, which may be felt to play best into the hands of those with educational advantage or other high stocks of social capital, randomness may well seem an attractive, 'fairer' option. An extension of this argument is to suggest that the use or introduction of random methods may not only increase perceptions of fairness, but may also actually serve to reduce the impact of pre-existing social advantage in how school places are allocated. This is perhaps what underlies the *Mail on Sunday*'s description of lotteries in this context as 'a frightening new experiment in social engineering'.

Reflection on 'experiments' with the use of lotteries in school admissions in a limited form, such as that in Brighton and Hove, discussed previously, suggests that far-reaching social consequences seem unlikely. Evidence to date seems to indicate that while the use of lotteries may have some potential to reduce the degree of certainty of reproduction of social advantage, by weakening the linkage between the ability of the affluent to buy houses in certain areas and access to the most popular schools, they do not, at least as employed in this context to date, go as far as to break such connections completely. As such, while random methods may offer marginal improvements in terms of reducing the tendency of school admission systems to reproduce social stratification or segregation, they do not, at least when employed primarily as tie-breaks, offer a mechanism likely to result in any dramatic shift in admission patterns. In this context, lotteries are much less radical than they might appear. This is not to say that random methods do not have potential to create change in this context, but rather to emphasise that as used in the limited ways they presently are, their impact is likely to be marginal. As such, debate is necessary concerning whether such schemes should be maintained, dropped, or adopted in an extended or more radical form to increase their impact, the latter course being that strongly supported by the SMF.

To an extent, any decision to maintain, drop or extend the use of random methods in school admissions processes will depend on the priority given to various factors or values, and the (party) political agendas of those in power. Prioritising concerns such as 'fairness' (however defined, or indeed undefined), or parental choice, or reducing social stratification, may well result in different responses to the use, or possible extension, of random methods. Such responses are likely to relate far more to the outcomes of processes in relation to the factors or values prioritised rather than the procedures adopted in and of themselves. Of particular significance in the present context is Stone's observation (Stone, 2011, p 106) that the process used to apply standards is a very different question to that of what standards ought to be applied, and his vision of a 'just lottery rule' includes a requirement that it should apply only where claims have been determined to be qualitatively the same (Stone, 2011, p 50); thus, substantial prior attention is still required for determining the strength of claims in relation to pre-established criteria before randomness can legitimately be resorted to. It is perhaps worth at this point concretising the argument again by reference to the approach taken by a recent British government. Worth noting in passing in this connection is the prohibition in the 2009 Code of Practice of 'oversubscription criteria that give priority to children according to their first name or surname or their date of birth' (para 2.16(o)). Though clearly potentially subject to some manipulation by particularly persistent parents, and maybe subject to inbuilt bias towards or against certain social or linguistic groups depending on typical names, in some ways such criteria seem more open to reasoned explanation than do the mysteries of 'blind chance' in the form of lottery, yet clearly constitute criteria which the then Minister considered illegitimate in the allocation process.

As just noted, lotteries for school places will likely seem attractive if fairness deriving from procedural purity is prioritised, but they may seem much less attractive if a premium is placed on an objective of actively seeking to reduce significantly the reproduction of social stratification in the school system. It may be thought that more positive action than, in Lawton's terms, 'treating unequals as equals' (Lawton, 1977, p 8) is required. In terms of parental choice, lotteries may be viewed as an aid or an obstacle, which for individuals will possibly depend simply on the outcome they achieve in the lottery. Thus, it has to be considered impossible to reach an authoritative position on the worth or appropriateness of random methods in this context without properly relating the question to the values which underlie debate about school admissions, and the extent to which the reality of outcomes match the priorities adopted. As proved to be the case when considering LEA-centred admissions policies in Chapter Three, and policies based on parental choice in Chapters Four and Five, the problem in analysing lotteries in this context, or at least in reaching a definitive conclusion, is the absence of a clear over-arching vision of purpose or priorities for the school system, or at least the failure of dominant political groups generally to specify such purpose or priority with honesty and reasonable clarity. In the absence of clarity about purposes for the school system, it is difficult to reach substantive conclusions regarding the success or failure, or the appropriateness, of administrative arrangements for allocating places. A situation such as this might be considered to highlight a need for, or render appropriate, or at least allow space for scrutinising such processes against underlying constitutional norms and expectations rather than just utilising the various criteria referred to in political debate or the specific legal framework relating to admissions. This as true in terms of discussing arguments in favour of random methods as it is for those against their use.

While arguments about random allocation incorporate elements of both education-specific and constitutional reasoning, many arguments against the use of lotteries for allocating school places start from very specific examples or pragmatic considerations which highlight what might be termed absurdities potentially arising from their use. The then Secretary of State, Ed Balls, was quoted as describing as 'ridiculous' the possibility that twins might be sent to separate schools as a result of a lottery (BBC, 1 March 2009), and similar arguments might be raised in relation to siblings more generally, or to the child living next door to a school who is randomly allocated a place some considerable distance away. Such arguments about absurdity immediately reveal a position based on rational criteria, yet, as Stone observes, while 'the lottery functions as a sort of surrogate reason' (Stone, 2011, p 33), 'Lotteries represent the polar opposite of reasoned decision-making' (Stone, 2011, p 13). For those making such arguments against the use of lottery, human and practical concerns relating to family life are considered relevant factors which require some priority in deciding how school places will be allocated. From there, argument may proceed down a range of avenues, incorporating values such as localism and/ or environmental considerations relating to home-school transport, but it is important to retain a high degree of awareness that they all relate to values, claims or arguments, which can be presented as having more resonance with the values which underpin our polity than do the outcomes of the operation of chance.

In a similar vein, the impersonal nature of decision making by lottery can be presented as problematic or inappropriate, given the very real human values and concerns at stake for the individual, and the broader social concerns also implicated. In response to the argument presented by Barbara Goodwin (2005, p 41), that lotteries should be considered appropriate distributive mechanisms in the absence of compelling reasons for the adoption of non-random distribution, we might point towards the pragmatic points just made, but should also consider the argument raised by Duxbury, that 'To argue that, in general, social goods and burdens ought to be distributed randomly is to take no account of criteria such as merit, desert, competence, and need' (Duxbury, 1999, p 15). Duxbury's list of criteria is clearly not intended to be exhaustive, and, depending on our political perspective, we may wish to add (or add emphasis to) a very large number of different criteria, in widely varying priorities, many of which will be related to fundamental expectations and values embedded in our constitutional arrangements. Though such values will be inherently contestable, they should be capable of being argued and prioritised by reason, the outcomes of this process being reflected in the methods adopted for allocating 'goods' such as school places. In adopting random methods and enjoying the benefits of procedural purity which they seem to offer, we engage in a trade-off in which certain values are marginalised or neglected entirely. Such potentially marginalised values include not only a fundamental expectation of rational discourse, but also those of individual human need and social priorities. As such, we should take careful note of Stone's proper limitation of the appropriate use of lotteries to those situations where it is not possible to distinguish qualitatively between claims.

A persistent problem in arguing against the use of lotteries in this context, however, is that their supporters will frequently and readily point towards the failure of society to agree any clear and universally accepted set of values which should inform a reason-based system of allocating school places. We are here in the realm of what Sunstein terms 'incompletely theorized agreements', which he argues have a legitimate and important role to play in judicial decision making and in the administration of any deliberative democracy properly-so-called, in which emphasis is placed on 'adhering to the original belief in governmental processes as one of deliberation oriented to the public good rather than a series of interest-group tradeoffs' (Sunstein, 1990, p 12). Duxbury offers some clear critique of Sunstein's position in the context of judicial decision making, but also explicitly suggests that 'Should it be considered desirable to encourage incomplete theorization in legal decision-making – and it is crucial to emphasize that it is by no means obvious that such encouragement is desirable – the requirement that adjudication be subject to a time limit and the possible imposition of a lottery might be one way of creating an appropriate incentive for decision-makers' (Duxbury, 1999, p 173). Decision making 'in the shadow of a lottery' may well serve to focus the decision maker's mind, and may contribute to speedier, possibly more 'efficient' decision making, but at the expense of reasoning. However, there is at least an arguable case that even incompletely theorised agreements might, from a constitutional perspective drawing on the basic tenets of liberal democracy, still be preferable to randomness given the potential for rational discourse to engage with outcomes of the former but not the latter.

For those struck by its procedural purity, the detachment of decision making by lottery from the complexities of rational discourse is presented as an inherent attraction rather than a pragmatic response to the difficulties of reaching definitive agreement on matters such as the priorities for a school admissions system. Yet there is a simple and absolute truth about *any* system of allocating places within a system in which schools are deemed to be of unequal quality and hence considered not to be equally desirable: as noted in Chapter Five, there will be winners and losers. In some ways, the bluntness of lotteries serves to highlight this issue, but also serves simultaneously to marginalise it. In Duxbury's terms, the outcomes of blind chance as manifested in lotteries 'do not guarantee benefits for the deserving' and also 'do not guarantee withholding of benefits from the undeserving', and can 'simultaneously ignore social worth and reward vice' (Duxbury, 1999, p 58). Most relevant for present purposes, 'lotteries are indifferent to losers' (Duxbury, 1999, p 52), and indifference to losers may seem problematic in relation to a matter as important as schooling.

While we might have general concerns regarding ever accepting the existence of winners and losers in relation to a vital public good such as high-quality schooling, this is of course a broad and unwieldy question relating to expectations of equality, and may result in counsels of perfection, requiring all schools to be of equally high quality. But while the detached and impersonal nature of decision making by lottery may in this context seem an attraction, especially perhaps for those charged with taking such difficult decisions, two obvious issues arise at this point in relation to the use of such devices in school admissions decisions. The first is that those parents whose choice is denied by lottery may well feel the outcome to be 'unfair' or irrational, even if they accept that the procedure is fundamentally fair – and in that situation, they will have nothing rational to engage with in seeking to address such unfairness. Rather than being able to view the outcome as a consequence of human endeavour, they must learn to accept that it is the outcome of pure chance, detached from any reasoning relating to the decision, and the crucial decision being taken on grounds which incorporate increased uncertainty when compared with alternative allocation mechanisms (see OSA, 2009a, para 22). In the face of a 'chance' decision, there is a significant likelihood that winners will find the process much more acceptable, and 'fair', than will the losers (see OSA, 2009a, para 23). What parents have to accept here, though, may be something fundamental to their child's future as a human being. The children who are the losers in this lottery may have their life chances significantly diminished as a result of this exercise of pure chance. The exercise of pure chance might be thought to be less alarming when there is subsequent potential for rotation or redistribution of outcomes. However, children 'playing' in the lottery of school allocation are effectively playing a once-and-for-all-time game, and it can be powerfully argued, from either an individualistic or collective standpoint, that such decisions are simply too important to leave to chance. Such an argument does depend on explicit recognition of the significance of school for the individual, and also inevitably returns us to a question of on what reasoned basis such a decision, with such profound consequences, should be taken, if not by chance. Inevitably, those in the habit of engaging in debate about decisions on the basis of discussion of reasons will have some difficulty in engaging in discussion about chance, and will draw comparisons between the perspective of randomness and alternative approaches to the subject under debate.

Though it need not detain us substantially at this point in our particular context, it is important to recognise a further issue which Stone (2011, pp 57–8) points towards in relation to consent to random allocation by those with an interest in the outcome of decisions. It can reasonably be stated that an underlying assumption exists within our polity that decisions will be taken on a rational and reasoned basis. There is therefore a substantial burden to discharge for those seeking to pursue random methods, in justifying a process which explicitly excludes reason. Though it will not be easy to justify to or obtain consent from the collective or the individual for the abandonment of reasoned decision making, Stone makes a persuasive case for utilising random methods in the limited circumstances and manner he suggests.

A further obvious issue here relates not to the impact of random decisions on rational discourse revolving around the purposes and values of the education system, but its impact on the rhetoric of parental choice, which has centrally informed school policy and debate since the late 1980s. In this connection, and bearing in mind the relatively high, and arguably reasonable, satisfaction rates arising both from LEA-planned admission schemes noted in Chapter Three, and from parental choice mechanisms in Chapter Five, it might be reasonable to assume that widespread use of lotteries, and certainly their use as anything more than a tie-break, could easily result in a *decrease* in satisfaction rates among those parents actively seeking to make a choice of their child's school, especially perhaps among that well-educated, well-informed and well-resourced group of parents which is presently best placed to articulate and pursue its preference via existing choice mechanisms. Interestingly, however, when scrutiny is made of opposition to lotteries in media outlets such as *The Telegraph* (25 February 2011), which might be considered representative of such group interests, it becomes apparent that concerns over the use of lotteries are possibly outweighed by other concerns relating to admissions policies based on reasoned rather than wholly random methods. The newspaper notes with concern the fact that 'Families ... face a potential fall in house prices if an oversubscribed school decides to employ a random admissions policy', where 'They have often paid a premium of tens of thousands of pounds to do so'. But of at least equal concern for *The Telegraph* is the use of 'fair banding', 'encouraged by Michael Gove, the Education Secretary, who has said that it could help make schools "truly comprehensive" '. The threat to sectional interests of its readers is summarised by *The Telegraph* in the following terms: 'The rise of lotteries and so-called "fair banding" –

where test results are used to select a proportion of pupils with lower ability – could thwart affluent families who have bought homes within the catchment areas of successful schools'. The policy of 'fair banding', a method requiring schools to take a cross-section of pupils by reference to ability levels, will be returned to in Chapter Seven, but in the present context it is worth noting that objections to outcomes relating to admissions which 'thwart' sectional interests will inevitably be opposed by those adversely affected, whether such outcomes derive from reasons or randomness. Interestingly, the Institute for Public Policy Research notes that 'Fair banding actually has very similar effects to the random allocation of pupils', but concludes that 'while from a technical point of view the random allocations determined by lotteries can be considered fair, they may not be perceived to be so by the public because they lack apparent rationale. We therefore prefer the use of fair banding by ability, in conjunction with other criteria such as parental preference, to the use of random lotteries' (IPPR, 2007, p 20).

In this context, it might be surprising to find support for the extended use of lottery mechanisms from an organisation such as the SMF, coming from a perspective which explicitly emphasises individual choice. Yet it quickly becomes apparent that the use of lotteries seems unlikely to interfere significantly with the ability of already socially advantaged parents to reproduce their advantage via obtaining places for their children at the most desirable schools; in the absence of readily available home-to-school transport, or heavy public subsidy for it, only those with the financial means to provide it will be able to exercise meaningful choice of school. For less affluent parents, no meaningful choice of school beyond those in their immediate area will be available. In the absence of free and thoroughly designed home–school transport schemes specifically tailored to the needs of children without parents able to fund it privately, choice will only be realistically available, or certainly disproportionately available, to the relatively affluent. Thus, while the lottery process may offer equal chances of success for all participants, the likelihood of taking part in that lottery in pursuit of places at the most attractive schools will presumably relate, *inter alia*, to an assessment by parents of whether travel to such schools is realistic, and hence will be closely related to parental income. This is a manifestation of the phenomenon that Goodwin observes, that 'Lotteries unrealistically assume equality on the part of their participants' (Goodwin, 2005, p 56); the 'equal chance' element of the lottery relates only to those who are in a realistic position to enter it. Whether allocated by mechanisms of choice or by lottery, local schools will remain the only realistic option for those financially unable to fund the potentially substantial costs of daily home–school transport – the extent of practical choice will continue to be inextricably and directly linked to the extent of disposable income. In addition to such criticism from those concerned with the potential for choice mechanisms simply to serve to reproduce social hierarchy, such measures that cut substantially across attendance at local schools might also be subject to criticism from perspectives which emphasise the negative environmental consequences of large-scale, long–distance transport of children to school.

This latter perspective tends to bring the potentially highly individualistic perspective of parental choice together with collective concerns. Such matters raise questions not only of individual legal rights, including those characterised as 'human rights', but also raise collective questions which might be expected to have constitutional and democratic aspects. While collective concerns about the environment are not to be underestimated or neglected, a broader range of collective values also seem to be at stake when consideration is given to the possibility of any greatly increased use of random methods in relation to allocation of school places. While such values might be thought to be inherently contested, one peculiarly persistent element of debate in the context of school admissions, both in relation to local authority based planning models and the current system centred on parental choice, is the tendency for the school system to reproduce social hierarchy or stratification. While apparently offering some real potential for addressing such in-built advantage within a system in which all schools are not considered equally desirable, as already noted, the sort of random methods adopted to date do not seem likely to result in any dramatic reduction in the reproduction of social stratification in the school system. Thus, in as far as such an agenda might be central to any collectively agreed planning objectives, the adoption of random methods might be thought to be too blunt or ineffective a tool to bring about radical or substantial reform.

If, and it is a large 'if', a central objective for the school admissions system was to be to make substantial inroads into the reproduction of social stratification and segregation in schooling, admission lotteries, certainly if used only as tie-breaks, should not be expected necessarily to achieve much in and of themselves. They might properly be viewed as a crude, and rather limited method for addressing inequalities in access to the most desirable schools, making only marginal differences in this regard while excluding reasoned debate about decisions. Yet if the real concern underlying debate about school admissions is thought to relate to matters of social equity or concerns about equality, it is correct to ask directly whether random methods of allocating school places actually fare any better or worse, or should be considered more or less preferable, when compared with the uncertainties of the present process, whether in terms of outcomes or criteria, and the negative consequences which may flow from such a situation for the parties involved.

6.5 Conclusions – on randomness and reason ...

In effect, the overarching question might now become framed in terms parallel to those used by Duxbury in the context of judicial decision making: 'Might there ... be a case for replacing a decision-making process which is driven by indeterminacy with one which is driven by randomness?' (Duxbury, 1999, p 92). Rather than delve into the niceties of exactly where indeterminacy stands on any risk continuum, it might prove more helpful to think in terms of an alternative dichotomy, pointed towards by Stone (2011, p 23) between risk and uncertainty – are the known and quantifiable 'risks' for any applicant involved in a lottery process preferable to the uncertainties, and inequalities in exercise of claim and likely outcomes, which result from choice models within schooling?

Certainly the OSA has noted how local authorities commented expressly on the concern that the introduction of random methods 'Would create uncertainty for parents who still look to their local school' (OSA, 2009a, para 18), and indeed how parents themselves have expressed precisely such concerns (para 22). The concern of uncertainty and unpredictability of outcome are exactly those which underlie much criticism of existing arrangements. Thus, while the use of lottery may, from an academic perspective, seem no better or worse an option than the existing alternative administrative decision-making processes, the practical outcomes, in terms of any additional uncertainty, would also need to be factored in when considering the options. Yet it seems possible to argue that the risks associated with random allocation are at least quantifiable, while the uncertainties of choice mechanisms are more substantial and more difficult to quantify, given the potential for a wide range of factors, extending far beyond what might be considered 'good reasons', to be brought into play at the initiative of parents or school admissions authorities.

Resort to random methods in allocating school places may derive from a variety of reasons. These may relate to pragmatic acknowledgement of the difficulties of addressing oversubscription in popular schools, a possible consequent desire on the part of politicians to distance themselves from difficult and potentially unpopular decisions, or from a genuine belief that randomness in this context leads to greater 'fairness'. While 'fairness' in the absence of explication and definition is a fundamentally problematic concept, there is little doubt that the way those introducing lotteries for school places, for example in Brighton and Hove, justify the move is in terms of a construct of fairness which relates to concerns about the reproduction of social stratification in the school system. Yet, for reasons that have been noted, there is little evidence to suggest that random methods in and of themselves, unless utilised on a more radical basis, will make more than a marginal difference in relation to such matters. Meanwhile parental perceptions of fairness do not seem to be changed significantly by the use of lotteries: just as with other systems, individual perceptions of fairness seem to relate closely to getting, or failing to get, the desired outcome, while surveying group attitudes to randomness in this context will, as Boyle (2010, pp 51–6) indicates, produce different responses depending on how the issue or question is framed. In this respect, the use of random methods, though readily (perhaps surprisingly readily) accepted, does not seem to feel more legitimate, certainly not significantly more legitimate, to those on the receiving end of the process than other processes based on criteria and reasons which were previously utilised.

While examples of cases in which random methods would result in siblings or even twins being separated, or in which great proximity to a local school does not result in a place at that school, might not in themselves seem decisive in terms of arguing for or against the use of random methods, the apparent absurdity of such outcomes will immediately cause many to seek immediately to overlay, or subvert, the use of randomness with policy decisions based on rational, normative criteria. Otherwise, the risk is that random allocation will simultaneously undermine expectations of the admissions system which derive from the model of parental choice within a quasi-market, and also those expectations arising from the democratic promise of rationality. In reality, though, as Stone (2011, p 153) indicates, situations where genuine indeterminacy exist, and hence where randomness should properly be prescribed, will be relatively rare – in most such situations of apparent indeterminacy it should be possible for the decision maker to obtain more information to allow reasoned decisions to be reached.

Crucially, in terms of this latter set of expectations, it returns us to Duxbury's observation in the context of judicial decision making, but arguably of equal application in the context of administrative decision making regarding school places, 'The provision of reasons tends to render decision-makers accountable and to satisfy the expectation that disputants be subjected to an adjudicative system which exhibits procedural fairness' (Duxbury, 1999, p 4). The potential for 'fit' between conventional administrative decision-making processes and our constitutional/democratic expectations is clear, and even if in practice the processes adopted may fail wholly to fulfil such promise, they may be capable of refinement or improvement, and they will be potentially subjected to further scrutiny, on a reasoned basis, by the judiciary, should decisions be challenged. Meanwhile, the legitimacy claims of random methods derive entirely from procedural purity rather than any premise in debate about values in the education system or reasoning which can be scrutinised or challenged, though if we are sceptical about the legitimacy of some factors (such as inherent class advantage) which (as the evidence in Chapter Five indicates) are clearly prominent factors in decision making within choice mechanisms, the sanitising effect of random allocation in screening out what could be considered 'bad reasons' for allocation might again appear to have attractions

Yet the question raised by the likes of Duxbury and Goodwin still hangs over us: if existing decision-making processes are imperfect to the extent of lacking legitimacy, and/or if they are over-complex, is there any good reason why they should not be replaced by chance? Stone's conclusion is relatively clear: there will be limited situations in which indeterminacy exists as a result of claims which are qualitatively indistinguishable, and where the lottery's 'sanitizing' effect of excluding 'bad reasons' is desirable, and in such cases it would be proper to conclude that a lottery would be normatively superior to alternative decision-making strategies. Ultimately, it seems that the most reasonable response to this question is that, *in general*, there is little to choose between a system based on indeterminacy and one based on randomness. Neither meshes readily with expectations of rationality or predictability in decision making on specific cases.

Given the significance of schooling to subsequent life chances, rather than adopting indeterminate or uncertain conventional decision-making processes or random methods, it seems far preferable to continue the Enlightenment project via an ongoing quest for objective criteria on which reasoned decisions can be made and justified. To do otherwise, in other words is to refuse either to establish good reasons for allocating school places sufficient to distinguish between applicants or to permit tacitly the application of reasons such as pre-existing social advantage, could be considered in democratic terms to be both lazy and cowardly.

Yet if as a society, collectively, our political processes fail to determine clearly priorities or purposes in the context of a system for allocating social goods such as school admissions, and if processes appear unduly complex or opaque, and if judicial reasoning in relation to such matters is not based on a clear enough structure of reasoned principle to give us confidence in the accountability of the system, the case for reform is strong. This is not, however, the same as saying that the case is necessarily established for use of random methods.

To return to the hypothetical approach posed earlier, if a central objective for the school admissions system was to be to make substantial inroads into the reproduction of social stratification and segregation in schooling, there are numerous alternative approaches which could be adopted that would seem likely to have at least as much impact, and possibly more, than would the adoption of lotteries for school places. More direct interventions such as the 'pupil premium' attaching to pupils from households with low incomes (if administered in such a way that the premium is spent in order to further the scheme's objectives), or the provision of free or heavily subsidised home–school transport, or requiring 'fair banding' in schools, could all be posited as direct and targeted measures aimed at the reduction of such perceived problems. Of course, alternative priorities compete with what can be characterised as an equality-driven agenda. Parental choice, whether as an aspect of consumerism or citizenship, is well established as a central feature of the quasi-market in schooling, while agendas of localism and environmental concerns about unnecessary travel (see OSA, 2009a, para 18) also have some profile. One possible response to this congeries of issues and priorities, which might be proposed by proponents of lotteries, is to introduce weighted lotteries, retaining an element of randomness in the ultimate process, but offering additional likelihood of success to some participants' entries; the immediately apparent problem here is that of determining the criteria that will result in additional weighting, and the degree of weighting to be added in accordance with different priorities – it requires a process of listing and prioritising criteria which seems close to conventional administrative allocation processes, and hence subject to the same difficulties. At the most practical level in relation to the parental choice agenda, in which perceptions of legitimacy of process are likely to relate closely to individual satisfaction with outcomes, it seems very unlikely that the widespread and far-reaching adoption of lotteries would deliver as high a parental satisfaction rate as either planned or quasi-market-based systems.

Much of the current uncertainty and/or indeterminacy in the school admissions system seems to derive from a failure, noted in Chapter One, of any of the settlements or re-settlements of the education system to tackle sufficiently directly the prioritisation of the many and varied factors that can be in play in this context. Meanwhile, it can be argued that fundamental democratic expectations, relating to rationality and accountability in decision making by public bodies, in the modern era at least, should be seen as transcending and surviving any such new settlements. From this perspective, simply put, it may well seem intellectually lazy and democratically unsatisfactory to resort to randomness.

In situations where the political process has resulted in criteria having been established with reasonable clarity and openly prioritised, and where processes have been transparent and operate in a manner which results in overall predictability of outcome which is consistent with the pre-determined priorities, a high degree of accountability should exist, and the process will have a strong claim to be meeting the requirements necessary for democratic legitimacy. In such a scenario, idealistic as it may seem, there may be a place for utilising random methods as a tie-break, but only when judgements based on criteria determined through reason and democratic processes and linked to the values at stake have been exhausted.

The works of the likes of Duxbury and Goodwin are helpful, in establishing that consideration of the use of random methods can serve as an extremely valid and worthwhile heuristic, challenging assumptions about the adequacy, appropriateness and legitimacy of existing decision-making processes. If a high degree of uncertainty of outcome exists, and if the reasoning involved in reality reveals (or masks) a high level of indeterminacy, or if compelling reasons cannot be identified for non-random distribution, then it is proper to consider whether lotteries are at least as appropriate an allocation method as more conventional administrative or judicial processes.

The conclusions to be drawn from the discussion in this chapter must be that using lottery as a tie-break, or requiring decision makers to act 'in the shadow of a lottery' is one thing; to opt actively for more extensive use of random methods in the context of school admissions would be quite another. To choose to utilise random methods rather than reasoned decision making where rational criteria *could* be selected and applied is quite different from using lottery as a last-resort tie-break. To actively prefer randomness in and of itself is to argue that the outcomes of random distribution of school places would be preferable to, or at least as satisfactory as, any reasoned system, and hence is to choose to demote reason, a value generally fundamental to our polity. Among possible objections to the use of lotteries in socially significant situations observed by Goodwin are that lotteries 'neglect human need', 'ignore personal merit and desert', 'circumvent the processes of rational thought and deliberation' and 'unrealistically assume equality on the part of their participants' (Goodwin, 2005, p 56). As is suggested by approaches such as that adopted in the SMF paper (SMF, 2004), it can certainly provide the appearance of a system with the attraction of it being 'blind to social class and largely immune to parental influence' (*TES*, 7 October 2005). The question which such a position raises, however, is whether blindness to inherent class advantage or disadvantage should be viewed as a strength or a weakness in arguments about the advisability of using random methods. If the principal concerns informing the school admissions system were to be related to social justice, and if lotteries as presently used (primarily as tie-breaks) produce only marginal impact on reducing the reproduction of social stratification in the state-funded school system, more radical prescriptions may be indicated. One such would be to choose to use lotteries at a much earlier stage than tie-break, while another would be to return to a task of actively and explicitly choosing and prioritising some values over others in pursuit of an admissions system legitimated by reasons derived from deliberation and rational discourse. Among such values might be thought to be expectations of equality of citizenship and hence equality of access to essentials for effective citizenship such as schooling. It should be expected that such values should be reflected strongly in the constitutional settlement, and in the legislative framework within which decision making, in whatever form, takes place.

SEVEN

Conclusions

7.1 Reviewing the realities

In the preceding chapters, we have considered three approaches to school admissions based on planning, quasi-markets and randomness. As should be apparent, each of the approaches tends to result in a certain set of outcomes which relate as much or more to the processes utilised to allocate places as to any specified educational outcomes or objectives. Our analysis has been informed by two lines of questioning: first, does each approach deliver what it claims to, and second does each approach meet democratic expectations relating, for example, to equality of citizenship, and, constitutional expectations relating to accountability?

Simply put, the evidence we have considered on the outcomes of each approach leads to the conclusion that the democratic expectations at stake in education are too important to be left to either quasi-markets or randomness. The reality emerging, from Chapter Five especially, is an increasing potential for schools to choose pupils rather than parents choosing schools. Given the market-driven interest of individual schools to attract and retain the 'best' pupils, while 'excluding' less desirable children via the admissions processes or via subsequent action (see Children's Commissioner, 2012), the interests of already vulnerable groups such as children with special educational needs (SEN), or with the highest socio-economic deprivation indicators, might be thought to be especially at risk.

Allen and Burgess (2010, p 6) observe that different 'admissions policies will simply alter the set of parents who are able to achieve their choice of school'. In such a situation it is worrying to find think-tanks of very different political orientation reaching remarkably similar conclusions: SMF (2004, p 6) conclude, 'School admissions in England and Wales do not sit well with equity and fairness', while IPPR (2007, p 4) note that 'the current admissions system is a cause of segregation by social class and ability across our schools system ... [and] ... is likely to lead to systematic unfairness in terms of whose preferences can be satisfied'. In Chapter Five we pointed towards strong evidence that such choice as parents enjoy in practice depends crucially on the family's income and social capital – 'some parents are ... better equipped to work the system to make sure they get what they want' (IPPR, 2007, p 17). The 'voice' of parents in expressing a preference is greatly amplified if they have the income required to move house, while the potential for 'exit' of the state-schooling system (purchasing private schooling), in circumstances where their preferences are not met, equally depends on having the necessary financial resources. As noted in Chapter Four, Wiborg (2010), drawing on experience in Sweden, suggests that within the current context in England, a further increase in socio-economic segregation seems the probable consequence of introduction of new school types such as Free Schools.

West et al (2004, p 347) have reported that in 1988, 15% of state schools were their own admissions authorities and, by 2004, this had grown to 30%. Extrapolating from statistics presented in the 2011 OSA Annual Report (see OSA, 2011, pp 11–12) concerning the number of schools that are their own admissions authorities and the DfE's projections for approved Academy transfers (DfE, 2012b), it is likely that around 60% of secondary schools will be their own admissions authorities in the academic year of 2012/13. This means that schools managing their own admissions will be the norm, not the exception. For social policy researchers and for government policy planners, especially those most concerned with the long-term educational and social development of children and young people, the challenge as the Coalition government progresses through its term of office will be to assess how reforms of the systems of housing and other welfare benefits will interact with an unprecedented acceleration in the number of schools managing their own admissions, to affect the life chances of the most vulnerable pupils.

Though parental choice would not be without some attractions in an ideal world (as choice is almost always attractive in principle), it needs to be exercised in a meaningful, informed and equitable manner, within a system which responds to such demand efficiently, in terms of public finances, and accountably, and the outcomes should relate to pre-determined educational values. The present system, by relying heavily on quasi-market forces, produces a particular and predictable set of outcomes which must be considered a political choice (a preference for a system which produces these outcomes) while masking this overarching preference under the guise of the exercise of individual choice in which the outcomes have the appearance of being determined in a marketplace. The evidence we have considered and presented suggests strongly that this approach fails in four ways. First, it fails on its own terms in relation to delivering substantial degrees of meaningful choice for parents; in reality, while many schools are able to exercise a power of choice, many parents are not. Second, it fails in terms of equality of citizenship, in providing effective choice only for some rather than all. As such, it can be seen to contribute to, rather than restrict or redress, segregation and the reproduction of social stratification. Third, in fragmenting and privatising decision making over admissions, while placing a premium on the need for accountability it simultaneously takes decision making outside conventional constitutional mechanisms of accountability, without installing suitable alternative devices. Fourth, the approach fails to relate to any specified educational values, as opposed to a general belief in the efficacy of market forces.

7.2 From choice to chance?

Such concerns explain why we have given extensive consideration to random allocation of school places which, *prima facie*, has an attractive potential to disrupt the exercise of social and financial advantage. While experiments to date, such as those in Brighton and Hove (discussed in Chapter Six), have not resulted in radical change of outcomes in terms of admissions, it is clear that the impact of the adoption of random methods in this context was always likely to be strictly limited by virtue of the continuing prominence of proximity criteria within the admissions policy. In themselves, experiments in England to date have not resulted in clear evidence for or against the use of random methods of allocation of school places. But there is little if any evidence to suggest that, in relation to the concerns regarding equity and fairness, the wider application of random methods would produce worse results than those deriving from the quasi-market or the former LEA-planned model. It is worth noting that random methods appear to share a fundamental characteristic with the quasi-market model – an assumption of equality between those applying. In the former case, a lottery, such a (false) assumption seems relatively unproblematic, and indeed its ability to screen out inbuilt social advantage may seem a positive feature, while in the latter case, the quasi-market, the assumption of equality has clear adverse effects in terms of equity of outcome. IPPR (2007, p 20) concludes that 'Fair banding actually has very similar effects to the random allocation of pupils ... as any random sample of sufficient size is likely to reflect the characteristics of its population'. Despite this serving as what might be considered an endorsement of random allocation, we are reluctant to recommend wholeheartedly the use of random methods.

Ultimately, we believe that the inability of random methods to incorporate substantive values or reasoning relating to education is problematic, at least to the extent of leading us not to advocate their wider or wholesale use in this context. While it is tempting to suggest that randomness is appropriate where rational deliberation has failed to produce a clear outcome, using randomness in the context of school admissions feels like applying a rather flimsy bandage to a gaping wound, as it remains clear that the political process has failed to sufficiently consider the determination and application of rational criteria prior to resort to random methods.

We have two main reasons for expressing reservations about resorting to random methods for allocating school places. First, opting for random methods involves a decision to focus on the process for allocating places, and relies for its legitimacy primarily on its procedural purity, rather than outcome-related consideration of values relating to the schooling system. Arising from this is our second reservation, which we share with IPPR (2007, p 20): that the lack of reasoning which necessarily attaches to random allocation runs counter to the deliberative and value-laden considerations which we believe are fundamental to democracy and citizenship. A requirement of reasoned decisions also provides scope for legal challenge on matters of substance, which otherwise can offer only a meagre, procedural mechanism for review.

The major attraction of considering more widespread use of randomness is its potential to mitigate the tendency of existing choice-driven mechanisms to result in segregation and reproduction of hierarchy. In respect of such concerns, random allocation seems significantly preferable to existing quasi-market mechanisms. But we believe it is necessary to determine priorities for schooling via political deliberation, and then to design systems for admissions which contribute to achieving the educational priorities and objectives which have been determined. In this context 'parental choice' is manifestly not an educational priority or objective, but rather no more than a device for super-imposing a particular view of society onto the school admissions system. Thus, approaches based around devices of randomness and choice both emphasise the mechanism for allocation of school places rather than educational values or associated social values, and neither of them is oriented towards systemic objectives or objectives arising from a prioritisation of substantive values. We believe that a deliberative approach is required, and difficult political choices have to be made, and then given effect via appropriate structures, if a system of school admissions is to be developed which reflects properly collective interests rather than simply the concerns of those parents best able to play the system, and of individual schools.

7.3 Values, institutions and accountability

From any perspective that seeks to critique or validate approaches to school admissions by reference to their purposes, a problem becomes quickly apparent: in general, engaging in analysis of such a system cannot begin and end with critique of the outcomes in the absence of consideration of prior factors. Rather, analysis of outcomes must be based upon scrutiny of the institutions and the mechanisms that deliver them, which in turn must be reviewed in relation to the justificatory rationales and principles that inform them, and the goals that derive from such rationales. Only when this full range of factors has been considered can meaningful conclusions be drawn as to whether the outcomes being produced are satisfactory or not in relation to the system's objectives and justifications. The fundamental problem here is that, in relation to schools and admission to them, the rationales, in terms of political and social values and the objectives that derive from them, are, as noted in Chapter One, complex and very rarely articulated clearly by those determining policy or institutional design or reform. While the very contestability of such values demands that they be articulated so that informed choices between them can be made and institutions designed which best mesh with the values chosen, the nature of the party political fray often tends in practice to militate against the development and statement of the value base underlying policy-making in fields such as education. As a result, 're-settlements' of education policy, such as that brought about from the 1980s onwards which re-oriented the school system towards quasi-market structures, too often seem to be focused on reform of institutional structures and mechanisms, and assertion of better outcomes to follow, without adequate specificity regarding the education-related values which are deemed appropriate as justificatory foundations for the reforms. For these reasons, it is difficult to judge the outcomes of a system against any over-arching value base for that system. As argued in Chapter Two, the reforms brought about from the Education Reform Act 1988 (ERA) onwards can be seen as relating more to the application of a general theory about the appropriate relationship between citizen and state rather than any education-specific values. In combination with the broader ongoing ideological struggle, as manifested in radical reform of central-local government relations, and a more managerial/ presidential style in central government resulting in shifts of power over education agendas from the DES to Downing Street (see Chapter Three), this inhibited the development of meaningful discourse on education-related goals or objectives for the school system as a whole, and admissions in particular.

In the value vacuum created by such an approach to school policy, it can seem difficult to gain any critical purchase in debate about admissions policy. Each of the possible approaches to admissions considered in earlier chapters – LEA-planned, quasi-markets and use of random methods – results in, and hence implies preference for, a particular set of outcomes but, as it is exceedingly difficult to relate them to education-specific values explicitly attached to the school system, it can be difficult to reach firm conclusions about their suitability or acceptability in the context of any values or objectives internal to the school admissions system. Yet it remains the case that adoption of any particular systemic approach to school admissions equates to, and hence does imply preference and/or approval for, the particular set of outcomes that the system will tend to result in. Each of the approaches to school admissions considered in previous chapters prioritises certain process criteria while simultaneously neglecting or marginalising other values competing for priority. As such, each of the approaches can reasonably be viewed as constituting social engineering in the sense that certain outcomes appear inevitable, or at least very likely, being engineered into the system that produces them.

The introduction of choice after ERA, the diminishment of local authority influence, the proliferation of schools lying outside the local authority system, and the near-impossibility of a central government department (the DfE) having the capacity to control the admissions practices of thousands of individual schools has provoked a crisis of accountability at both a constitutional level and at a practical, administrative level. The model of accountability promoted or prioritised within the quasi-market system is a narrow one, based on scrutiny and choice by actual or potential individual service-users in relation to a particular range of factors that will be individualistic to the exclusion of collective concerns. The model relates to the choices of individual parents and the actions and priorities of individual schools, it may be non-educational, and the criteria applied tend to value the measurable rather than measure the valuable. Such a model will be likely to neglect substantially the systemic needs of schooling in a locale.

While we do not necessarily argue for a return to a pre-1988 model of local government planning for the school admissions system, we do identify a pressing need to install institutional features which recognise the concerns often encompassed within concepts of 'social justice', including in particular equality of citizenship, which meet constitutional expectations of accountability, and which incorporate the expectations of rational discourse and deliberation into both high-level decision making regarding the school system as a whole, and individual decisions regarding admissions. The introduction by the Coalition government of the 'pupil premium' (discussed in Chapter Four) and consideration of 'fair banding' (discussed in Chapter Six) indicates recognition of the need to incorporate values into the administration of schooling beyond those that the quasi-market serves or reflects. Such concessions to a planning approach as these and indeed the School Admissions Forums introduced by New Labour (though now withdrawn as a mandatory requirement by the Coalition administration) indicate some acknowledgement of the need for processes oriented towards planning in pursuit of collective objectives and values, even if such mechanisms are to operate outside conventional local democratic structures. Reference here to a 'system' of schools, and for admissions to them, imply of necessity a degree of planning and control if it is to deliver whatever objectives are determined for it.

Decisions regarding schooling and allocation of places within it are too important to be left to the quasi-market or to random methods. Rather, a 'system' of schools implies the need for deliberation over priorities, and subsequently the engineering-in of processes and institutions to deliver on those priorities. It implies both a planning role in relation to this public service and an expectation that the processes relating to schooling will meet constitutional expectations of accountability. Such a deliberative approach implies for us a poly-centred approach to formation of education policy in which a range of interested and democratically legitimate bodies, including local politicians and education professionals have an input into decision making, rather than decision making resting only with the central state and individuals. And note here that we refer not to 'individual consumers', but to 'individuals' – for the strong indication of much of the evidence that we have considered in Chapters Four and Five has been that the reality of choice rests more with individual schools and those who run them, rather than with individual parents as citizens or even as effectively empowered potential or actual 'consumers'. In this sense, privatisation of decision-making power has occurred, rendering accountability via mechanisms conventionally utilised in relation to public bodies much more difficult.

The evidence we have considered and presented suggests strongly some likely issues for education policy makers in the next few years. It seems reasonable to predict a movement towards the creation of a more delineated two-tier system, split between those schools that act as their own admissions authority and those that do not, with some schools suffering and entering a spiral of decline as a result of the effects of local competition and the new permission, under the 2012 Admissions Code, for popular schools to expand without reference to the local authority. In such circumstances, in the absence of intervention in 'the market', it seems reasonable to expect that there will be an increase in inequality in the way school places are allocated, both in terms of differences in resources between different schools and the ability of groups of parents to exercise effective choice equally; as a result, social segregation and reproduction of social hierarchy can be expected to increase. We are already seeing the first stage of a response to such phenomena, in the form of adoption of 'fair banding' and 'pupil premium' policies, constituting something of an admission by government and its agencies that administering a market-oriented system requires a substantial infrastructure of support and intervention if socially undesirable or unacceptable outcomes are not to result. They clearly imply a need, albeit one not fully expressed, for intervention in pursuit of a system-related approach to allocation of school places. The test for such interventions will be to examine them to see whether they result in more equitable outcomes, and whether the mechanisms themselves meet expectations of democratic accountability.

7.4 Law and its limits

Shortly following 'National Offer Day' in 2012, the day when school admission decisions were communicated to parents, *The Independent* (5 March 2012) reported the likelihood of a 'boom year' for lawyers in the 'annual scramble for coveted secondary school places'. Further, it was reported that there were 'concerns that the appeals process could be thrown into chaos with the rapid rise in Academies and new regulations'.

Law has a proper but limited role to play here, but the constitutional settlement tends to encourage an approach to public law that focuses on procedure rather than substance of decision making, especially where the statutory framework fails to establish, or require decision makers to establish, clear priorities or criteria which can subsequently be judged. Clarity, consistency and transparency of operation will all contribute to an agenda of accountability in this context, in terms of permitting effective scrutiny of decision making. But such an approach may serve only to reconfirm the primacy of procedural justice rather than lending direct support to any substantive values. The judicial system will not autonomously produce substantive values relevant to school admissions, but rather will result in at most only minor variations within the framework established by legislation.

The 'liberalisation' of the school system post-ERA has been accompanied by a somewhat incongruous growth in legislation and the imposition of other modes of regulation (whether under legislation, or by Ministerial 'Code' under delegated powers) which schools are required to abide by when admitting pupils. The most striking characteristic of this trend, especially when compared with the 1944 settlement, is not the mere existence of such regulation but also its origins in a political vision imposed from the centre rather than the result of discourse between a range of perspectives represented by a diverse range of interested parties. Tony Blair's decision on assuming power in 1997 to build on the market-driven legacy of the Thatcher years has resulted in the absence of any alternative and compelling vision for schooling being developed or articulated at the level of national politics, while the marginalisation of local authorities and the teaching profession has left no intermediate body between central government and individual schools and parents which has the power or legitimacy to challenge the diarchy of central state and the individual.

Noted in Chapter Two was the observation by Booth et al (2011) of a divergence of policy and the legal framework in the context of addressing SEN. We believe that such issues are of wider concern than this specific context, and illustrate a fundamental problem in relying on the law to resolve disputes regarding education generally and school admissions specifically. Ultimately, the underlying questions that inform this area, and our consideration of it, imply the need for consideration of whether there are any identifiable substantive and/or collective values in play in this area and if so, what they are. Inevitably any such values will be contestable, and as such there is a democratic and constitutional necessity to debate, define, refine and protect them. It would be unwise to choose or expect a judicial system premised on individual causes and adversarial process to be an appropriate forum in which such matters can be addressed effectively. It may be thought that enshrining values in the form of 'human rights' may offer a way forward in this context. But it is necessary to note Tambakaki's argument that enshrining human rights in legal form does not in and of itself revitalise democratic practice (Tambakaki, 2010, p 136), and indeed risks further emphasising the centrality of individual rights and claims. Rather, it seems necessary to have the expectations of citizenship centre-stage, as these serve, helpfully, to re-emphasise collective institutions and values.

It is neither reasonable nor sensible to expect the legal system to act autonomously to identify or achieve desirable objectives in relation to school admissions. The absence of a clear statement of policies, priorities and objectives emerging from the political system, other than constant reaffirmation of the rhetoric of consumer choice, makes the quest for substantive accountability all but impossible. Even utilising the law to ensure the limited objective of procedural propriety becomes much more difficult when decision making is located not at the level of large-scale local planning authorities but at innumerable semi-independent individual schools. Meanwhile, despite allowing greater recourse to the Office of the Schools Adjudicator (OSA), the Coalition's restriction of the OSA's powers to work at a systemic level seems to serve only to reconfirm the centrality of individuals, and responses to individual cases, rather than permitting the (re)introduction of collective or systemic values into debates about admissions processes. In any case, the legal and administrative mechanisms of challenge can only be expected to have a useful role to play in explicating or stating authoritatively, and in a context rendering them enforceable, the principles and objectives which have been determined previously. Again, deliberative political processes need to have been utilised in accordance with democratic expectations, as a prior step, to determine those objectives and to establish administrative mechanisms for working towards them.

We have referred repeatedly to the desirability of an effective deliberative element in relation to decision making relating to school admissions policy; crucial as a distinguishing feature between the passive roles and expectations of consumer, and the active expectations of citizenship. The application of quasi-market forces tends to erode the democratic determination of values – the 'rationality' of market based choice does not equate with deliberative approaches which encourage reasoned decisions drawing on a wider set of social values, ranging beyond market-individualism – a deliberative approach contrasts with a mere aggregation of individual choices as a result of implying values often associated with 'social justice' such as inclusion, equality and reasonableness. And reasoned decision making is fundamental to the ability to engage both in prior discussion and *ex post facto* challenge of decisions.

The values informing the various settlements of the school system remain generally weakly, arguably inadequately, specified, though exceptions do exist – recent initiatives such as fair banding and 'pupil premium' actually acknowledge underlying values, though they are exceptions to the norm, which is premised on quasi-market mechanisms. But, crucially, we need to note the word 'system' – more readily associated with, and apparent in, the pre-ERA context than recent or current times. The recent revision by the Coalition government of the OSA role and the 'releasing' of the local authorities from the mandatory requirement to set up Admissions Forums, together with the rapid increase in Academies and the introduction of Free Schools, all seem to reconfirm a move away from systemic considerations and towards atomisation of schooling and decisions relating to it. We do not offer a prescription for an institutional framework in which systemic concerns will be adequately recognised and incorporated, though we do note the IPPR (2007) view that 'The obvious conclusion is to prevent any school from being its own admission authority, and instead for this function to be performed by an organisation whose primary concern is for pupil outcomes over a reasonably wide geographical area. The most obvious candidate is the local authority'. Unfortunately, it is evident that none of the major political parties show a clear intention of pursuing such an approach.

Under the New Labour administrations there was a discernible general trend towards increased transparency and structure in the discretion exercised by schools acting as their own admissions authorities, via mechanisms such as the 2009 Admissions Code and the OSA. As discussed in Chapter Four, the recent Coalition moves in limiting some aspects of the OSA's role and the revised 2012 Code's introduction of the right of the Secretary of State to vary the admissions requirements for Academies and Free Schools if there is 'demonstrable need' (despite the Code's claim that such schools should 'comply with the code and the law relating to admissions'), are not positive signs in terms of ensuring accountability of decision making by admissions authorities. Legal challenges, which tend to be procedural and individualistic, are likely to add little, if anything, to our understanding of the values in play, or to challenge the fundamental basis of the underlying approach to school admissions. Neither administrative routes of appeal nor the application of general legal principles in the course of judicial review will help to develop substantive principles related to the values or priorities associated with schooling, though the pursuit of individual claims via such routes can, as Tweedie (1986) noted more than 25 years ago, serve to cut across and substantially undermine legitimate planning objectives related to collective interests. The process of 'governance by contract' in relation to Academies, which we noted in Chapter Four, seems to confirm and indeed epitomise the problem of the individualised approach to the administration of schooling.

7.5 A last word

The legal system is manifestly not the place to seek to determine the relative strengths and weaknesses of the different claims of legitimacy made by LEA-planned, quasi-markets and random allocation in the context of school admissions. In any event, all three of those approaches to allocating school places share a common problem: they are all driven by differing views of the appropriate mechanisms for allocating school places, while avoiding addressing much more difficult questions relating to the identification of what should be the substantive values, priorities and outcomes against which we should judge the processes. It is clear that, for anyone concerned with the consequences that flow from the allocation of school places, it is necessary to engage in widespread and explicit deliberation of the values that underlie school admission processes. Only when such values have been identified with reasonable clarity can we expect to build institutional arrangements for allocating places that are designed effectively to deliver such priorities.

The increasingly fragmented nature of what was previously a system of schools reflects a particular view of how society should operate; a view brought into mainstream politics in Britain via 'Thatcherism' and which has ever since been unchallenged by the major political parties. As Chapter Five demonstrated, the school admissions processes now used can encourage an individualistic and self-serving approach, on the part of both parents and schools. Such an approach marginalises any collective or systemic values. The tension here, between the 'common good' function of schooling and the interests of individual children and individual schools is palpable, and may seem irreconcilable. The issues involved were summarised powerfully by Jonathan (1989) in the early days of the quasi-market in schooling:

> A policy which gives individuals the opportunity for each to maximise her own holding in a competitive or market situation might indeed be expected to have harmful consequences for those individuals who, for whatever reason, are less effective in exploiting that opportunity. Whether or not such an outcome is considered detrimental to society as a whole, rather than simply to its less fortunate members, depends upon the adequacy of competing social and economic theories, as well as upon further moral debate. (Jonathan, 1989, p 338)

This telling observation relating to the fundamental basis for allocating social goods such as school places serves to re-emphasise a theme we have returned to repeatedly in this book: the need for widespread, open and considered discourse in pursuit of the establishment of a clear value-base against which such policies can be judged, and on which opposition to inequitable policies which reproduce social stratification and segregation can be founded. Overall, our conclusion must be that there is a pressing need for an effective and accountable element of planning in the school admissions process, operating within a deliberative context in which mechanisms for school admissions are clearly related to objectives for the school system identified, as a prior task, by the political process. Within such a system, those charged with decision making in relation to admissions must operate subject to effective mechanisms of accountability, in accordance with democratic and legal principles. We would argue that these concerns should be central to reviews of past and present processes relating to allocation of school places, and advance scrutiny of proposed future measures.

References

Adler, M., Petch, A. and Tweedie, J. (1989) *Parental choice and educational policy*, Edinburgh: Edinburgh University Press.

Administrative Justice and Tribunals Council (AJTC) (2011) *Securing fairness and redress: Administrative justice at risk?*, London: AJTC, October.

Adonis, A. and Pollard, S. (1997) *A class act: The myth of Britain's classless society*, London: Hamish Hamilton.

Allen, R. and Burgess, S. (2010) 'The future of competition and accountability in education', *http://www.bristol.ac.uk/cmpo/publications/other/competition.pdf.*

Allen, R., Burgess, S. and McKenna, L. (2010a) 'The early impact of Brighton and Hove's school admission reforms', *Centre for Market and Public Organisation Working Paper*, No 10/244, Bristol: University of Bristol.

Allen, R., Coldron, J. and West, A. (2010b) *The effect of changes in published secondary schools admissions on pupil composition* (Research Report DFE-RR038), London: DfE.

Atherton, M. (2006) *Gambling*, London: Hodder and Stoughton.

Auby, J-B. (2007) 'Comparative approaches to the rise of contract in the public law', *Public Law*, Spring, pp 40–57.

Audit Commission (1989) *Losing an empire, finding a role: the LEA of the future,* London: HMSO.

Audit Commission (1996) *Trading places: the supply and allocation of school places*, London: Audit Commission Publications.

Audit Commission (2002) *Special educational needs: a mainstream issue*, London: Audit Commission Publications.

Ball, S. (1990) *Politics and policymaking in education*, London: Routledge.

Ball, S. (1993) 'Education markets, choice and social class: the market as a class strategy in the UK and the USA', *British Journal of Sociology of Education*, vol 14, no 1, pp 3–19.

Ball, S. (2008) *The education debate*, Bristol: The Policy Press.

Bangs, J., Galton, M. and MacBeath, J. (2010) *Reinventing schools, reforming teaching: from political visions to classrooms*, London: Routledge.

Barnes, C. (1991) *Disabled people in Britain and discrimination: a case for anti-discrimination legislation*, London: Hurst and Co.

Baron, S. and Centre for Contemporary Cultural Studies Education Group (1981) *Unpopular education: Schooling and social democracy in England since 1944*, London: Hutchinson in association with the Centre for Contemporary Cultural Studies, University of Birmingham.

Beetham, D. and Weir, S. (1999) *Political power and democratic control in Britain*, London: Routledge.

Benn, C. and Simon, B. (1972) *Half way there: report on the British comprehensive school reform* (2nd edn), London: Penguin.

Birkinshaw, P. (1995) *Grievances, remedies and the state* (2nd edn), London: Sweet and Maxwell.

Board of Education (1943) *White Paper on Education Reconstruction*, Cmnd 6458, London: Board of Education.

Bogdanor, V. (2003) *The British constitution in the twentieth century*, Oxford: Oxford University Press.

Booth C., Bush, M. and Scott, R. (2011) 'Complex needs, divergent frameworks: challenges disabled children face in accessing appropriate support services and inclusive educational opportunities', in S. Haines and D. Ruebain (eds) *Education, disability and social policy*, Bristol: Policy Press, pp 23–46.

Borsay, A. (2005) *Disability and social policy in Britain since 1750: a history of exclusion*, London: Palgrave Macmillan.

Boulton, P. and Coldron, J. (1996) 'Does the rhetoric work? Parental responses to new right policy assumptions', *British Journal of Educational Studies*, vol 44, no 3, pp 296–306.

Boyle, C. (2010) *Lotteries for education: sortition and public policy*, Exeter: Imprint Academic.

Bradley, A. and Ewing, K. (2011) *Constitutional and administrative law* (15th edn), Harlow: Pearson Education.

Brighouse, T., Tooley, J. and Howe, K. (2010) *Educational equality*, London: Continuum.

Bunar, N. (2008) 'The Free Schools "Riddle": between traditional social democratic, neo-liberal and multicultural tenets', *Scandinavian Journal of Educational Research*, vol 52, no 4, pp 423–8.

Bunar, N. (2009) 'Choosing for quality or inequality: current perspectives on the implementation of school choice policy in Sweden', *Journal of Educational Policy*, vol 25, no 1, pp 1–18.

Burchardt, T. (2005) *The education and employment of disabled young people: frustrated ambition*, Bristol: The Policy Press, pp 145–66.

Burgess, S., McConnell, B., Propper, C. and Wilson, D. (2004) 'Sorting out choice in English Secondary schools', *Centre for Market and Public Organisation Working Paper*, No 04/111, Bristol: University of Bristol.

Burgess, S., Briggs, A., McConnell, B. and Slater, H. (2006) 'School choice in England: background facts', *Centre for Market and Public Organisation Working Paper*, No 06/159, Bristol: University of Bristol.

Burgess, S., Greaves, E., Vignoles, A. and Wilson, D. (2009) 'What parents want: School preferences and school choice', *Centre for Market and Public Organisation Working Paper*, No 09/222, Bristol: University of Bristol.

Bush, T. and Kogan, M. (1982) *Directors of Education*, London: George Allen and Unwin.

Byrne, T. (1994) *Local government in Britain* (6th edn), Harmondsworth: Penguin.

Carr, W. and Hartnett, A. (1996) *Education and the struggle for democracy: the politics of educational ideas*, Buckingham: Open University Press.

Carroll, S. and Walford, G. (1997) 'The child's voice in school choice', *Educational Management and Administration*, vol 25, no 2, pp 169–80.

Children's Commissioner (2012) *'They never give up on you': Office of the Children's Commissioner School Exclusions Inquiry*, London: Office of the Children's Commissioner.

Chitty, C. (1992) *The education system transformed*, Manchester: Baseline Books.

Chitty, C. (2009) *Education policy in Britain* (2nd edn), London: Basingstoke: Palgrave Macmillan.

Christensen, C. and Rizvi, F. (eds) (1996) *Disability and the dilemmas of education and justice*, Buckingham: Open University Press.

Clarke, J. and Newman, J. (1997) *The managerial state*, London: Sage.

Clough, N., Lee, V., Menter, I., Trodd, T. and Whitty, G. (1989) 'Restructuring the Education System?' in L. Bash and D. Coulby (eds), *The Education Reform Act: Competition and control*, London: Cassell, pp 31–53.

Coldron, J., Stephenson, K., Williams, J., Shipton, L. and Demack, S. (2002) *Admission appeal panels: research study into the operation of appeal panels, use of the Code of Practice and training for panel members*, School of Education, Sheffield Hallam University, Research Paper 344, London: DfES.

Coldron, J., Tanner, E., Finch, S., Shipton, L., Wolstenholme, C., Willis, B., Demack, S. and Stiell, B. (2008) *Secondary school admissions*, London: DCSF.

Crowther, N. (2011) 'From SEN to Sen: could the "capabilities" approach transform the educational opportunities for disabled children?' in S. Haines and D. Ruebain (eds), *Education, disability and social policy*, Bristol: The Policy Press, pp 47–64.

Dahl, R. (1967) *Pluralist democracy in the United States: conflict and consent*, Chicago: Rand McNally.

Dale, R. (1989) *The state and education policy*, Milton Keynes: Open University Press.

Delannoi, G. and Dowlen, O. (eds) (2010) *Sortition: theory and practice,* Exeter: Imprint Academic.

DCSF (2009a) *School Admissions Code,* London: DCSF.

DCSF (2009b) *The Lamb Inquiry: Special educational needs and parental confidence,* Nottingham: DCSF Publications.

DfE (1992) *Choice and diversity: a new framework for schools,* Cmnd 2021, London: HMSO.

DfE (2010a) *Academies Act 2010: equality assessment,* London: DfE.

DfE (2010b) *http://www.data.parliament.uk/DepositedPapers/Files// DEP2010-1403.pdf*

DfE (2010c) *http://www.data.parliament.uk/DepositedPapers/Files/ DEP2010-1396.pdf*

DfE (2010d) *The importance of teaching: the schools White Paper,* DfE: The Stationery Office.

DfE (2011a) *Support and aspiration: a new approach to special educational needs and disability – a consultation,* Coalition Green Paper, Norwich: TSO.

DfE (2011b) *http://www.education.gov.uk/schools/adminandfinance/ schooladmissions/a0075929/choice-advisers*

DfE (2012a) *School Admissions Code,* London: DfE.

DfE (2012b) *http://www.education.gov.uk/schools/leadership/typesofschools/ academies*

DfE (2012c) *http://www.education.gov.uk/schools/leadership/typesofschools/ freeschools/b0066077/free-school-proposals*

DfE (2012d) *http://media.education.gov.uk/assets/files/pdf/l/letter%20 to%20new%20schools%20network%20%20%2018%20june%202010. pdf*

DfE (2012e) *http://www.education.gov.uk/schools/leadership/typesofschools/ freeschools/b0061428/free-schools/who*

DfE (2012f) *http://www.education.gov.uk/schools/leadership/typesofschools/ freeschools/b0061428/free-schools/what*

DfE (2012g) *http://www.education.gov.uk/schools/pupilsupport/premium/ b0076063/pp/notes*

DfEE (1999) *Code of Practice on School Admissions,* London: DfEE.

DfEE (2001) *Building on success: raising standards and promoting diversity,* Cm 5050, London: TSO.

DfES (2001) *Code of Practice on the Assessment and Identification of Special Needs,* London: DfES.

DfES (2003) *Code of Practice on School Admissions,* London: DfES.

DfES (2005) *Higher standards: Better schools for all – More choice for parents and pupils,* White Paper, Cmnd 6677, London: DfES.

DfES (2007) *Code of Practice on School Admissions,* London: DfES.

Duxbury, N. (1999) *Random justice: on lotteries and legal decision-making*, Oxford: Oxford University Press.

Feintuck, M. (1994) *Accountability and choice in schooling*, Milton Keynes: Open University Press.

Feintuck, M. (2004) *'The public interest' in regulation*, Oxford: Oxford University Press.

Feintuck, M. (2005) 'Precautionary maybe but what's the principle? The precautionary principle, the regulation of risk, and the public domain', *Journal of Law and Society*, vol 32, no 3, pp 371–98.

Finch, J. (1984) *Education as social policy*, London: Longman.

Floud, J., Halsey, A. and Martin, F. (1957) *Social class and educational opportunity*, London: Heinemann.

Flude, M. and Hammer, M. (eds) (1990) *The Education Reform Act 1988: its origins and implications*, Basingstoke: Falmer.

Forsey, M., Davies, S. and Walford, G. (eds) (2008) *The globalisation of school choice?*, Oxford: Symposium Books.

Freedland, M. (1994) 'Government by contract and public law', *Public Law*, vol 32, pp 86–104.

Gamble, A. (1994) *The free economy and the strong state* (2nd edn), Basingstoke: Palgrave Macmillan.

Gerber, M. (1996) 'Reforming special education: beyond "inclusion" ' in C. Christensen and F. Rizvi (eds), *Disability and the dilemmas of education and justice*, Buckingham: Open University Press, pp 156–74.

Gerwirtz, S., Ball, S. and Bowe, R. (1995) *Markets, choice and equity in education*, Buckingham: Open University Press.

Gibbons, S. and Machin, S. (2006) 'Paying for primary schools: supply constraints, school popularity or congestion?', *Economic Journal*, vol 116, no 510, pp C77–C92.

Gibbons, S. and Machin, S. (2007) 'Valuing school quality, better transport and lower crime: evidence from house prices', *Oxford Review of Economic Policy*, Housing Markets Seminar, Said Business School, 12 September.

Glennerster, H. (1991) 'Quasi-markets for education?', *Economic Journal*, vol 101, no 408, pp 1268–76.

Goodie, J. and Wickham, G. (2002) 'Calculating "public interest": Common law and the legal governance of the environment', *Social and Legal Studies*, vol 11, no 1, pp 37–60.

Goodwin, B. (2005) *Justice by lottery* (2nd edn), Exeter: Imprint Academic.

Goodwin, B. (2010) 'Lotteries, markets and fair competition', in G. Delannoi and O. Dowlen (eds), *Sortition: theory and practice*, Exeter: Imprint Academic, pp 105–18.

Goodwin, M. (2009) 'Choice in public services: Crying "wolf" in the school choice debate', *The Political Quarterly*, vol 80, no 2, pp 270–81.

Gorard, S., Taylor, C. and Fitz, J. (2003) *Schools, markets and choice policies*, London: Routledge Falmer.

Gould, P. (1998) *The unfinished revolution*, London: Little, Brown & Co.

Gray, C. (1994) *Government beyond the centre: sub-national politics in Britain*, Basingstoke: Macmillan.

Haines, S. and Ruebain, D. (eds) (2011) *Education, disability and social policy*, Bristol: The Policy Press.

Halsey, A., Heath, A. and Ridge, J. (1980) *Origins and destinations: family, class and education in modern Britain*, Oxford: Clarendon Press.

Harden, I. (1992) *The contracting state*, Buckingham: The Open University Press.

Harden, I. and Lewis, N. (1986) *The noble lie: the British Constitution and the rule of law*, London: Hutchinson.

Harris, N. (1990) *The law relating to schools*, London: Fourmat.

Harris, N. (1993) *Law and education: regulation, consumerism and the education system, London:* Sweet & Maxwell.

Harris, N. (2007) *Education, law and diversity*, Oxford: Hart.

Harris, N. and Riddell, S. (2011) *Resolving disputes about educational provision: a comparative perspective on special educational needs*, London: Ashgate.

Haviland, J. (ed) (1988) *Take care, Mr Baker! The advice on education reform which the government collected but withheld*, London: Fourth Estate Limited.

Held, D. (1996) *Models of democracy*, Cambridge: Polity Press.

Hirschman, A. (1970) *Exit, voice and loyalty: Responses to decline in firms, organizations, and states*, Cambridge, MA: Harvard University Press.

House of Commons (HOC) (2004) Education and Skills Select Committee, *Fourth Report of the Education and Skills Select Committee, 2003-04, Secondary education: School admissions* (HC 58 –1), London: The Stationery Office.

House of Commons (HOC) (2011a) *Public Bill Committee, Education Bill, 18th sitting (afternoon), 29 March*.

House of Commons (HOC) (2011b) Education Select Committee, *Inquiry into the new admissions and appeals code*, 16 October, London: The Stationery Office.

House of Commons (HOC) (2011c) *Education Committee*, 12 October 2011, *http://www.publications.parliament.uk/pa/cm201012/cmselect/cmeduc/uc1513-i/uc151301.htm*

House of Lords/House of Commons (HOL) (2010) *Joint Committee on Human Rights: Children's Rights, Twenty-fifth report of sessions, 2008–09*, 13 October, London: The Stationery Office.

Independent Schools Council (2011) *ISC Census, 2011*, ISC Research and Intelligence Team, London: ISC, January.

Institute of Fiscal Studies (IFS) (2010) (authors: Chowdry, H., Greaves, H. and Sibieta, L.) *The pupil premium: Assessing the options*, IFS: London, March (funded by ERSC).

Institute for Public Policy Research (IPPR) (2007) (authors: Tough, S. and Brooks, R.) *School admissions: Fair choice for parents and pupils*, London: IPPR.

Jenkins, S. (2007) *Thatcher & Sons*, London: Penguin.

Jenkins, S., Micklewright, J. and Schnepf, S. (2006) 'Social segregation in secondary schools: How does England compare with other countries?' Institute for Social and Economic Research (ISER) Working Paper, 2006-2, University of Essex, and S3RI Working Paper, AO6/01, University of Southampton.

Jonathan, R. (1989) 'Choice and control in education: parental rights, individual liberties and social justice', *British Journal of Educational Studies*, vol XXXVII, no 4, pp 321–38.

Jones, B., Kavanagh, D., Moran, N. and Norton, P. (2007) *Politics UK* (6th edn), Harlow: Pearson Education Ltd.

Jones, K. (2003) *Education in Britain: 1944 to present*, Cambridge: Polity Press.

Jowell, J. (2011) 'The rule of law and its underlying values', in J. Jowell and D. Oliver (eds) *The changing constitution* (7th edn), Oxford: Oxford University Press, chapter 1.

Keane, J. (2009) *The life and death of democracy*, London: Simon and Schuster.

Knights, S. (2005) 'Religious symbols in the school: freedom of religion, minorities and education', *European Human Rights Law Review*, vol 5, pp 499–516.

Kogan, M. (1975) *The politics of education: Edward Boyle and Anthony Crosland in conversation with Maurice Kogan*, Harmondsworth: Penguin.

Lawton, D. (1977) *Education and social justice*, London: Sage.

Lawton, D. (ed) (1989) *The Education Reform Act: Choice and control*, Sevenoaks: Hodder and Stoughton.

Leach, S. and Stoker, G. (1988) 'The transformation of central-local government relationships' in C. Graham and T. Prosser (eds) *Waiving the rules: The constitution under Thatcherism*, Milton Keynes: Open University Press, pp 95–115.

Le Grand, J. (1982) *The strategy of equality*, London: Allen & Unwin.

Le Grand, J. (1991) 'Quasi-markets and social policy', *Economic Journal*, vol 101, pp 1256–67.

Le Grand, J. and Bartlett, W. (eds) (1993) *Quasi-markets and social policy*, Basingstoke: Macmillan.

Leigh, I. (2011) 'The changing nature of local and regional democracy', in J. Jowell and D. Oliver (eds) *The changing constitution* (7th edn), Oxford: Oxford University Press.

Leslie, C. and Skidmore, C. (2008) *SEN: The truth about inclusion*, London: Bow Group, 10 January.

Lester, A. (Lord) and Beattie, K. (2011) 'Human rights and the British Constitution', in J. Jowell and D. Oliver (eds) *The changing constitution* (7th edn), Oxford: Oxford University Press, pp 59–83.

Loughlin, M. (1996) *Legality and locality: The role of law in central-local relations*, Oxford: Oxford University Press.

Loughlin, M. (2003) 'The demise of local government', in V. Bogdanor (ed) *The British constitution in the twentieth century*, Oxford, Oxford University Press, pp 521–56.

Maclure, S. (1988) *Education re-formed*, Sevenoaks: Hodder and Stoughton.

Marquand, D. (2004) *Decline of the public: The hollowing-out of citizenship*, Cambridge: Polity.

Marshall, T.H. (1950) *Citizenship and social class, and other essays*, Cambridge: Cambridge University Press.

Mauger, P. (1970) 'Selection for secondary education', in D. Rubinstein (ed) *Education for democracy*, Harmondsworth: Penguin Books, pp 131–8.

Mellors, C. (1978) *The British MP: A socio-economic study of the House of Commons*, London: Saxon House.

Meredith, P. (1995) 'The future of local education authorities as strategic planners', *Public Law*, Summer, pp 234–43.

Middlemas, K. (1986) *Power, competition and the state, Vol. 1: Britain in search of balance*, London: Macmillan, pp 1940–61.

National Audit Office (NAO) (1986) *Department of Education and Science: Falling school rolls, Report by the Comptroller and Auditor General*, London: HMSO.

National Audit Office (NAO) (2010) *Department for Education: The Academies programme,* London: NAO.

National Foundation for Educational Research (NFER) (2006) (authors: Chamberlain, T., Rutt. S. and Fletcher-Campbell, F.) *Admissions: who goes where? Messages from the statistics*, LGA Research Report 4/06, Slough: NFER, August.

Newsom Report (1963) *Half our future: a report of the Central Advisory Council for Education (England)*, London: HMSO, August.

Noden, P. and West, A. (2009) *Secondary school admissions in England: admissions forums, local authorities and schools*, London: Research and Information on State Education, London, December.

Office of the Schools Adjudicator (OSA) (2009a) *Report to the Secretary of State for Children, Schools and Families on the use of random allocation in admission arrangements for schools in England*, 1 September.

Office of the Schools Adjudicator (OSA) (2009b) *Report to the Secretary of State for Children, Schools and Families on fraudulent or misleading applications for admission to schools*, 1 October.

Office of the Schools Adjudicator (OSA) (2011) *OSA Annual Report 2011*, Darlington: Office of the Schools Adjudicator.

Ofsted (2010) *The special educational needs and disability review*, Manchester: Ofsted, September.

Oplatka, I. (2008) 'The introduction of controlled school choice in Tel Aviv, Israel: An attempt to attain a balance between integration and pluralism', in M. Forsey, S. Davies and G. Walford (eds) *The globalisation of school choice?*, Oxford: Symposium Books, pp 111–30.

Organisation for Economic Co-operation and Development (OECD) (1994) *School: A matter of choice*, Paris: OECD Publishing.

Pollard, S. (2005) *David Blunkett*, London: Hodder & Stoughton.

Rallings, C. and Thrasher, M. (1994) 'Community identity and participation in local democracy', in C. Rallings, M. Temple and M. Thrasher (eds) *Commission for Local Democracy*, London: Commission for Local Democracy.

Ranson, S. (1990) 'From 1944 to 1988: education, citizenship and democracy', in Flude, M. and Hammer, M. (eds) (1990) *The Education Reform Act 1988: Its origins and implications*, Basingstoke: Falmer, pp 1–19.

Roulstone, A. and Prideaux, S. (2012) *Understanding disability policy*, Bristol: The Policy Press.

Ruff, A. (2002) *Education Law: text, cases and materials*, London: Butterworths LexisNexis.

Rustemier, S. and Vaughan, M. (2005) *Segregation trends – LEAs in England 2002–2004*, Bristol: Centre for Studies on Inclusive Education.

Sagoff, M. (2004) *Price, principle and the environment*, Cambridge: Cambridge University Press.

Sandland, R. (2008) 'Developing a jurisprudence of difference: the protection of the human rights of travelling peoples by the European Court of Human rights', *Human Rights Law Review*, vol 8, no 3, pp 475–516.

Sayer, A. (1995) *Radical political economy: A critique*, Oxford: Basil Blackwell.

Seaward, P. and Silk, P. (2003) 'The House of Commons', in V. Bogdanor (ed) *The British constitution in the twentieth century*, Oxford, Oxford University Press, pp 139–88.

Seldon, A. and Lodge, G. (2011) *Brown at 10*, London: Biteback Publishing.

Shaw, E. (2007) *Losing Labour's soul: New Labour and the Blair Government 1997–2007*, London: Routledge.

Simon, B. (1991) *Education and the social order, 1940–1990*, London: Lawrence & Wishart.

Social Market Foundation (SMF) (2004) (editor: Haddad, M.) *School admissions: A report of the Social Market Foundation Commission*, London: Social Market Foundation.

Social Market Foundation (SMF) (2005) (author: Wood, C.) *Making choice a reality in secondary education*, London: Social Market Foundation.

Stevens, R. (2011) *The development of the academies policy, 2000–2010: The influence of democratic values and constitutional practice*, Unpublished doctoral thesis, University of Hull.

Stewart, R. (1983) 'Regulation in a liberal state: the role of non-commodity values', *Yale Law Journal*, vol 92, no 8, pp 1537–90.

Stillman, A. (1990) 'Legislating for choice' in M. Flude and M. Hammer (eds) *The Education Reform Act 1988: its origins and implications*, Basingstoke: Falmer.

Stillman, A. and Maychell, K. (1986) *Choosing schools: Parents, LEAs and the 1980 Education Act*, London: Routledge.

Stone, P. (2011) *The luck of the draw: The role of lotteries in decision making*, Oxford: Oxford University Press.

Sunstein, C. (1990) *After the rights revolution: Reconceiving the regulatory state*, Cambridge, MA: Harvard University Press.

Sutton Trust (2008) (with the IoE) 'The Academies programme: Progress, problems and possibilities', London, The Sutton Trust, December.

Sutton Trust (2010a) 'The educational background of Members of Parliament in 2010', London: The Sutton Trust, May.

Sutton Trust (2010b) (with University of Buckingham, authors: Smithers, A. and Robinson, P.) 'Choice and selection in admissions: The experience of other countries', Sutton Trust, November.

Swedish National Agency for Education (Skolverket) (2006) 'School like any other? Free schools as part of the system 1991–2004', Stockholm: Swedish National Agency for Education.

Tambakaki, P. (2010) *Human rights or citizenship?*, Oxford: Birkbeck Law Press.

Taylor, C. (2009) *A good school for every child*, Abingdon: Routledge.

Taylor, J., Fitz, J. and Gorard, S. (2001) 'Market frustration: admission appeals in the UK education market', unpublished paper, University of Cardiff.

Todd, L. (2011) 'Multi-agency working and disabled children and young people: From "what works" to "active becoming" ', in S. Haines and D. Ruebain (eds) (2011) *Education, disability and social policy*, Bristol: The Policy Press, pp 65–87.

Tomlinson, S. (1982) *A sociology of special education*, London: Routledge and Kogan Page.

Tomlinson, S. (2005) *Education in a post-welfare society* (2nd edn), Milton Keynes: Open University Press.

Tweedie, J. (1986) 'Rights in social programmes: the case of parental choice of school', *Public Law*, Autumn, pp 407–36

Walford, G. (1994) *Choice and equity in education*, London: Cassell.

Walford, G. (1996) 'School choice in England and Wales', *Oxford Studies in Comparative Education,* vol 6, no 1, pp 49–61.

Walford, G. (2000) 'From City Technology Colleges to sponsored grant-maintained schools, *Oxford Review of Education*, vol 26, no 2, pp 145–8.

Walford, G. (2008) 'School choice in England: globalisation, policy borrowing or policy corruption?' in M. Forsey, S. Davies and G. Walford (eds) *The globalisation of school choice?*, Oxford: Symposium Books, pp 95–109.

Walters, R. (2003) 'The House of Lords', in V. Bogdanor (ed) *The British constitution in the twentieth century*, Oxford, Oxford University Press, pp 189–237.

Warnock, M. (1978) *Report of the Commission of Enquiry into the Education of Handicapped Children and Young People* (the Warnock Report), London: HMSO.

West, A., Barham, E. and Hind, A. (2009) 'Secondary school admissions in England: Policy and practice', London: RISE (Research and Information on State Education)/LSE, March.

West, A., Hind, A. and Pennell, H. (2004) 'School admissions and "selection" in comprehensive schools: Policy and practice', *Oxford Review of Education*, vol 30, no 3, pp 347-69.

West, A., Pennell, H. and Hind, A. (2003) 'Secondary school admissions in England: selection by stealth', *Management in Education*, vol 17, no 4, pp 18–22.

Whitty, G. (2001) 'Education, social class and social exclusion', *Journal of Education Policy*, vol 16, no 4, pp 287–95.

Whitty, G. (2002) *Making sense of education policy*, London: Paul Chapman Publishing.

Wiborg. S. (2010) *Swedish Free Schools: Do they work?*, Centre for Learning and Life Chances in Knowledge Economics and Societies, Research paper 18, London: Institute of Education.

Willetts, D. (1997) *Why vote Conservative?*, London: Penguin.

Wilson, D. (2010) 'School choice: what do parents want?', *Research in Public Policy* (Summer 2010), p 11.

Wolfe, D. (2010) 'Academies and the law', in H. Gunter (ed), *Education policy and the state: The Academies programme*, London: Continuum Publishing Group, pp 19-38.

Wolfe, D. (2011) 'The Act in a nutshell', *CASEnotes*, Issue 45, December 2011, London: CASE.

Woods, P., Bagley, C. and Glatter, R. (1998) *School choice and competition: Markets in the public interest?*, London: Routledge.

Wooldridge, A. (1996) 'The English state and educational theory', in S. Green and R. Whiting (eds) *The boundaries of the state in modern Britain*, Cambridge: Cambridge University Press, pp 231–60.

Young, I. (2000) *Inclusion and democracy*, Oxford: Oxford University Press.

Index